New York by Area

Essentials

Published by Time Out Guides Ltd
Universal House
251 Tottenham Court Road
London W1T 7AB
Tel: + 44 (0)20 7813 3000
Fax: + 44 (0)20 7813 6001
Email: guides@timeout.com
www.timeout.com

Editorial Director Sarah Guy
Management Accountant Margaret Wright

Time Out Guides is a wholly owned subsidiary of Time Out Group Ltd.

© Time Out Group Ltd
Chairman & Founder Tony Elliott
Chief Executive Officer Aksel Van der Wal
Editor-in-Chief Tim Arthur
UK Chief Commercial Officer David Pepper
International Managing Director Cathy Runciman
Group IT Director Simon Chappell
Group Marketing Director Carolyn Sims

Time Out and the Time Out logo are trademarks of Time Out Group Ltd.

This edition first published in Great Britain in 2013 by Ebury Publishing
A Random House Group Company
Company information can be found on www.randomhouse.co.uk
Random House UK Limited Reg. No. 954009
10 9 8 7 6 5 4 3 2 1

Distributed in the US and Latin America by Publishers Group West (1-510-809-3700)

For further distribution details, see www.timeout.com

ISBN: 978-1-84670-378-2

A CIP catalogue record for this book is available from the British Library.

Printed and bound in Germany by Appl.

The Random House Group Limited supports the Forest Stewardship Council® (FSC®), the leading international forest-certification organisation. Our books carrying the FSC label are printed on FSC® - certified paper. FSC is the only forest-certification scheme supported by the leading environmental organisations, including Greenpeace. Our paper procurement policy can be found at www.randomhouse.co.uk/environment

New York Shortlist

The **Time Out New York Shortlist 2014** is one of a series of annual guides that draws on Time Out's background as a magazine publisher to keep you current with everything that's going on in town. As well as 2014's key sights and the best of its eating, drinking and leisure options, it picks out the most exciting venues to have opened in the last year and gives a full calendar of annual events from October 2013 to December 2014. It also includes features on the important news, trends and openings, all compiled by locally based editors and writers. Whether you're visiting for the first time in your life or the first time this year, you'll find the *Time Out New York Shortlist* contains all you need to know, in a portable and easy-to-use format.

The guide divides central New York into four areas, each containing listings for Sights & Museums, Eating & Drinking, Shopping, Nightlife and Arts & Leisure, and maps pinpointing their locations. At the front of the book are chapters rounding up these scenes city-wide, and giving a shortlist of our overall picks. We also include itineraries for days out, plus essentials such as transport information and hotels.

Our listings give phone numbers as dialled within the US. Within New York you need to use the initial 1 and the three-digit area code even if you're calling from within that area code. From abroad, use your country's exit code followed by the number (the initial 1 is the US's country code).

We have noted price categories by using one to four $ signs ($-$$$$), representing budget, moderate, expensive and luxury. Major credit cards are accepted unless otherwise stated. We also indicate when a venue is **NEW**, and give **Event highlights**.

All our listings are double-checked, but places do sometimes close or change their hours or prices, so it's a good idea to call a venue before visiting. While every effort has been made to ensure accuracy, the publishers cannot accept responsibility for any errors that this guide may contain.

Venues are marked on the maps using symbols numbered according to their order within the chapter and colour-coded as follows:

❶ Sights & Museums
❶ Eating & Drinking
❶ Shopping
❶ Nightlife
❶ Arts & Leisure

Map Key	
Major sight or landmark	
Hospital or college	
Railway station	
Park	
River	
Freeway	═478═
Main road	
Main road tunnel	
Pedestrian road	
Airport	✈
Church	✚
Subway station	Ⓜ
Area name	SOHO

Time Out **New York** Shortlist 2014

EDITORIAL
Editor Lisa Ritchie
Copy Editor Ros Sales
Listings Editors Julianna Flamio,
  Alex Schechter
Proofreader Marion Moisy

DESIGN
Senior Designer Kei Ishimaru
Designer Darryl Bell
Picture Editor Jael Marschner
Deputy Picture Editor Ben Rowe

ADVERTISING
Sales Director St John Betteridge
Advertising Sales
  Christine Legnaman, Deborah Maclaren

MARKETING
Senior Publishing Brand Manager
  Luthfa Begum
Head of Circulation Dan Collins

PRODUCTION
Production Controller
  Katie Mulhern-Bhudia

CONTRIBUTORS
This guide was researched and written by Adam Feldman, Julianna Flamio, Howard Halle, Sophie Harris, Christina Izzo, Gia Kourlas, Ethan LaCroix, Lee Magill, Amy Plitt, Lisa Ritchie, Jenna Scherer, Steve Smith, Bruce Tantum, Mari Uyehara, Carl Williott, Jennifer M Wood and the writers of *Time Out New York*.

PHOTOGRAPHY
Photography: pages 8 Michael Kirby; 14 Andrey Bayda/Shutterstock.com; 15 Filip Wolak; 16 Benoit Linero; 19 Anna Simonak; 25 Francine Daveta; 27 Sez Devres; 29 Songquan Den/Shutterstock.com; 32 Gary Yim/Shutterstock.com; 34 Virginia Rollison; 37, 41 Lev Radin/Shutterstock.com; 39 Jack Vartoogian/FrontRowPhotos; 40 Jolie Ruben; 42 Andrew F. Kazmierski/Shutterstock.com; 43 Ilenia Martini; 44 Wendy Connett; 47 Robert Polidori for The Skyscraper; 48 Lucian Mortula/Shutterstock.com; 52 Vvoe/Shutterstock.com; 54 Sean Pavone/Shutterstock.com; 61 Lee Magill; 69 (top) 99, 119 Alys Tomlinson; 69 (bottom) Ben Rosenzweig; 76, 109 Caroline Voagen Nelson; 83 Paul Wagtouicz; 87 Duane Park; 97 Loren Wohl; 110, 126, Jessica Lin; 51, 53, 54, 62, 155, Shuterstock.com; 141 Paula Court; 143 Evan Sung; 151 Getty Images; 158, 165, Jolie Ruben; 169, 170 Matthew Williams.

The following images were supplied by the featured establishments: Pages, 9, 50, 66, 131, 166, 177, 180.

Cover photograph: Midtown Manhattan by Ben Leshchinsky.

MAPS
JS Graphics (john@jsgraphics.co.uk).

About **Time Out**

Founded in 1968, Time Out has expanded from humble London beginnings into the leading resource for those wanting to know what's happening in the world's greatest cities. As well as our influential what's-on weeklies in London, New York and Chicago, we publish nearly 30 other listings magazines in cities as varied as Beijing and Mumbai. The magazines established Time Out's trademark style: sharp writing, informed reviewing and bang up-to-date inside knowledge of every scene.

Time Out made the natural leap into travel guides in the 1980s with the City Guide series, which now extends to over 50 destinations around the world. Written and researched by expert local writers and generously illustrated with original photography, the full-size guides cover a larger area than our Shortlist guides and include many more venue reviews, along with additional background features and a full set of maps.

Throughout this rapid growth, the company has remained proudly independent, still owned by Tony Elliott four decades after he started Time Out London as a single fold-out sheet of A5 paper. This independence extends to the editorial content of all our publications, this Shortlist included. No establishment has been featured because it has advertised, and no payment has influenced any of our reviews. And, for our critics, there's definitely no such thing as a free lunch: all restaurants and bars are visited and reviewed anonymously, and Time Out always picks up the bill. For more about the company, see www.timeout.com.

Don't Miss 2014

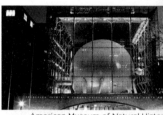

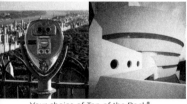

Metropolitan Museum of Art

WHAT'S BEST
Sights & Museums

Most visitors are aware of New York's massive Metropolitan Museum of Art (p137) – at two million square feet, it houses more than that number of objects. But you may not have heard about the city's smallest cultural institution. Launched by a trio of filmmakers, the 60-square-foot cabinet of curiosities known simply as Museum (see box p66) occupies an elevator shaft in Tribeca. In between, there are institutions devoted to just about everything you can think of, from erotica (p107) to the first national Museum of Mathematics (p107). Spring 2014 will see a major debut when the long-anticipated National September 11 Museum opens in the memorial plaza (see box p61).

Another long-term project due to wrap up is the High Line (see p93),

a 1.5-mile defunct elevated train track on the West Side that's being converted into a stylish, slender park. Since the first stretch (from Gansevoort Street in the Meatpacking District to 20th Street in Chelsea) made its debut in 2009, it has joined the ranks of the city's most popular attractions. The second leg, continuing up to 30th Street, opened in spring 2011, and the third and final section, which skirts a rail yard that's being developed into a mixed-use complex, is tipped for completion in 2014.

The elevated park-cum-promenade cuts through the city's prime gallery district, so it's fitting that the Whitney Museum of American Art (p139), which hosts a high-profile biennial of current creative talent, is building its new base alongside it. The Renzo

Piano-designed museum broke ground in 2011 and is expected to open in 2015, with 50,000 square feet of indoor gallery space as well as a rooftop that will be used for exhibitions. Together with the New Museum of Contemporary Art (see p75), a striking off-kilter structure built on the Bowery five years ago, it represents a considerable culture shift downtown.

Although many of the city's venerable institutions have been in place for decades, even the stateliest are moving with the times. Uptown on the Upper West Side, the city's oldest museum, the New-York Historical Society (p146), has embraced the digital age with a high-tech revamp that brings its extraordinary trove of artefacts, art and documents to vivid life. Across the park on Museum Mile, the Cooper-Hewitt, National Design Museum, housed in the elegant Carnegie mansion, will reopen in autumn 2014 after a $64 million renovation and expansion.

Of course, a priority for first-time visitors will be to see some of the world-class collections for which the city is famous. The Metropolitan Museum of Art (p137) is renowned for its European painting and sculpture, Islamic art, Greek and Roman collections and an ever-changing array of blockbuster travelling shows. The Museum of Modern Art (p125) contains some of the most famous artworks of the 19th century to the present; it's also worth checking out its cutting-edge affiliate, MoMA PS1 (p164) in Queens. And in autumn 2013, the borough will debut a major revamp of the Queens Museum (see box p166), which occupies a former World's Fair pavilion and contains the remarkable scale model of the metropolis, the *Panorama of the City of New York.*

DON'T MISS: 2014

SHORTLIST

Best new/revamped
- MoMath (p107)
- Museum (p66)
- National September 11 Memorial & Museum (p60)
- Queens Museum (p167)

Best for local insight
- Lower East Side Tenement Museum (p74)
- Museum of the City of New York (p139)
- New-York Historical Society (p146)

New York icons
- Chrysler Building (p129)
- Empire State Building (p124)
- Statue of Liberty (p63)

Best free
- Brooklyn Bridge (p157)
- Governors Island (p55)
- National Museum of the American Indian (p60)
- National September 11 Memorial & Museum (p60)
- Staten Island Ferry (p63)

Best urban oases
- Central Park (p131)
- The Cloisters (p153)
- High Line (p93)
- New York Botanical Garden (p156)

The 'big three' museums
- American Museum of Natural History (p143)
- Metropolitan Museum of Art (p137)
- Museum of Modern Art (p125)

Best museum buildings
- New Museum of Contemporary Art (p75)
- Solomon R Guggenheim Museum (p139)

BROADWAY'S HIGHEST-FLYING SPECTACULAR!
SPIDER-MAN
TURN OFF THE DARK
Photos by Henry Hargreaves
ONLY ON BROADWAY ONLY IN NEW YORK
TICKETMASTER.COM 877-250-2929
FOXWOODS THEATRE 213 W. 42ND ST. SpiderManOnBroadway.com
*Restrictions and black-out dates may apply.
MARVEL
OFFICIAL AIRLINE
American Airlines

The Guggenheim (p139), in Frank Lloyd Wright's Upper East Side landmark building, is another New York essential. If you want a bit of background, then the Museum of the City of New York (see p139) provides fascinating insight, while the Lower East Side Tenement Museum (see p74) brings New York's immigrant history to life.

It may have been surpassed by 1 World Trade Center in height, but the Empire State Building (p124) is still New York's most famous skyscraper. There can be a long wait to ascend to the observation deck, but the building is now open until 2am and late-night viewings are usually less crowded – and the illuminated cityscape is spectacular. Another option for panoramas is the Top of the Rock observation deck, perched above midtown's Rockefeller Center (p127). The art deco tower gets one up on the Empire State by allowing a view of that iconic structure. And, on the subject of spectacular views, after being closed for nearly a year following 2012's Superstorm Sandy, the interior of the Statue of Liberty (p63), including the crown, reopened to visitors in summer 2013.

Slicing up the Apple

This book is divided by neighbourhood. Downtown is the oldest part of Manhattan and also the most happening. At the tip of the island, the Financial District contains the seat of local government and the epicentre of capitalism. Elsewhere, the character of many downtown neighbourhoods is in a state of continual evolution as the forces of gentrification and fashion take hold. Over the past decade, trendy bars, boutiques and galleries have been moving into erstwhile immigrant neighbourhood the Lower East Side. Former bohemian stomping ground Greenwich Village still resounds with cultural associations, but today is more moneyed and has the restaurants to prove it; to the west, leafy, winding streets give way to the Meatpacking District's warehouses, now colonised by designer stores, eateries and nightspots. The once-radical East Village brims with bars and restaurants. Former art enclave Soho is now a prime shopping and dining destination, along with well-heeled neighbour Tribeca, while Little Italy is being crowded out by ever-expanding Chinatown and, to the north, boutique-studded Nolita.

In midtown, Chelsea contains New York's main contemporary-gallery district. Rivalled only by rapidly gentrifying Hell's Kitchen to the North, it is also one of the city's most prominent gay enclaves. Once mainly commercial, the Flatiron District has evolved into a fine-dining destination and nearby Union Square attracts foodies four days a week to New York's biggest farmers' market. Among the skyscrapers of midtown's prime commercial stretch are some of NYC's most iconic attractions. Here, Fifth Avenue is home to some of the city's poshest retail, while Broadway is the world's most famous theatreland. Love it or loathe it, garish Times Square (p118) is a must-gawp spectacle.

Uptown, bucolic Central Park (p131), with its picturesque lakes, expansive lawns and famous zoo, is the green divider between the patrician Upper East Side and the less conservative but equally well-heeled Upper West Side. Between them, these wealthy locales contain the lion's share of the city's cultural institutions: most museums are on the UES – the Metropolitan Museum of Art and others on Fifth Avenue's Museum Mile, in the stately former mansions of the early 20th-century elite – but the UWS has the Metropolitan Opera, the New York Philharmonic and the New York City Ballet at Lincoln Center (see p149). Further north, regenerated Harlem offers vibrant nightlife, soul food and plenty of cultural history.

Making the most of it

First, accept that you can never see it all. The typical week's visit to the city will involve some tough choices. Similarly, it's self-defeating to attempt to hit all the major collections in one visit to an institution as large as the Met or the American Museum of Natural History. So plan, pace yourself and take time to enjoy aimless wandering in picturesque areas like the West Village or Central Park.

Because the city's museums are privately funded, and receive little or no government support, admission prices can be steep. However, these usually include entry to temporary as well as the permanent collections, and many institutions offer one day or evening a week when admission fees are either waived or switched to a voluntary donation (and remember, 'suggested donation' prices are just that). Be warned that many museums are closed on Mondays – except on some holidays, such as Columbus Day and Presidents' Day.

Despite recent budget cuts, the subway (p184) is still highly efficient and runs 24 hours a day. It is generally well populated, clean and relatively easy to navigate. It will often get you from one end of the city to another more quickly (not to mention more cheaply) than a cab. Charge up a MetroCard and you can travel seamlessly by subway and bus. Of course, you should keep your wits about you and take basic precautions, but New York these days is a pretty safe place. However, the very best way to get to know the city is by walking. Manhattan is a mere 13.4 miles long and 2.3 miles across at its widest point, and once you've mastered the grid, it's easy to find your way (although it gets a little trickier downtown).

National September 11 Memorial p9

Carbone

WHAT'S BEST
Eating & Drinking

In Gotham, where apartments are as tight as sardine cans, restaurants serve as vibrant second living rooms and top chefs are elevated to rock-star status. For visitors, there's no better way to tap into the city's zeitgeist than soaking up the scene at its most beloved culinary destinations. One of the most exciting restaurants to open in recent years comes courtesy of Italian-American food evangelists Rich Torrisi and Mario Carbone, the duo behind lauded tasting-menu spot Torrisi Italian Specialties and its casual follow-up Parm (p73). In early 2013, the pair forged ahead with blockbuster (and wallet-busting) Carbone (p90), a *Godfather* hangout on steroids, with elegant riffs on red-sauce classics and waitstaff nattily outfitted in red velvet tuxes designed by Zac Posen.

Culinary fusion has an obvious appeal in a city that prides itself on being an ethnic melting pot. Korean-American superstar David Chang continues to draw fans to his cadre of buzzy restaurants, including Momofuku Ssäm Bar (p84). But, more recently, a new cast of gastronomic renegades has come to the fore. At Mission Chinese Food (p77), white-hot San Francisco import Daniel Bowien tantalises diners with gutsy, inventive takes on Far East dishes like *kung pao* pastrami at his wildly popular hipster haunt. And restaurateur Ed Schoenfeld and chef Joe Ng bring farm-to-table zeal to the art of dim sum at RedFarm (p95).

Nouveau scene-maker Gabriel Stulman has built a mini empire in a stretch of the West Village affectionately named Little

Wisco (a nod to his home state of Wisconsin). The latest addition to his stable, Montmartre (158 Eighth Avenue, at 18th Street (1-646 596 8838, www.montmartrenyc.com), expands his holdings to Chelsea, with creative Asian-accented French fare from longtime David Chang lieutenant Tien Ho.

New Yorkers love Italian food, whether eaten in humble pizzerias or Michelin-starred white-tablecloth gems. Even in a crowded market, Michael White stands above the fray. Over the past few years he's criss-crossed Gotham, erecting standard-bearing beacons of Italian cuisine, including gleaming seafood temple Marea (p128) on Central Park South and the raucous Bolognese trattoria Osteria Morini (p68).

There was a time, in the early 20th century, when grand hotels were the place to find the best restaurants in New York. You'll find a return to form at the NoMad (p112), an opulent throwback from chef Daniel Humm and Will Guidara of Eleven Madison Park (p111) renown. No meal is complete without the show-stopping chicken for two – amber-hued, with foie gras, brioche and black truffle stuffing under its skin. Boutique hotels – and their restaurants – have also arrived in Williamsburg, where Andrew Tarlow, empire builder behind fan favourites Diner and Marlow & Sons (p160), debuted seasonal brasserie Reynard in the Wythe Hotel (p182), and haute technician Paul Liebrandt (of the acclaimed fine-dining affair Corton, p67) turned to more casual eats with the Elm at King & Grove (160 North 12th Street, between Bedford Avenue & Berry Street, 1-718 218 1088, www.theelmnyc.com).

The East Village has a knack for sprouting reasonably priced eateries that draw big followings. Tuck into some of the city's best burritos at the Cal-Mex-style Dos Toros (p82) and superlative smoked meats at barbecue booster Mighty Quinn's (p84). The always-packed Japanese transplant Ippudo NY (p82) has long been king of the city's ramen ranks, but at press time Tokyo wunderkind Ivan Orkin was poised to challenge its supremacy with a Lower East Side outpost. The East Village is also the location of Lafayette (380 Lafayette Street, at Great Jones

NoMad

Street (1-212 533 3000), the new French café from Andrew Carmellini of boisterous Italian tavern Locanda Verde in the Greenwich Hotel (p172) and cross-cultural American canteen the Dutch (p67).

While gastronomes take pride in haute cuisine temples like Per Se (p148) and Daniel (p140), you'll find equal devotion to more humble classics. The city's best burger is a source of constant debate, with many critics giving their budget-patty nod to celebrated restaurateur Danny Meyer's Shake Shack chain (p148). The Neapolitan pizza craze has shown no sign of flagging, either, though the latest trend to take hold is the *montanara* – a puffy, golden-crusted pie that's flash-fried before hitting the oven. Find standout examples at Don Antonio by Starita (p120).

New York's farm-to-table movement is perhaps most robust in Brooklyn, where cheaper rents and a DIY spirit have made the borough a refuge for young, risk-taking chefs. The nerve centre of the movement is Roberta's in Bushwick (see p161), which grows some of its own produce, plays host to the Heritage Food Network's sustainable-eats radio station, and recently spun off reservations-only restaurant Blanca, serving chef Carlo Mirarchi's artful tasting menu, in the back garden. In 2012, Andy Ricker turned Red Hook into a Thai food destination with Pok Pok NY (p160), soon to be joined by South-east Asian-style drinkery Whiskey Soda Lounge.

Elsewhere, there are cheek-by-jowl Asian restaurants in Chinatown, while Koreatown, the stretch of West 32nd Street between Fifth Avenue and Broadway, is lined with Korean barbecue joints and other eateries. Further afield, Harlem offers soul food and West African cooking, while the most diverse borough,

SHORTLIST

Best new
- Carbone (p90)
- Chez Sardine (p94)
- Mighty Quinn's (p84)
- Mission Chinese Food (p77)
- Proletariat (p85)

Best cheap eats
- Cafe Edison (p120)
- Dos Toros (p82)
- Pok Pok NY (p160)
- Shake Shack (p148)

Where to blow the budget
- Corton (p67)
- Per Se (p148)
- The NoMad (p112)

The classics
- Bemelmans Bar (p140)
- Grand Central Oyster Bar & Restaurant (p130)
- Katz's Delicatessen (p77)

New twists on NYC faves
- Dominique Ansel Bakery (doughnuts) (p18)
- Don Antonio by Starita (pizza) (p120)
- RedFarm (dim sum) (p95)

Best seasonal fare
- ABC Kitchen (p108)
- Blue Hill (p90)
- Roberta's (p161)

Best for carnivores
- The Breslin Bar & Dining Room (p111)
- BrisketTown (p159)
- The Cannibal (p114)

Best cocktails
- Attaboy (p75)
- Pegu Club (p68)

Best local brews
- Blind Tiger Ale House (p93)
- Jimmy's No 43 (p84)

DON'T MISS: 2014

Queens, counts Greek (in Astoria), Thai (in Elmhurst) and Indian (in Jackson Heights) among its globe-spanning cuisines.

Some of these further-flung locales are now attracting big-name chefs. In 2011, Quebecois toque Hugue Dufour put Queens on the food map with his snout-to-tail cooking at the short-lived M Wells, which he followed up with M Wells Dinette at MoMA PS1 (p168), plus a steakhouse-cum-boathouse, which should be open by the time you read this.

Veg out

In spite of the city's obsession with locally sourced produce, new vegetarian restaurants are few and far between. Dirt Candy (p82), from talented chef Amanda Cohen, serves sometimes sinful, always sophisticated meat-free eats, while Kajitsu (p115) draws reverent devotees for shojin cuisine, a type of hyperseasonal vegan cooking that originated in Zen Buddhism.

Sweet spots

If something sweet is what you're after, look no further than Soho's Dominique Ansel Bakery (189 Spring Street, between Sullivan & Thompson Streets, 1-212 219 2773, www.dominiqueansel.com), which launched international phenom the Cronut, a doughnut-croissant hybrid. At another cultishly beloved bakeshop, Momofuku Milk Bar (p84), which has several locations in the city, you can sate your sweet tooth with Christina Tosi's madcap creations, such as Cereal Milk soft-serve ice-cream and the addictively creamy Crack Pie.

The big tipple

New York continues to be a cradle of cocktail culture. Standard bearers like Audrey Saunders' renowned Pegu Club (p68) still offer fine drinks, but new life is brought to the scene by newcomers, including Attaboy (p75), a sultry den in the former Milk and Honey space from two of its longtime bartenders, and the Dead Rabbit (p64), a Financial District barroom with a sprawling historical menu. Thoughtful drinking also thrives in Brooklyn, most notably in Williamsburg at spots such as Maison Premiere (p160) – a throwback New Orleans-Style *boîte* specialising in absinthe-based tipples.

The craft-beer revolution that's swept the country has a firm foothold in NYC, too. Scrappy producers like Sixpoint and Barrier Brewing Co have brought attention to the local brewing scene. The most dependable spots to sample the local offerings are hops-head havens like Jimmy's No 43 (p84) and Blind Tiger Ale House (p93), while the pint-size den Proletariat (p85) offers an intimate beer-geek experience.

While wine doesn't drive the boozing scene like cocktails and beer, a new breed of vino bars is tossing out the pretence and putting an emphasis on well-chosen but affordable lists. The poster child of this movement is Terroir (p85), which recently opened its fourth location in Park Slope, Brooklyn, after conquering the East Village, Tribeca and Murray Hill.

Where there's smoke...

The only legal places to smoke indoors are venues that cater largely to cigar smokers (and sell tobacco products) and those that have created areas for smokers. Try Circa Tabac (32 Watts Street, between Sixth Avenue & Thompson Street, Soho, 1-212 941 1781) or Hudson Bar & Books (636 Hudson Street, at Horatio Street, 1-212 229 2642).

Fine and Dandy

WHAT'S BEST
Shopping

One of the best cities in the world to drop some of your hard-earned cash, New York offers anything you could possibly want to buy, and – as long as you're prepared to shop around or hit some sample sales – at the best prices. Locals may complain about the 'mallification' of certain neighbourhoods such as Soho, but for visitors (and, if they're honest, many New Yorkers), these retail-rich areas are intoxicating consumer playgrounds. As America's fashion capital, and the site of the prestigious Fashion Institute of Technology and other high-profile art colleges, the metropolis is a magnet for creative young designers from around the country. This ensures that the shops and markets are stuffed with unique finds, and it also

means that the Garment District is a hotbed of open-to-the-public showroom sales (p23).

While the recession hit the retail sector hard, it has been a boon for bargain-hunters. Shopkeepers have become more creative in order to survive, launching pop-up shops that in some cases take root in permanent digs, such as new Hell's Kitchen men's accessories trove Fine and Dandy (p121). Others hedge their bets with mixed-use businesses, such as the Dressing Room (p78), which combines a bar and a boutique. Increasingly, small shops are selling a combination of goods, and the vintage trend, appealing to the environmentally aware and budget-conscious alike, is stronger than ever. In indie-music hub Williamsburg, Brooklyn, Tiger Blanket Records & Vintage

Boutique (p162) is a hybrid venture launched by a fashion-loving singer-songwriter.

Retail hotspots

Although many of the city's retail-rich districts are within walking distance of one another, and you can zip quickly between others on the subway, because of the dense concentration of shops in some areas (for example, the Lower East Side or Madison Avenue), you might want to limit yourself to a couple of areas in a day out. Generally speaking, you'll find the most unusual shops downtown and in parts of Brooklyn.

Although Soho has been heavily commercialised, especially the main thoroughfares, this once edgy, arty enclave still has some idiosyncratic survivors and numerous top-notch shops – don't miss tucked-away design store Kiosk (p70). Urban fashion abounds on Lafayette Street, while Broome Street is becoming an enclave for chic home design. To the east, Nolita has been colonised by indie designers, especially along Mott and Mulberry Streets.

Once the centre of the 'rag' trade, the Lower East Side used to be associated with bargain outlets and bagels. Now a bar- and boutique-laden patch, it's especially good for vintage, streetwear and local designers, such as secretive sneaker store Alife Rivington Club (p77) and Chuck Guarino's rockin' clothing label the Cast (p77). Orchard, Ludlow and Rivington Streets are hotspots. North of here, in the East Village, you'll find a highly browsable mix of vintage clothing, streetwear and records alongside stylish home and kids' goods, but shops are more scattered than on the Lower East Side.

Over on the other side of the island, the one-time down-at-heel wholesale meat market, stretching

S H O R T L I S T

Best new
- Fine and Dandy (p121)
- Owen (p96)
- Tiger Blanket Records & Vintage Boutique (p162)
- Warm (p74)

Best vintage and antiques
- Doyle & Doyle (p78)
- Mantiques Modern (p105)
- What Goes Around Comes Around (p70)

Best for bargains
- Century 21 (p65)
- Loehmann's (p105)

Taste of New York
- Russ & Daughters (p79)
- Smorgasburg (p40)
- Zabar's (p149)

Best books and music
- Downtown Music Gallery (p73)
- Other Music (p88)
- Strand Book Store (p88)

Local lines
- The Cast (p77)
- Erica Weiner (p73)
- In God We Trust (p70)
- Obsessive Compulsive Cosmetics (p78)

Best for gifts
- Bond Street Chocolate (p86)
- By Brooklyn (p161)
- Kiosk (p70)
- Magpie (p148)

Best home goods
- ABC Carpet & Home (p112)
- The Future Perfect (p86)
- Modern Anthology (p162)

Best for designer labels
- Barneys New York (p142)
- Fivestory (p143)
- Opening Ceremony (p70)

south from 14th Street, has become a high-end consumer playground; the warehouses of the Meatpacking District are now populated by a clutch of upscale stores, including newcomer Owen (p96), which was launched by a FIT graduate and showcases both established and emerging labels. Meanwhile, the western strip of Bleecker Street is lined with a further cache of designer boutiques.

Most of the city's department stores can be found on Fifth Avenue between 38th and 59th Streets, in the company of chain stores and designer flagships (the parade of lofty names continues east on 57th Street). The exceptions are Macy's, in Herald Square, and Bloomingdale's and Barneys, which are both on the Upper East Side. The Uptown stretch of Madison Avenue has long been synonymous with the crème de la crème of international fashion.

It's also well worth venturing across the East River. Williamsburg abounds with idiosyncratic shops and one-off buys. As well as the main drag, Bedford Avenue, North 6th and Grand Streets are good hunting grounds for vintage clothes, arty housewares and record stores. There are further treasures in Cobble Hill, Carroll Gardens and Boerum Hill, especially on Court and Smith Streets and Atlantic Avenue; the latter has been known mainly for antiques, but cool clothiers have started to move in.

Keep it local

Of course, many of the country's most popular designers are based in New York, from established names like Diane von Furstenberg and Marc Jacobs to newer contemporary stars such as Phillip Lim, Thakoon Panichgul, and Marcus Wainwright and David Neville of Rag & Bone (p96). Made-in-NYC items –

jewellery by Erica Weiner (p73), make-up from Obsessive Compulsive Cosmetics (p78), accessories from In God We Trust (p70) or cards printed at Bowne & Co Stationers (p65) – are chic souvenirs. Stores that stock local designs among their wares include Castor & Pollux (p96), Honey in the Rough (p78), Opening Ceremony (p70) and The Future perfect (p86) for interior items. There are also opportunities to buy goods direct from emerging designers at popular weekend markets such as the Brooklyn Flea (see box p40).

Famous names

Of course, many visitors to New York will simply be looking to make the most of the incredible variety of big brands on offer in the city. For young, casual and streetwear labels, head to Broadway in Soho. Fifth Avenue heaves with a mix of designer showcases and mall-level megastores. Madison Avenue is more consistently posh, with a further line-up of deluxe labels.

If you prefer to do all your shopping under one roof, famous department stores Macy's (good for mid-range brands), Bloomingdale's (a mix of mid-range and designer), Barneys (cutting-edge and high-fashion) and Bergdorf Goodman (luxury goods and international designer) are all stuffed with desirable items.

Sniffing out sales

New York is fertile bargain-hunting territory. The traditional post-season sales (which usually start just after Christmas and in early to mid June) have given way to frequent markdowns throughout the year: look for sale racks in boutiques, chain and department stores. The twice-a-year warehouse sale held by Barneys New York (p142) has long been an important fixture on the bargain hound's calendar, but as this guide went to press it was uncertain whether the event would continue in 2014 – the designer department store now operates a year-round online sale at www.barneyswarehouse.com.

Of course, as New York is home to numerous designer studios and showrooms, there is a weekly spate of sample sales. The best are listed in the Shopping & Style section of *Time Out New York* magazine and www.timeout.com/newyork. Other terrific resources are Racked (www.ny.racked.com), Top Button (www.topbutton.com) and Clothing Line (1-212 947 8748, www.clothing line.com), which holds sales for a variety of labels – from J Crew and Theory to Helmut Lang and Rag & Bone, at its Garment District showroom (Second Floor, 261 W 36th Street, between Seventh & Eighth Avenues).

Chief among the permanent sale stores is the famous Century 21 (p65) – it's beloved by rummagers, but detested by those with little patience for sifting through less than fabulous merchandise for the prize finds. A second Manhattan location opened on the Upper West Side in 2011, but we recommend braving the original for breadth of stock and, sometimes, deeper discounts. Loehmann's (see p105) can also come up trumps. Union Square's Nordstrom Rack (60 E 14th Street, between Broadway & Fourth Avenue, 1-212 220 2080, www.nordstromrack.com), the discount arm of the department store, is worth checking out too.

Have a rummage

Flea market browsing is a popular weekend pastime among New Yorkers. Chelsea's Annex Antiques Fair & Flea Market may be consigned to history, but the area retains the covered market Antiques Garage (p104), although there have been longstanding rumours it might relocate; it has a sibling outdoor market in Hell's Kitchen. There are also some worthwhile antiques stores in the neighbourhood, including the wonderfully eclectic Mantiques Modern (p105). Make the pilgrimage to one of the deservedly popular Brooklyn Fleas (see box p40) to browse everything from vintage jewellery and crafts to salvage and locally made foodstuffs. For fine antiques, with prices to match, head for Madison Avenue in the 60s and 70s.

Consumer culture

Chain retailer Barnes & Noble (www.barnesandnoble.com) still dominates the book scene, but well-loved independents, such as the Strand Book Store (p88), home to 18 miles of books, have been holding their own for years. Housing Works Bookstore Café (p70) doubles as a popular Soho hangout. For art books, as well as cool souvenirs, don't forget museum shops – MoMA Design & Book Store, attached to the Museum of Modern Art (p125) and the New Museum of Contemporary Art store (p75) are both excellent.

When Other Music (p88) opened opposite Tower Records in the East Village in the mid 1990s, it boldly stood as a small pocket of resistance to corporate music. Its Goliath now shuttered, Other Music rolls on, offering a well-curated selection of indie-rock, world music and experimental sounds. Tucked away in a Chinatown basement, the Downtown Music Gallery (p73) is an essential stop for seekers of avant-garde jazz and new classical.

Slipper Room p26

WHAT'S BEST
Nightlife

The discotheque may have had its origins in occupied Paris during World War II – apparently, the Nazis weren't too keen on jazz, dancing and high times, driving such pursuits underground – but it was in New York City that the modern concept of clubbing came into being. Hallowed halls such as the Loft, Studio 54, the Paradise Garage and Area are imbedded in nightlife's collective consciousness as near-mythic ideals. But in this millennium? Well, the city can no longer claim to be the world's clubbing capital; the balance of power has shifted eastward to cities like London and Berlin. Still, with this much history (not to mention eight million people ready to party), New York nightlife can never be counted out – and the scene today is as strong as it's been in years.

This is largely thanks to a burst of roving shindigs, often held in out-of-the-way warehouses and lofts. Some of the best – particularly if you're a fan of underground house, techno or bass music – are run by the teams at Blkmarket Membership (www.blkmarketmembership.com), ReSolute (www.resolutenyc.com), Rinsed (rinsed.it) and Mister Saturday Night (www.mister saturdaynight.com); a visit to www.timeout.com/newyork should help to clue you in.

Don't rule out the clubs themselves, though, as there are still plenty of fabulous DJs playing music of all persuasions. Cielo (see p96), an intimate and beautiful Meatpacking District venue, boasts underground jocks playing over one of the city's best sound systems. At the other end of the spectrum,

Pacha (p122) is the club of choice for followers of big-name superstars, with the likes of Axwell, Afrojack and Fedde Le Grand regularly presiding over the dancefloor. Brooklyn's new Output (p162) attracts the underground scene's best jocks to play outer-limits house, techno and bass music over its monster of a sound system. Santos Party House (p71) is another good bet, particularly when Danny Krivit takes the spot over for the soulful house and classics-oriented 718 Sessions (www.dannykrivit.net).

Some of the city's best parties take place only occasionally or are seasonal. Warm Up, a summertime soirée held every Saturday during July and August in the courtyard at MoMA PS1 in Queens (see p164), attracts kids who like to boogie down to some pretty twisted DJs and bands. The (usually) monthly Bunker bash, one of New York's top techno get-togethers, has been nomadic of late, but you can follow the party at www.beyondbooking. com/thebunker. Likewise, the house-music-loving Verboten crew tosses top-shelf, one-off affairs all over the city (www.verbotennewyork.com). And, of course, there's the Sunday-night tea dance Body & Soul (www. bodyandsoul-nyc.com), helmed by the DJ holy trinity of Danny Krivit, Joe Claussell and François K. The formerly weekly affair now pops up only a few times each year – but it's still a spectacle, with a few thousand sweaty revellers dancing their hearts out from start till finish.

For those who like a bit of bump-and-grind in their after-dark activities, the city's burlesque scene is as strong as it's ever been. Some of the best producers and performers – they often cross over – are Doc Wasabassco (www.wasabassco.com), Shien Lee (www.dancesofvice.com), Jen Gapay's Thirsty Girl Productions

(www.thirstygirlproductions.com),
Angie Pontani of the World Famous
Pontani Sisters (www.angiepontani.
com) and Calamity Chang, 'the Asian
Sexation'(www.calamitychang.com).
After a two-year absence from
the scene, Gotham's burly-Q
headquarters, the Slipper Room
(p79) has returned with a spiffed-
up space on the Lower East Side.

Live action

New York is among the greatest
cities in the world in which to see
live music. Manhattan and Brooklyn
are packed with venues, from hole-
in-the-wall dives to resplendent
concert halls. Plan accordingly and
you can catch more than one world-
class show on any given night.

For larger seated shows, try
the posh theatres in midtown and
further north. The palatial art deco
Radio City Music Hall (p128) gives
grandeur to pop performances, while
Harlem's Apollo Theater (p154) still
hosts its legendary Amateur Night
competition. In addition to classical
performances, Carnegie Hall (p123)
hosts jazz mavericks like Keith
Jarrett, and Jazz at Lincoln Center's
Allen Room (p149) has a million-
dollar view that threatens to
upstage even the good shows.

Some of music's biggest acts –
Jay-Z, Lady Gaga, Rod Stewart
– play at Madison Square Garden
(p117), which wraps up its facelift
around the time of publication of this
guide. After 45 years, Manhattan's
legendary music and sports hub has
got some serious competition – from
a Brooklyn contender. The Barclays
Center (p163) opened its doors in
autumn 2012, and its debut could not
have been more dazzling. Jay-Z (who
has a share in the venue's basketball
team) played an unprecedented
week-long run and native daughter
Barbra Streisand performed two
sold-out concerts.

The rock scene's heart is in
downtown Manhattan and Brooklyn.
The clubs dotting the East Village
and Lower East Side are too many
to count, but don't miss the Mercury
Lounge (p79), the no-nonsense spot
that launched the career of the
Strokes, among others. Joe's Pub
(p88), the classy cabaret room tucked
inside the Public Theater, continues
to present great acts of all genres.
For medium-size acts, the Bowery
Ballroom (p79) is Manhattan's hub,
while its sister venue in Brooklyn,
Music Hall of Williamsburg (p162),
hosts bands such as Sonic Youth
and Hot Chip, often on the day after
they've played Bowery Ballroom.

Williamsburg is an essential stop
for indie-rock aficionados. Former
downtown Manhattan incubator of
experimental music Knitting Factory
moved its New York base here (361
Metropolitan Avenue, at Havemeyer
Street, 1-347 529 6696, www.knitting
factory.com) a few years ago. These
days, it's a well-managed club, with
solid indie and hip hop bills (Zola
Jesus, Black Milk) designed to suit
its hipster clientele. In addition, cute
local spot Pete's Candy Store (p163)
offers everything from whimsical
folk music to poetry readings.

Working the room

Few cities in the world, if any,
offer a cabaret scene as varied
as New York's. The genre offers
a confluence of opposites: the
heights of polish and the depths
of amateurism; intense honesty and
airy pretence; earnestness and camp.
At its best, it can provide a uniquely
intimate experience of musical
communication. For a classic, high-
end New York cabaret experience,
visit the speakeasy-style 54 Below
(p121), whose line-up of performers
leans towards A-list Broadway
stars, or the elegant but pricey Café
Carlyle in the plush Upper East Side

hotel (35 E 76th Street, at Madison Avenue, 1-212 744 1600, www.the carlyle.com); the Flatiron District venue Metropolitan Room (p113) is easier on the wallet. In recent years, an edgier alt-cabaret scene – with a more subversive style – has sprouted up in spots like Joe's Pub and the newly renovated Cutting Room (44 E 32nd Street, between Madison Avenue & Park Avenue South, 1-212 691 1900, www.thecuttingroomnyc.com).

If it's laughs you're after, the city's myriad comedy clubs serve both as platforms for big names and as launchpads for stars of tomorrow. The looming presence of TV sketch giant *Saturday Night Live*, which has been filmed at Rockefeller Center since 1975, helps to ensure the continued presence of theatrical comedy; more influential in the day-to-day landscape, however, is the improv and sketch troupe Upright Citizens Brigade. Its theatre (p106) has been the most visible catalyst in New York's current alternative comedy boom, and it expanded with a second space in the East Village in 2011. The Comedy Cellar (p92), another popular venue, spread out with a spin-off space nearby in summer 2013.

Out and about

Offering much more than drag and piano bars (though, delightfully, they still thrive), today's LGBT New York has popular venues devoted to rock and country music and an abundance of arty, pan-queer parties and events (you'll find the best at www.timeout.com/newyork). Each June, NYC Pride brings a whirl of parties and performances. The weekend-capping event, the NYC LGBT Pride March (p38), draws millions of spectators and participants. Other annual events include the notorious Black Party (March) and the Folsom Street East leather-and-fetish street fair (June).

Brooklyn – Williamsburg, in particular – is a home base for many young queers, resulting in a thriving scene outside the traditional Manhattan strongholds of the Village, Chelsea and the current It neighbourhood of Hell's Kitchen. The latter is the location of New York's first gay luxury hotel, the Out NYC (p179), which contains XL Nightclub – one of surprisingly few all-gay megaclubs in the city.

Warm Up p25

Bags packed, milk cancelled, house raised on stilts.

You've packed the suntan lotion, the snorkel set, the stay-pressed shirts. Just one more thing left to do – your bit for climate change. In some of the world's poorest countries, changing weather patterns are destroying lives.

You can help people to deal with the extreme effects of climate change. Raising houses in flood-prone regions is just one life-saving solution.

Climate change costs lives.
Give £5 and let's sort it *Here & Now*

www.oxfam.org.uk/climate-change

Be Humankind Oxfam

Broadway

WHAT'S BEST
Arts & Leisure

Given the impressive sweep of
New York's cultural life, it's easy
to be overwhelmed by the number
of events on offer. From enormous
stadia to tiny Off Broadway stages,
from revival cinemas to avant-
garde dance venues, the choices
are endless. With a little planning,
however, you can take in that game,
concert or show that will make
your visit more memorable. Consult
Time Out New York magazine or
www.timeout.com/newyork for
the latest listings.

Classical music & opera

In recent years, the primary story
of New York's classical music
scene has been the advent of
musical entrepreneurs such as
the International Contemporary
Ensemble (ICE), New Amsterdam

Records and Gotham Chamber
Opera, among others. Nowadays,
the real action is in watching how
mainstay institutions have adapted –
and in some ways adopted – lessons
taught by those grassroots upstarts.

Lincoln Center (p149), for
example, has been enriched
and enlivened with the kind of
ground-breaking, genre-flouting
programming that was once the
exclusive province of fledgling
institutions – not least the White
Light Festival, an ongoing autumn
exploration of spiritual dimensions
in art. At the Metropolitan Opera,
fresh productions and up-to-date
technologies continue to lure
newcomers while also giving longtime admirers fresh notions to
mull over. And the esteemed
New York Philharmonic, based
in Avery Fisher Hall, continues

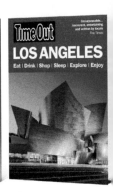

its steady march forward under the leadership of music director Alan Gilbert, with the orchestra's inaugural NY Phil Biennial taking place in May and June 2014.

The venerable Carnegie Hall (p123) continues to live up to its legendary status as the world's most prestigious concert hall. The Brooklyn Academy of Music (p163) is another invaluable player, hosting the perennially popular multidiscipline Next Wave Festival (p41), which includes a season-launching premiere from the New York City Opera – the local company continues to reassert its inventiveness under the leadership of general manager George Steel.

To catch the latest musical innovators in their native habitats, though, head to chic Greenwich Village nightclub Le Poisson Rouge (p92) or downtown Brooklyn's twin bastions of experimental music, Roulette (509 Atlantic Avenue, at Third Avenue, 1-917 267 0363, www.roulette.org) and Issue Project Room (22 Boerum Place, between Livingston & Schermerhorn Streets, 1-718 330 0313, www.issueprojectroom.org). In the second half of 2014, the organisation plans to renovate its 1926 theatre for a grand opening in 2015, but will continue to stage performances at other venues during closures. All three are playing a critical role in bringing classical music and opera to wider, hipper audiences.

Dance

With its uptown and downtown divide, New York dance includes both luminous tradition and daring experimentation. For classical dance, Lincoln Center is home to both the New York City Ballet and American Ballet Theatre. NYCB is known for staging works by George Balanchine and Jerome Robbins,

DON'T MISS: 2014

SHORTLIST

Best new/revamped
- Barclays Center (p163)
- BAM Richard B Fisher Building (p152)
- Madison Square Garden (p117)

Most experimental
- Anthology Film Archives (p89)
- The Kitchen (p106)

Best for unwinding
- Great Jones Spa (p89)
- Juvenex (p117)

Best for cinephiles
- Film Forum (p98)
- Film Society of Lincoln Center (p152)

Best long-running shows
- Book of Mormon (p123)
- Once (p123)
- Sleep No More (p107)

Best Off Broadway
- New York Theatre Workshop (p89)
- Playwrights Horizons (p124)
- Public Theater (p89)

Best free outdoor arts
- River to River Festival (p38)
- Shakespeare in the Park (p37)
- SummerStage (p37)

Essential high culture
- Carnegie Hall (p123)
- Metropolitan Opera House (p150)
- New York City Center (p123)

Best cheap tickets
- Lincoln Center Theater's Claire Tow Theater (p152)
- Soho Rep (p71)
- TKTS (p120)

Yankee Stadium

but in the 2013-14 season look out for premieres by French artistic director Angelin Preljocaj and young British choreographer Liam Scarlett as well as Justin Peck, a soloist in the company whose choreographic star is on the rise. ABT is the spot for story ballets, international guest artists and, if you're lucky, a new piece by the extraordinary Russian choreographer Alexei Ratmansky, who is also the company's artist in residence. His *Nutcracker* is unveiled each holiday season at the Brooklyn Academy of Music (p163).

While Lincoln Center's David H Koch Theater is officially NYCB's home, during its off seasons it hosts other big-name dance companies too, including the San Francisco Ballet in autumn 2013. Spring 2014 marks the return of the Paul Taylor Dance Company. And the Alvin Ailey American Dance Theater, which has been infused with new life by Robert Battle, is in residence at New York City Center (p123) each December.

Yet there's a world beyond traditional modern dance. Throughout New York, but especially in parts of Brooklyn and Queens, choreographers are intent on exploring the more complex notions of performance and the body; the internationally admired laboratory Movement Research (www.movementresearch.org) is devoted to the investigation of dance and movement-based forms and showcases works-in-progress at Greenwich Village's historic Judson Church. The art-world's continuing obsession with dance is reflected in programming at the Museum of Modern Art (p125) and the Whitney Museum of American Art (p139), where, in spring 2014, Sarah Michelson – winner of the 2012 Whitney Biennial's Bucksbaum Award – will premiere a new piece.

Film

Every corner of NYC has been immortalised in celluloid, so it's not surprising that the city has a special relationship with the movies. The calendar is packed with festivals, including Tribeca (p36), the New York Film Festival and several others organised by the excellent Film Society of Lincoln Center (p152), which a few years ago opened its new Elinor Bunin Monroe Film Center. Summer brings the great tradition of free outdoor screenings in midtown's Bryant Park and other green spaces (see box p39).

Cinephiles love Film Forum (p98) for its wide range of revivals and new indie features, while Anthology Film Archives (p89) specialises in experimental programming.

Sports

The professional sports scene has been marked by an edifice complex in the past few years, as several teams have built brand-new stadia. First it was baseball's turn with the 2009 openings of Citi Field in Queens and Yankee Stadium in the Bronx, the respective homes of the hapless Mets (newyork.mets. mlb.com) and the mighty Yankees (newyork.yankees.mlb.com).

Next came American fotball, when the Giants and Jets kicked off their 2010 seasons in the MetLife Stadium (www.metlifestadium.com) across the river in New Jersey.

Now Madison Square Garden (p117), home to basketball's Knicks and hockey's Rangers, is wrapping up a multi-million-dollar rolling revamp, and the new Barclays Center (p163) in Brooklyn welcomed basketball's Nets in autumn 2012.

Theatre

Broadway theatre is one of New York's crowning attractions. The oldest venues, such as the New Amsterdam and the Belasco, date back to the early 20th century, and unique architectural features enhance the experience.

Musicals continue to exert the strongest drawing power. Every season brings new spectacles to satisfy a wide range of tastes, from the outrageously funny *The Book of Mormon* to the bittersweet *Once*. Many new musicals slated for 2013-14 are adapted from well-known films, including *Rocky*, *Aladdin* and *The Bridges of Madison County*. Keep an eye out, too, for revivals of popular shows, such as the return of *Les Misérables* in spring 2014.

Straight plays tend to have shorter runs but can generate considerable excitement, especially when they include big stars. And serious theatre fans will want to visit the more intimate world of Off Broadway. You don't have to leave midtown to find Playwrights Horizons (p124) or the Pershing Square Signature Center, a new complex designed by Frank Gehry.

You can also find strong Off Broadway work at East Village institutions like New York Theatre Workshop (p89) and the Public Theater (p89), which mounts two free Shakespeare in the Park (p37) shows each summer. Brooklyn Academy of Music stages first-rate productions from around the world at its Harvey Theater (p163). In autumn 2013, Theatre for a New Audience (www.tfana. org) is opening its own new Brooklyn headquarters nearby with a production of Shakespeare's *A Midsummer Night's Dream*, directed by Julie Taymor, known for Broadway musicals *The Lion King* and *Spider-Man: Turn Off the Dark*.

It can be tough to score tickets for some of the more popular shows, so check www.theatermania.com and www.playbill.com for advance information. Nearly all Broadway and Off Broadway shows are served by big ticketing agencies, but for cheap seats to shows that aren't sold out, your best bet is the beloved TKTS Discount Booth (p120).

For theatre that is edgier and more adventurous – and less expensive – explore the Off-Off Broadway scene downtown and in Brooklyn, where the experimental impulse is alive and well, with troupes such as Elevator Repair Service (www.elevator.org), Radiohole (www.radiohole.com) and the Civilians (www.thecivilians.org), and venues like Soho Rep (p71).

DON'T MISS: 2014

WHAT'S ON
Calendar

Macy's Thanksgiving Day Parade

The following is our selection of annual events, plus the best one-offs confirmed when this guide went to press. For the latest information, check the listings in *Time Out New York* magazine or www.timeout.com/newyork, and always confirm dates before making any travel plans. Dates in **bold** indicate public holidays.

October 2013

Ongoing Next Wave Festival
(see Sept 2014)

11 Oct-23 Feb
The Armory Show at 100
New-York Historical Society, p146
www.nyhistory.org
Works by Duchamp, Picasso, et al are on display to commemorate the landmark modern art exhibition.

12, 13 **Open House New York**
Various locations
www.ohny.org
Architectural sites that are normally off-limits open their doors to the public.

14 Columbus Day

17-20 **New York City Wine & Food Festival**
Various locations
www.nycwff.org
Four belt-busting days of tasting events and celebrity-chef demos.

21 Oct-14 Nov **Two Boys**
The Metropolitan Opera, Lincoln Center, p150
www.metoperafamily.org
The US premiere of Nico Muhly's opera set in the internet age.

15-19 **CMJ Music Marathon & Film Festival**
Various locations
www.cmj.com
Showcase for new musical acts.

25, 26 **Manhattan Vintage Clothing Show**
Metropolitan Pavilion, Chelsea
www.manhattanvintage.com
Around 90 exhibitors sell all kinds of vintage garb dating from the 1800s through to the 1980s.

31 Village Halloween Parade
Sixth Avenue, from Spring to
16th Streets
www.halloween-nyc.com
An out-of-this-world costume display.

November 2013

Ongoing Next Wave Festival (see
Sept 2014); the Armory Show at
100 (see Oct); Two Boys (see Oct)

3 ING New York City Marathon
Various locations
www.ingnycmarathon.org
Starting on Staten Island, the runners
hotfoot it through all five boroughs, fin-
ishing in Central Park.

6-10 New York Comedy Festival
Various locations
www.nycomedyfestival.com
Presented in association with Comedy
Central, this five-day laugh fest fea-
tures big names and up-and-comers.

**8 Nov-30 Dec Radio City
Christmas Spectacular**
Radio City Music Hall, p128
www.radiocity.com
Precision dance troupe the Rockettes
star in this annual festive show.

11 Veterans' Day

28 Thanksgiving Day

**28 Macy's Thanksgiving
Day Parade**
Central Park West, at 77th Street,
to Broadway, at 34th Street
www.macys.com/parade
Gigantic balloons and elaborate floats
star in this annual parade.

December 2013

Ongoing Next Wave Festival (see
Sept 2014); The Armory Show at
100 (see Oct); Radio City Christmas
Spectacular (see Nov)

4 Rockefeller Center Tree-Lighting
Rockefeller Center, p127
www.rockefellercenter.com
The giant evergreen is illuminated
following a star-studded line-up.

19 Beyoncé
Barclays Center, p163
Queen B holds court in Brooklyn.

25 Christmas Day

31 Emerald Nuts Midnight Run
Naumburg Bandshell, middle of
Central Park
www.nyrr.org
A new year jog through Central Park.

**31 New Year's Eve
in Times Square**
Times Square, p118
www.timessquarenyc.org
Catch celeb performances and see the
giant illuminated ball drop at midnight.

January 2014

Ongoing The Armory Show at 100
(see Oct)

1 New Year's Day

**1 New Year's Day Marathon
Benefit Reading**
Poetry Project, St Mark's Church-in-
the-Bowery, East Village
www.poetryproject.org
Big-name bohos step up to the mic
in this spoken-word event.

7 Jan-9 Feb King Lear
BAM Harvey Theater, p163
www.bam.org
Frank Langella stars in a new production of the Shakespeare play.

**17, 18 Manhattan Vintage
Clothing Show**
Metropolitan Pavilion, Chelsea
www.manhattanvintage.com
See above Oct 2013.

20 Martin Luther King, Jr Day

late Jan-early Feb
Winter Restaurant Week
Various locations
www.nycgo.com/restaurantweek

Sample special set menus at top restaurants at highly palatable prices.

31 Jan, 2 Feb **Chinese New Year**
Around Mott Street, Chinatown
www.betterchinatown.com
The firecracker ceremony (31 Jan) and parade (2 Feb) are key events.

February 2014

Ongoing The Armory Show at 100 (see Oct); Chinese New Year (see Jan); King Lear (see Jan); Winter Restaurant Week (see Jan)

12 Presidents' Day

21 Feb-16 Mar
Vienna: City of Dreams
Various venues
www.carnegiehall.org
Carnegie Hall leads a citywide festival featuring the Vienna Philharmonic Orchestra and Vienna State Opera.

March 2014

Ongoing Vienna: City of Dreams (see Feb)

Mar-June **Whitney Biennial**
Whitney Museum of American Art, p139
www.whitney.org
See box p141.

6-9 **Armory Show**
Piers 92 & 94, Hell's Kitchen
www.thearmoryshow.com
A huge contemporary art mart.

17 **St Patrick's Day Parade**
Fifth Avenue, from 44th to 86th Streets
www.nycstpatricksparade.org
March of green-clad merrymakers.

18 Mar-13 Oct **Inspired**
Museum of Arts & Design, p145
www.madmuseum.org
The museum celebrates five years in its Columbus Circle digs with this show illuminating the creative process.

April 2014

Ongoing Whitney Biennial (see Mar); Inspired (see Mar)

18 Apr-10 Aug **Ai Weiwei: According to What?**
Brooklyn Museum, p157
www.brooklynmuseum.org
This touring exhibition is the first US survey of the Chinese artist-activist.

20 **Easter Parade**
Fifth Avenue, from 49th to 57th Streets
Admire myriad creative Easter bonnets.

26, 27 **Sakura Matsuri (Cherry Blossom Festival)**
Brooklyn Botanic Garden, p156
www.bbg.org
The climax to the cherry blossom season celebrates Japanese culture with a weekend of events, such as concerts, dance and tea ceremonies.

late Apr **Tribeca Film Festival**
Various locations
www.tribecafilm.com/festival
Robert De Niro's two-week downtown showcase of indie flicks.

May 2014

Ongoing Whitney Biennial (see Mar); Inspired (see Mar); Ai Weiwei: According to What? (see Apr)

4 **TD Five Boro Bike Tour**
Battery Park to Staten Island
www.bikenewyork.org
A 42-mile Tour de New York.

9-12 **Frieze Art Fair New York**
Randalls Island Park
www.friezenewyork.com
This superfair features more than 180 international galleries.

24-26, 31, 1 June **Washington Square Outdoor Art Exhibit**
Greenwich Village
www.washingtonsquareoutdoorart exhibit.org
See art in streets around the park.

Tribeca Film Festival

26 Memorial Day

late May Lower East Side Festival of the Arts
Theater for the New City, 155 First Avenue, between 9th & 10th Streets
www.theaterforthenewcity.net
Three days of theatre, poetry readings, and family-friendly programming.

late May-Aug Shakespeare in the Park
Delacorte Theater, Central Park
www.publictheater.org
Join the queue for free alfresco performances of Shakespeare plays.

June 2014

Ongoing Whitney Biennial (see Mar); Inspired (see Mar); Ai Weiwei: According to What? (see Apr); Washington Square Outdoor Art Exhibit (see May); Shakespeare in the Park (see May)

June-Aug SummerStage
Rumsey Playfield, Central Park & parks across the city
www.summerstage.org
Rockers, orchestras, authors and dance companies take to the stage.

6-8 June Howl! Festival
East Village
www.howlfestival.com
A reading of Allen Ginsberg's seminal poem kicks off this three-day festival of the arts.

8 National Puerto Rican Day Parade
Fifth Avenue, from 44th to 86th Streets
www.nationalpuertoricandayparade.org
Celebrate the city's largest Hispanic community, and its culture.

10 Museum Mile Festival
Fifth Avenue, from 82nd to 110th Streets, Upper East Side
www.museummilefestival.org
Nine major museums are free of charge for one day of the year.

early June Governors Ball Music Festival
Randalls Island Park
www.governorsballmusicfestival.com
Catch big names in rock, pop and hip hop at this three-day outdoor festival.

early June Egg Rolls & Egg Creams Festival
Eldridge Street Synagogue, p74
www.eldridgestreet.org

The nabe's Jewish and Chinese traditions converge, with klezmer music, tea ceremonies and more.

early June **Big Apple Barbecue Block Party**
Madison Square Park, p107
www.bigapplebbq.org
This meat blowout features top pit masters from all over the country.

early June-mid Aug **Celebrate Brooklyn!**
Prospect Park Bandshell, Brooklyn
www.bricartsmedia.org
Brooklyn's premier summer fête offers music, dance, film and spoken word.

mid June **Broadway Bares**
Roseland Ballroom, Theater District
www.broadwaycares.org/broadwaybares
Some of Broadway's hottest bodies *sans* costumes feature in this fundraiser.

mid-late June **River to River Festival**
Various downtown venues
www.rivertorivernyc.com
Catch hundreds of free outdoor arts events at waterside venues.

21 **Mermaid Parade**
Coney Island, Brooklyn
www.coneyisland.com
Decked-out mermaids, mermen and elaborate, kitschy floats.

late June **NYC LGBT Pride March**
From Fifth Avenue, at 36th Street, to Christopher Street
www.nycpride.org

late June-mid July **Midsummer Night Swing**
Lincoln Center Plaza, p149
www.lincolncenter.org
Dance under the stars to salsa, Cajun, swing and other music for three weeks.

late June-early Sept **Warm Up**
MoMA PS1, p164
www.ps1.org
Thousands make the pilgrimage to Long Island City on summer Saturdays for this underground clubbing event.

July 2014

Ongoing Ai Weiwei: According to What? (see Apr); Shakespeare in the Park (see May); SummerStage (see June); Midsummer Night Swing (see June); Celebrate Brooklyn! (see June); River to River Festival (see June); Warm Up (see June)

4 Independence Day

4 Macy's Fourth of July Fireworks
Waterfront locations
www.macys.com/fireworks

4 Nathan's Famous International Hot Dog Eating Contest
Nathan's Famous, 1310 Surf Avenue, at Stillwell Avenue, Coney Island, Brooklyn
www.nathansfamous.com
Eaters gather from all over the world for the granddaddy of all pig-out contests.

mid July **New York Philharmonic Concerts in the Parks**
Various locations
www.nyphil.org

mid July-Aug **Harlem Week**
Various Harlem locations
www.harlemweek.com
'Week' is a misnomer: in addition to a weekend street fair, events are spread over more than a month.

late July/early Aug **Summer Restaurant Week**
Various locations
www.nycgo.com/restaurantweek
See Jan Winter Restaurant Week.

late July-mid Aug **Lincoln Center Out of Doors**
Lincoln Center, p149
www.lincolncenter.org
Free alfresco music, dance and other performances take over the complex.

August 2014

Ongoing Ai Weiwei: According to What? (see Apr); Shakespeare in the Park (see May); SummerStage

Summer in the city

Get outside and soak up some free culture.

SummerStage

While many New Yorkers escape to the coast for summer weekends, there are many advantages to visiting NYC in July and August. For one thing, hotel rates are at their lowest, apart from chilly January–March. Yes, it will be hot and humid, but there is less competition for tickets to Broadway shows and tables at hyped restaurants. Summer Streets (www.nyc.gov/summerstreets) – which creates a car-free route from Brooklyn Bridge to Central Park for three Saturdays in August – offers a rare opportunity to stroll along Park Avenue sans traffic. But best of all, summer brings a roster of standout free events.

Shakespeare in the Park (p37)

Droves of theatre-lovers line up for hours in Central Park. Free tickets (two per person) are distributed at the Delacorte Theater at noon on the day of the show. The queue can start forming as early as 6am when big-name stars are on the bill. Bring a blanket and provisions (though many local eateries distribute menus and deliver to your spot).

SummerStage (p37)

This annual cultural behemoth brings more than 100 free shows to parks in all five boroughs, from concerts and DJ events to theatre, comedy and dance performances.

River to River (p38)

Though the 2014 festival won't span a full month as in previous years, lower Manhattan will host hundreds of free concerts, art installations, dance and theatrical performances for two to three weeks.

Lincoln Center Out of Doors (p38)

The sprawling campus comes alive with dozens of gratis shows by musicians, dancers and other artists from all over the world.

Outdoor movie festivals

Alfresco film series in city parks, including Bryant Park (www.bryantpark.org) and Central Park (www.centralparknyc.org) are a summer tradition. Arrive early to claim a prime patch of grass in front of the big screen.

Flea season

Shop and nosh outdoors throughout the year.

Smorgasburg

Rummaging in the city's outdoor flea markets has long been a favourite New York weekend pastime, but the past few years have seen the emergence of a more sophisticated breed of seasonal bazaar, offering high-quality crafts and gourmet snacks alongside vintage clothing, furniture and bric-a-brac. The popular **Brooklyn Flea** (www. brooklynflea.com) was launched in 2008 by Jonathan Butler, founder of Brooklyn real-estate blog Brownstoner.com, and Eric Demby, former PR man for the Brooklyn borough president, who identified Brooklyn as being ripe for a destination market. The original location (176 Lafayette Avenue, between Clermont & Vanderbilt Avenues, Fort Greene) is open from April to the third week of November on Saturdays, and includes around 150 vendors, selling a mix of vintage clothing, records, furnishings, locally designed fashion and crafts. A second location runs on Sundays in Williamsburg, along the waterfront at North 7th Street, which is also the site of a nosh-only Saturday spin-off, **Smorgasburg**; in winter, the flea market moves indoors, occupying a majestic old bank (Skylight One

Hanson, at Ashland Place, Fort Greene) on Saturday and Sunday through March.

On Saturdays from May through October, you can sample everything from locally made ice-cream to tacos as you browse vintage fashion, handmade jewellery and skincare at **Hester Street Fair** (Hester Street, at Essex Street, www.hesterstreet fair.com). Located on the site of a former Lower East Side pushcart market, it has around 60 vendors.

In winter, several holiday markets set up shop. From late October until early January, 125 glassed-in shoplets operate in Bryant Park (between Fifth & Sixth Avenues and 40th & 42nd Streets), forming a festive microcosm, the **Holiday Shops at Bryant Park** (1-212 661 6640, www.theholidayshopsat bryantpark.com), clustered around a seasonal skating rink. Although some of the wares skirt tourist-craft-shop territory, there are plenty of unusual finds, including jewellery and accessories, toys, foodstuffs and household devices. You'll find a similar mix at the **Union Square Holiday Market** at the south-west corner of Union Square, at 14th Street (1-212 529 9262, www. urbanspacenyc.com), open mid/ late November to late December.

(see June); Celebrate Brooklyn! (see June); Warm Up (see June); Harlem Week (see July); Summer Restaurant Week (see July); Lincoln Center Out of Doors (see July)

8-24 New York International Fringe Festival
Various locations
www.fringenyc.org
Wacky, weird and sometimes wonderful, the Fringe Festival – inspired by the Edinburgh original – crams hundreds of shows into 16 days.

26 Aug-9 Sept US Open
USTA Billie Jean King National Tennis Center, Flushing Meadows-Corona Park, Queens
www.usopen.org
New York becomes the capital of the tennis world as the sport's final Grand Slam thwacks its way into Queens.

30, 31; 1, 6-7 Sept Washington Square Outdoor Art Exhibit
See above May 2014.

September 2014

Ongoing Warm Up (see June); US Open (see Aug); Washington Square Outdoor Art Exhibit (see Aug)

1 Labor Day

mid Sept-Dec Next Wave Festival
Brooklyn Academy of Music, p163
www.bam.org
A showcase of the very best of avant-garde music, dance, theatre and opera at the Brooklyn Academy of Music.

mid Sept Feast of San Gennaro
Little Italy, p71
www.sangennaro.org
An eleven-day street fair with a marching band and plenty of Italian food stalls.

late Sept New York Burlesque Festival
Various venues
www.thenewyorkburlesquefestival.com
Catch more than 120 tassel-twirling, shimmying performances in this annual burlesque blowout.

late Sept Dumbo Arts Festival
Various locations in Dumbo, Brooklyn
www.dumboartsfestival.com
Concerts, forums, a short-film series, open studios and installations.

late Sept-mid Oct New York Film Festival
Lincoln Center, p149
www.filmlinc.com

US Open

October 2014

Ongoing Next Wave Festival
(see Sept); New York Film
Festival (see Sept)

early Oct **Open House New York**
See above Oct 2013.

early-mid Oct **New York City Wine
& Food Festival**
See above Oct 2013.

13 Columbus Day

mid-late Oct **CMJ Music Marathon
& FilmFest**
See above Oct 2013.

late Oct **Manhattan Vintage
Clothing Show**
See above Oct 2013.

31 **Village Halloween Parade**
See above Oct 2013.

November 2014

Ongoing Next Wave Festival
(see Sept)

early Nov **New York Comedy
Festival**
See above Nov 2013.

early Nov **ING New York
City Marathon**
See above Nov 2013.

11 Veterans' Day

early Nov-late Dec **Radio City
Christmas Spectacular**
See above Nov 2013.

27 Thanksgiving Day

27 **Macy's Thanksgiving
Day Parade**
See above Nov 2013.

December 2014

Ongoing Next Wave Festival
(see Sept); Radio City Christmas
Spectacular (see Nov)

early Dec **Rockefeller Center
Tree-Lighting**
See above Dec 2013.

25 Christmas Day

31 **Emerald Nuts Midnight Run**
See above Dec 2013.

31 **New Year's Eve in
Times Square**
See above Dec 2013.

Rockefeller Center Christmas tree

Itineraries

Elevated Pursuits

A disused freight train track reborn as a public park-cum-promenade, the High Line has existed in its current incarnation for only half a decade, but it is already one of the most popular spots with visitors and locals alike. The lush, landscaped green strip provides a verdant pathway between the somewhat hedonistic Meatpacking District and the still-evolving neighbourhood of Hell's Kitchen, cutting through the city's main gallery district in Chelsea. You could easily spend an entire day traversing its length, disembarking to enjoy attractions, eateries and bars along the way.

The urban sanctuary has a less-than-serene history. Back in the early days of the 20th century, the West Side had something in common with the Wild West. When freight-bearing trains competed with horses, carts and pedestrians on Tenth Avenue, the thoroughfare was so treacherous it earned the moniker 'Death Avenue'. In an attempt to counteract the carnage, mounted men known as 'West Side Cowboys' would ride in front of the train, waving red flags to warn of its imminent approach. These urban cowboys lost their jobs when the West Side Improvement Project finally raised the railway off street level and put it up on to an overhead trestle – the High Line – in 1934. Originally stretching from 34th Street to Spring Street, the line fell into disuse after World War II as trucks replaced trains. A southern chunk was torn down in the 1960s, and, after the last train ground to a halt in 1980, local property owners lobbied for its destruction. However, thanks to the efforts of railroad enthusiast Peter Obletz and, later, the Friends of the High Line, which was founded by local residents Joshua David and Robert Hammond, the industrial relic was saved. A decade after the group began advocating for its reuse

High Line

to be completed in 2015, will have 50,000 square feet of indoor exhibition space, plus alfresco rooftop galleries.

As you stroll north alongside trees, flowers and landscaped greenery, keep an eye out for several interesting features along the way. Commanding an expansive river view, the 'sun deck' between 14th and 15th Streets has wooden deck chairs that can be rolled along the original tracks, plus a water feature for cooling your feet. Just past 15th Street, the High Line cuts through the old loading dock of the former Nabisco factory, where the first Oreo cookie was made in 1912. This conglomeration of 18 structures, built between the 1890s and the 1930s, now houses Chelsea Market (75 Ninth Avenue, between 15th & 16th Streets, www.chelseamarket. com). Alight here if you want to shop in the ground-floor food arcade for artisanal bread, wine, baked goods and freshly made ice-cream, among other treats. From around late April until late October, however, food vendors set up on the High Line itself, and you can stop for a tipple at seasonal open-air café, the Porch, at 15th Street, which serves local wine and beer from cult vino spot **Terroir** (p85).

At 17th Street, steps descend into a sunken amphitheatre with a glassed-over 'window' in the steel structure overlooking the avenue. The elevated walkway provides a great vantage point for viewing the surrounding architecture; you will see not only iconic structures like the Statue of Liberty and the Empire State Building during your stroll, but also newer buildings such as Frank Gehry's 2007 headquarters for Barry Diller's InterActiveCorp (555 W 18th Street, at West Side Highway), which comprises tilting glass volumes that resemble a fully rigged tall ship.

as a public space, the first phase of New York's first elevated public park opened in summer 2009 (the second leg followed two years later).

Start your expedition in the Meatpacking District, where upscale shops include designer department store **Jeffrey New York** (p96), new independent boutique **Owen** (p96) and longtime local fixture **Diane von Furstenberg** (874 Washington Street, at W 14th Street, 1-646 486 4800, www.dvf.com). Combine retail therapy with a jolt of caffeine at the **Rag & Bone General Store** (425 W 13th Street, at Washington Street; 1-212 249 3331). The latest location of the rapidly growing New York-born boutique chain (see p96) has an on-site cult coffee bar courtesy of Jack's Stir Brew Coffee (p64).

From here, it's just a couple of blocks to the southernmost entrance to the High Line, on Washington Street, at Gansevoort Street. As you mount the stairs, you'll notice a building under construction to your left. The new home of the **Whitney Museum of American Art** (p139), due

By now it's probably time for brunch. Descend the stairs at 20th Street for **Cookshop** (p104), which serves baked eggs with applewood bacon and seasonal variations on French toast.

Fortified, you're ready for some cultural sustenance. Before you embark on a contemporary art crawl, note the block-long campus of the General Theological Seminary of the Episcopal Church across 20th Street. The land was once part of the estate known as Chelsea, owned by poet Clement Clarke Moore, author of 'A Visit from St Nicholas' (more commonly known as "Twas the Night Before Christmas'). The seminary's former guest wing is now the **High Line Hotel** (p176).

In the 1980s, many of New York's galleries left Soho for what was then an industrial wasteland on the western edge of Chelsea. Today, blue-chip spaces and numerous less exalted ones attract swarms of art aficionados to the area between Tenth and Eleventh Avenues from 19th to 29th Streets. If you have limited time, hit 24th Street, which has a concentration of high-profile spaces, including Mary Boone Gallery, Gagosian Gallery, Gladstone Gallery, Luhring Augustine and Matthew Marks Gallery. At its western corner, check out the 19-storey apartment building at 200 Eleventh Avenue. Designed by Annabelle Selldorf, it has a car elevator, allowing residents to bring their prized motor up to their door. A couple of blocks north is a notable example of industrial architecture, the 1929 Starrett-Lehigh Building (601 W 26th Street, at Eleventh Avenue).

It's also worth swinging by 22nd Street, between Tenth and Eleventh Avenues, to see the outdoor art installation *7000 Oaks* by German artist Joseph Beuys: 18 pairings of basalt stones and trees. Maintained by Dia Art Foundation (diaart.org), the piece is a spin-off of a five-year international effort, begun in 1982 at Germany's Documenta 7 exhibition, to enact social and environmental change by planting 7,000 trees. If you want to pick up a souvenir, stop by arty bookshop **Printed Matter** (p105).

Your art tour isn't over when you resume your High Line perambulation (there are stairs at 23rd and 26th Street). Befitting its location, the park itself is a platform for creativity and has a dedicated curator of temporary site-specific installations. Through to April 2014, look out for *Busted*, a series of figurative sculptures by various artists, including George Condo, Mark Grotjahn and Andra Ursuta.

On Thursdays, Fridays and Saturdays until May 2014, you can see Brooklyn-based artist Carol Bove's *Caterpillar*, seven large-scale, site-specific sculptures in a yet-to-be-developed section of the park (admission is free but advance reservations are required via www.thehighline.org).

Unless you're reading this in the latter half of 2014 or beyond, if you haven't booked, you'll reach the end of the line at 30th Street; the final section of the park, skirting the under-construction mixed-use complex of Hudson Yards, is tipped to open in the year ahead.

From here, you can walk or take a taxi to Hell's Kitchen. Ninth Avenue in the 40s and 50s is packed with inexpensive restaurants serving just about any ethnic cuisine you can think of – we like Mediterranean wine bar/fondue spot **Kashkaval** (p120). The bright lights of Broadway (and Off Broadway), a few blocks away, beckon. Catch an affordable show at the Gehry-designed **Pershing Square Signature Center** (p124) or score cut-price tickets at **TKTS** (p120).

Skyscraper Museum

High Points

In *Here is New York*, EB White wrote that the city 'is to the nation what the white church spire is to the village – the visible symbol of aspiration and faith, the white plume saying that the way is up.' Despite the irrevocable damage to the skyline from the 9/11 attacks, that comment still resonates – New York is constantly rebuilding itself and adding to its cache of cloudbusters.

The logical starting point for an architectural tour is a visit to the **Skyscraper Museum** (p60) in the Financial District. Here you can see large-scale photographs of lower Manhattan's skyscrapers from 1956, 1976 and 2004, and a 1931 silent film documenting the construction of the Empire State Building. You can also compare original models of the Twin Towers and the World Trade Center's new centrepiece skyscraper, in preparation for a subsequent stop.

Head out of the door, make a left and follow Battery Place across West Street and along the northern edge of Battery Park. Turn left up Greenwich Street, and at Morris Street walk along Trinity Place to make a brief stop at **Trinity Church** (p63). In stark contrast to the skyscrapers that surround it, Trinity – designed by Richard Upjohn, it's the third church to stand on this spot – remains frozen in Gothic Revival style, but it was the island's tallest structure when it was completed in 1846, thanks to its 281-foot spire. The churchyard, which dates back to 1697, is one of New York's oldest cemeteries. Alexander Hamilton (the nation's first secretary of the treasury – you can check out his mug on the $10 bill) is buried here.

Afterwards, it's time to visit one of the most powerfully moving sites in recent history: the site where the mighty Twin Towers once stood. From the church, continue to walk up Trinity Place for two more blocks and cross over Liberty Street. The World Trade

Center is to your left. The awe-inspiring **National September 11 Memorial**, comprising two 30-foot-deep waterfalls in the footprints of the towers, opened on the ten-year anniversary of the attacks, but until construction is completed on the site, you'll need to reserve a timed entry pass on the website or at the **9/11 Memorial Preview Site** (box p61) on Vesey Street, where you can also view renderings of the development. When complete, it will include a museum (expected to open in spring 2014), a striking transport hub designed by Santiago Calatrava, and five towers. Now the city's tallest building, **1 World Trade Center** topped out at 1,776 feet in spring 2013.

From the place where New York's tallest towers fell, it's onwards and upwards to the spot where the race to the heavens began. Walk up Vesey Street, then north on Broadway to the **Woolworth Building** (no.233, at Barclay Street). Note the flamboyant Gothic terracotta cladding designed by Cass Gilbert in 1913. The 55-storey, 793-foot 'Cathedral of Commerce' was the world's tallest structure for 16 years until it was topped by 40 Wall Street.

The Woolworth Building overlooks City Hall Park. Walk through the park and aim for the foot of the **Brooklyn Bridge** (p157). On the way, admire the curled and warped stainless-steel façade of the audaciously named, 870-foot **New York by Gehry** (8 Spruce Street, between Gold & Nassau Streets). Our sojourn is about buildings, not bridges – but we wouldn't mind if you made a detour here; it takes about half an hour to walk out to the middle of the bridge and back, but you'll want to allow plenty of time to gaze at the East River, the web of steel cables – and, of course, the panoramic view of the Manhattan skyline.

Back to the current plan: once you've passed through the park (bordered to the east by Park Row), look for a subway entrance to your left. Board the Uptown 4 or 5 train to Grand Central-42nd Street. On the subway, consider this: it took ten years of unflagging effort for Jacqueline Kennedy Onassis and others to save **Grand Central Terminal** (p129), your next destination. After the original Pennsylvania Station was demolished in 1963, developers unveiled plans to wreck the magnificent Beaux Arts edifice and erect an office tower in its place. Jackie O rallied politicians and celebrities to her cause. In 1978, her committee won a Supreme Court decision affirming landmark status for the beloved building, which celebrated its centennial in 2013.

By now you'll likely be famished. Head back downstairs to one of the city's most famous eateries, the **Grand Central Oyster Bar & Restaurant** (lower concourse, p130), for a late lunch. Before heading inside, linger a moment under the low ceramic arches, dubbed the

Chrysler Building

'whispering gallery'. Instruct a friend to stand in an opposite, diagonal corner from you and whisper to each other – they'll sound as clear as if you were face to face.

Revitalised, you're ready for the next stop: **Columbus Circle**. Either hop back on the subway (S to Times Square, transfer to the Uptown 1 train and get off at 59th Street-Columbus Circle) or, preferably, you can hoof it there in about 30 minutes. Exit Grand Central on 42nd Street and head west. At Fifth Avenue, you'll pass another Beaux Arts treasure from the city's grand metropolitan era, the **New York Public Library** (p125) with its sumptuous white-marble façade. Completed in 1911, the library now sits on the greensward known as Bryant Park. When you get to Broadway, make a right and head north into Times Square. Imposing, sentinel-like skyscrapers mark the southern entry to the electric carnival here; the 2000 **Condé Nast Building** (no.4) and the 2001 **Reuters Building** (no.3), both by Fox & Fowle, complement Kohn Pedersen Fox's 2002 postmodern **5 Times Square** and David Childs' 2004 **Times Square Tower** (no.7). Originally Longacre Square, the 'Crossroads of the World' was renamed after the *New York Times* moved here in the early 1900s; beneath its sheath of billboards and snaking news zipper, the broadsheet's old HQ, 1 Times Square, is an elegant 1904 structure. Take a detour if you want to see the paper's current home base, Renzo Piano's 2007 **New York Times Building** (620 Eighth Avenue, between W 40th & 41st Streets), one block west and a couple of blocks south. The glass-walled design represents the newspaper's desire for transparency in its reporting.

Back on Broadway, walk north on the pedestrian-packed sidewalks until you spot Christopher gazing out from his perch in the centre of Columbus Circle at 59th Street. The renovated traffic circle, with its ring of fountains and benches, is the perfect place to contemplate another set of twin towers, the 2003 **Time Warner Center**, also designed by David Childs.

Increasingly, skyscrapers are incorporating green design. Norman Foster's extraordinary 2006 **Hearst Magazine Building** (959 Eighth Avenue, at W 57th Street) is a shining example. Look south-west and you can't miss it; it's the one that resembles a giant greenhouse.

At this point you have two options. The first is to end the day at the Time Warner Center and enjoy the staggering view from the **Mandarin Oriental Hotel**'s Lobby Lounge, perched 35 floors up. The drinks prices here are equally staggering, but the Fifth Avenue and Central Park South skylines make it worth the splurge. Or, you can hail a cab and top off a day of skyscraper gazing with a panoramic view from either New York's most iconic tower, the **Empire State Building** (p124), or the **Top of the Rock** observation deck at **Rockefeller Center** (p127). The latter has an edge as it affords a great view of the former. Also look out for William Van Alen's silver-hooded **Chrysler Building** (p129). The acme of art deco design, it was part of a madcap three-way race to become the world's tallest building. The competitors were **40 Wall Street** (now the Trump Building) and the Empire State Building. Van Alen waited for the first to top out at 927 feet before unveiling his secret weapon – a spire assembled inside the Chrysler's dome and raised from within to bring the height to 1,046 feet. At 102 storeys and 1,250 feet, the Empire State Building surpassed it only 11 months later.

Woody Allen with the Eddy Davis New Orleans Jazz Band p52

Woody's Manhattan

You've seen the movies, now experience the city through the lens of quintessential New Yorker – and longtime Upper East Sider – Woody Allen. This full-day tour takes in locations from the director's 1970s masterpieces *Annie Hall* and *Manhattan*.

Alvy Singer and Annie Hall first meet at the now-defunct Wall Street Racquet Club on Pier 13, so start your voyage into Woody's world downtown – if you're feeling energetic you can even book a squash court at the nearby New York Health & Racquet Club (39 Whitehall Street, between Pearl & Water Streets, 1-212 269 9800). A day pass to the club costs $25-$50 per person, plus $14-$26 per hour to rent the court and $5 per racquet.

After your game, head for the waterfront. Walk south on Whitehall Street, left on Water Street and right on Old Slip, which will take you to the river.

Stroll north along the East River Esplanade; before you reach South Street Seaport's touristry Pier 17, you'll come to the recently developed Pier 15, which has a cool bi-level lawned viewing platform and deck chairs. Stop here to soak up a panorama of the Brooklyn Bridge, the gorgeous (or, as Annie might say, 'neat') backdrop for the scene in which Alvy and Annie profess their love to each other and kiss at dusk. Just a little foreshadowing for a certain other iconic bridge scene you may be familiar with…

You've probably worked up an appetite after your morning exertions, so it's time to stop for a cinematic bite. Walk up Wall Street to the subway stop of the same name – deep in the Financial District. You're sure to run into a few 'analysts', but not the kind Woody's neurotic characters typically rely on. Catch the 2 or 3 train, then change to the 1 at

Chambers Street and get off at Christopher Street-Sheridan Square. From here it's a two minute walk south to **John's of Bleecker Street** (278 Bleecker Street, at Jones Street, 1-212 243 1680, www.johns brickovenpizza.com), where Isaac Davis takes his 17-year-old girlfriend Tracy in *Manhattan* and learns she has won a place to study in London. There may be newer pizza places with more impressive foodie pedigrees, but John's, with its well-worn booths and divey vibe, has been a Village fixture since 1929.

Hop back on the subway and zip up to 59th Street-Columbus Circle to access **Central Park** (p131), where Tracy and Isaac take a horse-and-buggy ride for their 'corny' date (their last before they break up). Since horse-drawn carriages are a controversial subject these days, you may prefer to hire one of the prolific human-powered pedicabs; Manhattan Rickshaw Company (1-212 604 4729, www.manhattan rickshaw.com) is a good bet.

Diehard location spotters will want to take a detour to 63rd Street and Columbus Avenue, across the

street from Lincoln Center – the spot where Annie and Alvy part ways in *Annie Hall*'s final moments.

Ditch your ride at 81st Street and Central Park West and pay a visit to the Rose Center for Earth and Space at the **American Museum of Natural History** (p145), the updated version of the Hayden Planetarium, where, in *Manhattan*, Isaac and Mary take shelter during an electrical storm. Use your brain (that most overrated organ) to count Saturn's moons and maybe, if you're travelling with a partner, indulge in some interstellar canoodling.

But to really experience the character of the classic Upper West Side, head west to grab a snack at quintessential Jewish food store **Zabar's** (p149), which Isaac and Tracy pass in another scene. Order a sandwich of hand-sliced corned beef on fresh rye, and remember Isaac's comment: 'Corned beef should not be blue.'

Your next destination is Woody's home patch – the Upper East Side. Catch the crosstown bus at the corner of 79th and Broadway and get off at Fifth Avenue. Walk north

ITINERARIES

Central Park

for the **Solomon R Guggenheim Museum** (p139), site of Isaac's first, unpromising, meeting with Mary, whose views on art he finds pretentious. Even if you don't venture inside, admire Frank Lloyd Wright's dramatic 1959 spiral building – the architect's only NYC structure apart from a private house on Staten Island. The pair's second, more successful, meeting takes place at the **Museum of Modern Art** (p125) – but you won't be able to fit that into your schedule today.

If you fancy a stroll, explore Annie Hall's neighbourhood – the scene outside her apartment was shot on E 68th Street, between Madison and Park Avenues. (The director's townhouse is around the corner on E 70th Street.)

Make your way south-east to the new location of the **Beekman Theatre** (1271 Second Avenue, between 66th and 67th Streets, 1-212 585 4141, www.beekman theatre.com), which featured in *Annie Hall*. At the original cinema, which was across the street (1254 Second Avenue) but has since been torn down, two pushy fans pester Alvy for an autograph before Annie shows up for their date. 'Hey, dis is Alvy Singah!' (Since Annie is late for the start of Ingmar Bergman's *Face to Face*, Alvy insists on heading across town to the New Yorker Theater at Broadway and 88th, which has since closed. There, Alvy famously addresses the audience while arguing with a moviegoer about Marshall McLuhan – and happens to have Mr McLuhan on hand to prove his point. As Alvy says, 'Boy, if life were only like this'.

To recreate one of *Manhattan*'s most iconic scenes, continue south-east to Riverview Terrace at Sutton Square (E 58th Street, at the East River), where you can gaze at the view of the Queensboro Bridge that capped Isaac and Mary's unofficial first date, which lasted until dawn.

You'll have to drag yourself away from the stunning vista, though, for the grand finale of your itinerary – catch a cab to the Carlyle Hotel's swanky cabaret room, **Café Carlyle** (p26), at 76th Street and Madison Avenue, to see the man himself. Woody Allen plays clarinet with the Eddy Davis New Orleans Jazz Band, which has an ongoing Monday-night slot ($100-$195 per person, plus $25 minimum).

Solomon R Guggenheim Museum

New York by Area

Wall Street 1

Downtown

The southern tip of Manhattan has always been the city's financial, legal and political powerhouse. It's where New York began as a Dutch colony, and where the 19th-century influx of immigrants infused the city with new energy. Yet with much of it off the Big Apple's orderly grid, downtown doesn't conform to the standard. Here, the landscape shifts from block to block. In the Financial District, gleaming skyscrapers rub shoulders with 18th-century landmarks; Tribeca's top dining spots are only a short hop from Chinatown's frenetic food markets; and around the corner from the flashy nightspots of the Meatpacking District, affluent West Villagers reside in stately brownstones.

Financial District

Commerce has been the backbone of New York's prosperity since the city's earliest days. The southern point of Manhattan quickly evolved into the Financial District because, in the days before telecommunications, banks established their headquarters near the port. Wall Street, which took its name from a defensive wooden wall built in 1653 to mark the northern limit of Nieuw Amsterdam, is synonymous with the world's greatest den of capitalism. On the eastern shore of lower Manhattan, old buildings in the disused South Street Seaport area were redeveloped in the mid 1980s into restaurants, bars and stores. Also check out the views of Brooklyn Bridge (see p157).

Sights & museums

City Hall
City Hall Park, from Vesey to Chambers Street, between Broadway & Park Row (1-212 788 2656, www.nyc.gov/design commission). Subway J, Z to Chambers

Street; R to City Hall; 2, 3 to Park Place; 4, 5, 6 to Brooklyn Bridge-City Hall. **Open** *Tours* (individuals) noon Wed, 10am Thur; (groups) 10.30am Mon-Wed. **Admission** free. **Map** p56 C2 ❶

Designed by French émigré Joseph François Mangin and native New Yorker John McComb Jr, the fine, Federal-style City Hall was completed in 1812. Tours take in the rotunda, with its splendid coffered dome; the City Council Chamber; and the Governor's Room, which houses a collection of 19th-century American political portraits as well as historic furnishings (including George Washington's desk). Individuals can book for the Thursday-morning tour (at least two days in advance); alternatively, sign up before 11.45am on Wednesday at the NYC tourism kiosk at the southern end of City Hall Park on the east side of Broadway, at Barclay Street, for the first-come, first-served tour at noon. Group tours should be booked at least a week in advance.

Fraunces Tavern Museum

2nd & 3rd Floors, 54 Pearl Street, at Broad Street (1-212 425 1778, www.frauncestavernmuseum.org). Subway J, Z to Broad Street; 4, 5 to Bowling Green. **Open** noon-5pm daily. **Admission** $7; free-$4 reductions. **Map** p56 C4 ❷

True, George Washington slept here, but there's little left of the original 18th-century tavern that was favoured by Washington during the Revolution. Fire-damaged and rebuilt in the 19th century, it was reconstructed in its current Colonial Revival style in 1907. The museum itself features period rooms, a collection of 800 Revolutionary flags and such Washington relics as a lock of his hair. It was here, after the British had finally been defeated in 1783, that Washington took tearful farewell of his troops and vowed to retire from public life. Luckily, he had a change of heart six years later and became the country's

first president. You can still raise a pint in the bar, now run by Dublin's Porterhouse Brewing Company.

Governors Island

1-212 440 2202, www.govisland.com. Subway R to Whitehall Street-South Ferry; 1 to South Ferry; 4, 5 to Bowling Green; then take ferry from Battery Maritime Building at Slip no.7. **Open** late May-late Sept (see website for hours & ferry schedule). **Admission** free. **Map** p56 C5 ❸

A seven-minute ride on a free ferry takes you to this seasonal island sanctuary, a scant 800 yards from lower Manhattan. Because of its strategic position in the middle of New York Harbor, Governors Island was a military outpost and off-limits to the public for 200 years. It finally opened to summer visitors in 2006. The verdant, 172-acre isle still retains a significant chunk of its military-era architecture, including Fort Jay, started in 1776, and Castle Williams, completed in 1812 and for years used as a prison. Today, as well as providing a peaceful setting for cycling (bring a bike on the ferry, or rent from Bike & Roll once there), the island hosts a programme of events (see website for schedule). In 2012, construction began on a new park, and 30 acres of green space will open to the public for the 2014 season. A Hammock Grove of 1,500 trees will offer shady reclining and 14 acres of lawn will include two ball fields. Eventually, new hills constructed from the debris of demolished (non-historic) buildings will provide even more spectacular viewpoints for harbour panoramas.

Museum of American Finance

48 Wall Street, at William Street (1-212 908 4110, www.moaf.org). Subway 2, 3, 4, 5 to Wall Street; R, 1 to Rector Street. **Open** 10am-4pm Tue-Sat. **Admission** $8; free-$5 reductions; free Sat through 2013. **Map** p56 C4 ❹

A WATTS ST
DESBROSSES ST
VESTRY ST
HUDSON ST
LAIGHT ST
COLLISTER ST
HUBERT ST
ERICKSON PL
BEACH ST
NORTH MOORE ST
FRANKLIN ST

B ST JOHN'S LN
VARICK ST
J N A,C,E

CANAL ST
MERCER ST
HOWARD ST

C Museum of Chinese in America
33
39
BAXTER ST

See p58
LISPENARD ST
J,N, Q,R,6
WALKER ST
38
WHITE ST
FRANKLIN ST
LEONARD ST
19
CORTLANDT ALLEY
LAFAYETTE ST
33

WEST SIDE HWY
26
25

STAPLE ST
JAY ST
STAPLE ST
HARRISON ST
GREENWICH ST

WEST BROADWAY
WORTH ST
THOMAS ST
DUANE ST
21
READE ST

BROADWAY
CENTRE ST
CHINATOWN
Colu

ST ANDREWS PL
FOLEY SQ
HAMIL

CHINATOWN

TRIBECA
CHAMBERS ST
1,2,3

African Burial Ground

WARREN ST
PARK PL W
MURRAY ST
BARCLAY ST
VESEY PL
NORTH END AVE
15
VESEY ST

PARK PL
27
A,C
R
City Hall Park
1
City Hall

J,Z 4,5,6

PARK PL
2,3
PARK ROW
FRANK

River Terr

1 World Trade Center
VESEY ST
National September 11 Memorial & Museum
6
DEY ST
17
CORTLANDT
R
SPRUCE ST
BEEKMAN ST
ANN ST
A,C,J,Z

FULTON ST
4,5
2,3

World Financial Center
PUBLIC PL
LIBERTY ST
GREENWICH ST
CEDAR ST
Federal Reserve Bank
MAIDEN LN
WILLIAM ST
JOHN
PLATT S

BATTERY PARK CITY
CEDAR ST
THAMES ST
ALBANY ST
CARLISLE ST
WASHINGTON ST
Trinity Church
13
NASSAU ST
PINE ST
Museum o American Fin

RECTOR PL
S END AVE
W THAMES ST
RECTOR ST
NY Stock Exchange
4,5
J,Z 2,3
HANOVER
WA

EXCHANGE PL
BEAVER ST
WILLIAM ST
HAND SO

FINANCIAL DISTRICT
THIRD PL
MORRIS ST
NEW ST
BROAD ST
PEARL ST
S WILLIAM ST
WATER ST

SECOND PL
BNW PLAZA
Bowling Green
MARKETFIELD ST
STONE ST
BRIDGE ST
2,3
Fraunce Tavern

FIRST PL
Museum of Jewish Heritage
Skyscraper Museum
BATTERY PL
Museum of the American Indian
5
WHITEHALL ST
MOORE ST

Castle Clinton
Battery Park
10
1
Ferry to Statue of Liberty
Staten Is Ferry Ter

BROOKLYN-BATTERY TUNNEL

H u d s o n   R i v e r

Downtown 1

ELIZABETH ST

CHRYSTIE ST

FORSYTH ST

ALLEN ST

ORCHARD ST

LUDLOW ST

ESSEX ST

See p59

Seward Park

M F

CANAL ST

ELDRIDGE ST

HESTER ST

HENRY ST

MADISON ST

GOUVERNEUR ST

WATER ST

1

Eldridge St Synagogue 50

YARD ST

PELL ST

Confucius Plaza

44

CLINTON ST

JEFFERSON ST

MONTGOMERY ST

DIVISION ST

MADISON ST

RUTGERS ST

CHERRY ST

CHATHAM SQ

42

HENRY ST

MARKET ST

PIKE ST

Rutgers Park

OLIVER ST

CATHERINE ST

MONROE ST

46

Rutgers Park

K ROW

ST JAMES PL

First Shearith Israel Graveyard

WATER ST

SOUTH ST

ROOSEVELT DR

MANHATTAN BRIDGE

2

ST

WAGNER PL

D

DOVER ST

BROOKLYN BRIDGE

PECK SLIP

FRANKLIN

WATER

BEEKMAN ST

16

South Street Seaport

3

FULTON ST

9

South Street Seaport Museum

19

18

17

16

New York City Police Museum

PEYSTER ST

15

14

13

BROOKLYN

NEUR LN

11

9

0   200 m

0   200 yds

© Copyright Time Out Group 2013

4

5

❶	Sights & museums
❶	Eating & drinking
❶	Shopping
❶	Nightlife
❶	Arts & leisure

Downtown 2

High Line

CHELSEA

General Theological Seminary of the Episcopal Church

Joyce Theater

NINTH AVE
EIGHTH AVE
SEVENTH AVE

W 20TH ST
W 18TH ST
W 16TH ST

Flatiron Building

FLATIRON DISTRICT

Theodore Roosevelt Birthplace

BROADWAY
PARK AVE SOUTH

MIDTOWN
(pp99-130)

Union Square

139 W 14TH ST A,C,E,L 1,2,3 F,L,M

TENTH AVE

W 13TH ST
W 12TH ST
W 11TH ST
W 10TH ST
W 9TH ST
W 8TH ST

SIXTH AVE
FIFTH AVE
UNIVERSITY PL

L,N,Q,R,
4,5,6

115
118

MEAT-PACKING DISTRICT

126
142
140

LITTLE W 12TH ST
GANSEVOORT ST

130 W 12TH ST

HORATIO ST
JANE ST

GREENWICH AVE

110

WEST VILLAGE

146
132
129 144
145

WAVERLY PL

GREENWICH

WASHINGTON SQ EAST

New York University

BETHUNE ST
BANK ST
W 11TH ST
PERRY ST
CHARLES ST

136
135
131
141
138

HUDSON ST
GREENWICH ST
BLEECKER ST
W 4TH ST

WAVERLY PL
113
WASHINGTON PL
A,C,E
B,D,F,M

Washington Square

112

WASH SQ SOUTH
GREENE ST

W 3RD ST

W 10TH ST
CHRISTOPHER ST
BARROW ST
MORTON ST
LEROY ST
CLARKSON ST

50
46
45
42
40

BEDFORD ST
GROVE ST
BARROW ST
COMMERCE ST

123
143

SEVENTH AVE SOUTH

CORNELIA ST
LEROY ST
CARMINE ST
DOWNING ST

134
125
121
122
117
124
123
114

MINETTA LANE

LA GUARDIA PL

AIA Center for Architecture

BLEECKER ST

W HOUSTON ST
B,D,F,M

147
36

MACDOUGAL ST
SULLIVAN ST
THOMPSON ST

23
26

SOHO

BROADWAY
WOOSTER ST
GREENE ST
MERCER ST

32

KING ST
CHARLTON ST
VANDAM ST
SPRING ST

37

VARICK ST

PRINCE ST

SPRING ST
BROOME ST

31

WEST BROADWAY

HOLLAND TUNNEL

CANAL ST

New York City Fire Museum

WATTS ST
DESBROSSES ST

GRAND ST

28

HUDSON ST
VARICK ST

CANAL ST
A,C,E
HOW

34

WEST SIDE HWY

WATTS ST
DESBROSSES ST
VESTRY ST
LAIGHT ST
HUBERT ST
BEACH ST
NORTH MOORE ST
FRANKLIN ST

LISPENARD ST
WALKER ST

38

J.P

WHITE ST
FRANKLIN ST
LEONARD ST
WORTH ST
THOMAS ST

22

WEST BROADWAY

CHI

0   300 m
0   300 yds

© Copyright Time Out Group 2013

26

See
p56

TRIBECA

Situated in the old headquarters of the Bank of New York, the Museum of American Finance's permanent collection traces the history of Wall Street and America's financial markets. Displays in the august banking hall include a bearer bond made out to President George Washington and ticker tape from the morning of the stock market crash of 1929. A timeline, 'Tracking the Credit Crisis' helps to clarify the current global predicament, while themed temporary exhibitions bring the world of money to life.

National Museum of the American Indian

George Gustav Heye Center, Alexander Hamilton US Custom House, 1 Bowling Green, between State & Whitehall Streets (1-212 514 3700, www.nmai. si.edu). Subway R to Whitehall Street-South Ferry; 1 to South Ferry; 4, 5 to Bowling Green. **Open** 10am-5pm Mon-Wed, Fri-Sun; 10am-8pm Thur. **Admission** free. **Map** p56 C4 ⑤

The National Museum of the American Indian's George Gustav Heye Center, a branch of the Smithsonian Institution, displays its collection on the first two floors of Cass Gilbert's grand 1907 Custom House, one of the finest Beaux-Arts buildings in the city. On the second level, the life and culture of Native Americans is illuminated in three galleries radiating out from the rotunda. A permanent exhibition, 'Infinity of Nations', displays 700 items from the museum's wide-ranging collection of Native American art and objects, from decorated baskets to elaborate ceremonial headdresses, organised by region. On the ground floor, the Diker Pavilion for Native Arts & Culture is the city's only dedicated showcase for Native American performing arts.

National September 11 Memorial & Museum

NEW *Enter on Albany Street, at Greenwich Street (1-212 266 5211, www.911memorial.org). Subway A,* *C, J, Z, 2, 3, 4, 5 to Fulton Street; E to World Trade Center; R, 1 to Rector Street.* **Open** *Oct-Feb 10am-6pm daily. Mar-Sept 10am-8pm daily (see website for updates and extended holiday hours).* **Map** p56 B3 ⑥

Until construction is completed on the World Trade Center site, visitors must reserve timed entry passes to the memorial online or at the 9/11 Memorial Preview Site (20 Vesey Street, at Church Street), where you can also see renderings of the plans, artefacts, films and other displays; there are further exhibits at the 9/11 Memorial Visitor Center (90 West Street, at Albany Street). The 9/11 Memorial Museum is expected to open in spring 2014. See box p61.

Skyscraper Museum

39 Battery Place, between Little West Street & 1st Place (1-212 968 1961, www.skyscraper.org). Subway 4, 5 to Bowling Green. **Open** noon-6pm Wed-Sun. **Admission** $5; $2.50 reductions. **Map** p56 B4 ⑦

The only institution of its kind in the world, this modest space explores high-rise buildings as objects of design, products of technology, real-estate investments and places of work and residence. A large part of the single gallery (a mirrored ceiling gives the illusion of height) is devoted to temporary exhibitions – such as autumn 2013's 'Sky High', which looks at the construction of slender residential towers. A substantial chunk of the permanent collection relates to the Word Trade Center, including original models of the Twin Towers and the new 1,776ft 1 World Trade Center.

South Street Seaport Museum

12 Fulton Street, at South Street (1-212 748 8600, www.southstreet seaportmuseum.org). Subway A, C to Broadway-Nassau Street; J, Z, 2, 3, 4, 5 to Fulton Street. **Open** Call or see website. **Admission** Call or see website. **Map** p57 D3 ⑧

The new World Trade Center

Pay your respects, and be awed, at the 9/11 Memorial.

National September 11 Memorial

In spring 2013, the final piece of the World Trade Center site's centrepiece tower was hoisted into place. At 1,776 feet, 1 World Trade Center (formerly known as the Freedom Tower) has surpassed the Empire State Building in height and is the third highest skyscraper in the world. After years of stalled construction, the new WTC is almost complete.

For most of the decade following 9/11, those who made the pilgrimage to Ground Zero were confronted by an impenetrable fence, and although plans for the site's redevelopment were announced in 2003, there wasn't much evidence of progress. Yet, as the tenth anniversary of the attacks loomed, construction surged, and the 9/11 Memorial opened to visitors on 11 September 2011.

The **National September 11 Memorial & Museum** (*see p58*)

occupies half of the WTC site's 16 acres. The memorial itself, *Reflecting Absence*, designed by architects Michael Arad and Peter Walker, comprises two one-acre 'footprints' of the destroyed towers, with 30-foot man-made waterfalls – the country's largest – cascading down their sides. Bronze parapets around the edges are inscribed with the names of those who died. As the title makes clear, the intention is to convey a powerful sense of loss. The museum pavilion, designed by Snøhetta – the Oslo-based firm behind its home city's New Norwegian National Opera & Ballet building (2008) – rises between the waterfalls. Its web-like glass atrium houses two steel trident-shaped columns salvaged from the base of the Twin Towers.

Once the museum opens in spring 2014, visitors will be able to descend to the vast spaces of the original foundations alongside a remnant of the Vesey Street staircase known as the 'Survivors' Stairs', as it was used by hundreds escaping the carnage. The collection commemorates the victims of both the 1993 and 2001 attacks on the World Trade Center. Survivors and victims' families have donated items and helped to weave personal tales of people who died in the towers. One gallery will be devoted to artists' responses to the events, and items like the East Village's Ladder Company 3 fire truck, which was dispatched to the towers with 11 firefighters who died during the rescue, will be on display.

Statue of Liberty

As this guide went to press, the South Street Seaport Museum, founded in 1967, was closed for repairs in the aftermath of 2012's Hurricane Sandy. A reopening date hadn't been set; call or see website for updates. In addition to three floors of galleries devoted to changing exhibitions illuminating aspects of the city and its relationship with the sea, the museum encompasses historic ships and Bowne & Co Stationers (see p65).

Staten Island Ferry

Battery Park, South Street, at Whitehall Street (1-718 727 2508, www.siferry.com). Subway R to Whitehall Street-South Ferry; 1 to South Ferry; 4, 5 to Bowling Green. **Open** *ferry runs 24hrs daily.* **Tickets** *free.* **Map** p56 C5 **9**
During this commuter ferry's 25-minute crossing, you'll see superb panoramas of lower Manhattan and the Statue of Liberty.

Statue of Liberty & Ellis Island Immigration Museum

Liberty Island (1-212 363 3200, www.nps.gov/stli). Subway R to Whitehall Street-South Ferry; 1 to South Ferry; 4, 5 to Bowling Green; then take Statue of Liberty ferry (1-201 604 2800, 1-877 523 9849, www.statuecruises.com), departing roughly every 30mins from gangway 4 or 5 in southernmost Battery Park. **Open** *ferry runs 8.30am-4.30pm daily. Purchase tickets online, by phone or at Castle Clinton in Battery Park.* **Admission** *$17; free-$14 reductions.* **Map** p56 B5 **10**
The sole occupant of Liberty Island, *Liberty Enlightening the World* stands 305ft tall from the bottom of her base to the tip of her gold-leaf torch. Intended as a gift from France on America's 100th birthday, the statue was designed by Frédéric Auguste Bartholdi (1834-1904). Construction began in Paris in 1874, her skeletal iron framework crafted by Gustave Eiffel (the man behind the Tower), but only the arm with the torch was finished in time for the centennial in 1876. In 1884, the statue was finally completed – only to be taken apart to be shipped to New York, where it was unveiled in 1886. It served as a lighthouse until 1902, and as a welcoming beacon for millions of immigrants. These 'tired…poor…huddled masses' were evoked in Emma Lazarus's poem 'The New Colossus', written in 1883 to raise funds for the pedestal and engraved inside the statue in 1903. In autumn 2012, Hurricane Sandy caused significant damage to the statue's infrastructure, making it off limits to visitors, but it reopened on 4 July 2013. With a free Monument Pass, available only with ferry tickets reserved in advance, you can enter the pedestal and view the interior through a glass ceiling. Access to the crown costs an extra $3 and must be reserved in advance.

Usually, the ferry also stops at Ellis Island, a half-mile across the harbour from Liberty Island. However, at press time, a reopening date had not yet been set for the former immigration-processing centre, now a museum. Visit www.nps.gov/elis for updates.

Trinity Wall Street & St Paul's Chapel

Trinity Wall Street *89 Broadway, at Wall Street (1-212 602 0800, www.trinitywallstreet.org). Subway R, 1 to Rector Street; 2, 3, 4, 5 to Wall Street.* **Open** *7am-6pm Mon-Fri; 8am-4pm Sat; 7am-4pm Sun. See website for cemetery hours.*
St Paul's Chapel *209 Broadway, between Fulton & Vesey Streets (1-212 233 4164, www.trinitywallstreet.org). Subway A, C to Broadway-Nassau Street; J, Z, 2, 3, 4, 5 to Fulton Street.* **Open** *10am-6pm Mon-Sat; 7am-6pm Sun.*
Both **Admission** *free.* **Map** p56 B3 **11**
Trinity Church was the island's tallest structure when it was completed in 1846

(the original burned down in 1776; a second was demolished in 1839). A set of gates north of the church on Broadway allows access to the adjacent cemetery, where tombstones mark the final resting places of dozens of past city dwellers, including such notable New Yorkers as Founding Father Alexander Hamilton, business tycoon John Jacob Astor and steamboat inventor Robert Fulton. The church museum displays an assortment of historic diaries, photographs, sermons and burial records. Trinity Church also hosts the free seasonal music series Concerts at One (see website for details).

Six blocks north, Trinity's satellite, St Paul's Chapel (1766), is more important architecturally. The oldest building in New York still in continuous use, it is one of the nation's most valued Georgian structures.

Eating & drinking

Adrienne's Pizzabar

54 Stone Street, between Broad Street & Hanover Square (1-212 248 3838, www.adriennespizzabar.com). Subway R to Whitehall Street-South Ferry; 1 to South Ferry; 2, 3 to Wall Street. **Open** 11.30am-midnight Mon-Sat; 11.30am-10pm Sun. **$. Italian. Map** p56 C4 ⑫
Good, non-chain eateries are scarce in the Financial District, but this bright, modern pizzeria on quaint Stone Street provides a pleasant break from the crowded thoroughfares and skyscrapers – there are outside tables from April through November. The kitchen prepares nicely charred pies with delectable toppings, such as the rich quattro formaggi. If you're in a hurry, you can eat at the 12-seat bar, or opt for the sleek, wood-accented dining room to savour small plates and pasta dishes.

The Dead Rabbit

NEW 30 Water Street, at Broad Street (1-646 422 7906, www.deadrabbit nyc.com). Subway R to Whitehall Street-South Ferry. **Open** noon-4am daily. **Bar. Map** p56 C4 ⑬

At this time-capsule nook, you can drink like a boss – Boss Tweed, that is. Belfast bar vets Sean Muldoon and Jack McGarry have conjured up a rough-and-tumble 19th-century tavern in a red-brick landmark. Resurrecting long-forgotten quaffs is nothing new in NYC, but the Dead Rabbit's sheer breadth of mid-19th-century libations eclipses the competition, spanning 100-odd bishops, fixes, nogs and smashes. The fruit-forward Byrrh Wine Daisy, era-appropriate in its china teacup with moustache guard, is particularly well wrought.

Jack's Stir Brew Coffee

222 Front Street, between Beekman Street & Peck Slip (1-212 227 7631, www.jacksstirbrew.com). Subway A, C to Broadway-Nassau; J, Z, 2, 3, 4, 5 to Fulton Street. **Open** phone or see website. **$. Café. Map** p57 D3 ⑭
As we went to press, this award-winning caffeine spot was finally about to reopen following late 2012's devastating Hurricane Sandy. Coffee – made from organic, shade-grown beans – is served by espresso artisans with a knack for oddball concoctions, such as the super-silky Mountie latte, infused with maple syrup.

North End Grill

104 North End Avenue, at Murray Street (1-646 747 1600, www.northend grillnyc.com). Subway A, C to Chambers Street; E to World Trade Center; 2, 3 to Park Place. **Open** 11.30am-2pm, 5.30-9.30pm Mon-Thur; 11.30am-2pm, 5.30-10pm Fri; 11am-2pm, 5.30-10pm Sat; 11am-2.30pm, 5.30-9pm Sun. **$$$. American. Map** p56 A3 ⑮
Danny Meyer has brought his Midas touch to Battery Park City. This instant classic has all the hallmarks of a Meyer joint: effortless, affable service; a warm, buzzy space with top-notch acoustics; and cooking that's easy, accessible and tasty, too. Former Tabla toque Floyd Cardoz leaves his stamp on the menu, devoting an entire section to eggs and adding generous doses of fire and spice.

You might start with evanescent cod throats meunière before moving on to excellent composed plates such as wood-fired lamb loin shingled on a bed of stewed chickpeas seasoned with mint. Desserts are crowd-pleasing, but not predictably so – the sticky toffee pudding is elevated by a shot of Glenlivet.

Shopping

Bowne & Co Stationers

South Street Seaport Museum, 211 Water Street, at Fulton Street (1-646 628 2707). Subway A, C to Broadway-Nassau Street; J, Z, 2, 3, 4, 5 to Fulton Street. **Open** 11am-7pm daily. **Map** p57 D3 ⑯

South Street Seaport Museum's re-creation of an 1870s print shop, Bowne & Co Stationers, doesn't just look the part: the 19th-century platen presses – hand-set using antique type and powered by a treadle – turn out beautiful art prints and cards. The shop also stocks journals and other gifts.

Century 21

22 Cortlandt Street, between Broadway & Church Street (1-212 227 9092, www.c21stores.com). Subway A, C to Broadway-Nassau Street; E to World Trade Center; J, Z, 2, 3, 4, 5 to Fulton Street; N, R to Cortlandt Street. **Open** 7.45am-9pm Mon-Wed; 7.45am-9.30pm Thur, Fri; 10am-9pm Sat; 11am-8pm Sun. **Map** p56 C3 ⑰

A Gucci men's suit for $300? A Marc Jacobs cashmere sweater for less than $200? No, you're not dreaming – you're shopping at Century 21. You may have to rummage around to unearth a treasure, but with savings of up to 65% off regular prices, it's often worth it.

Tribeca & Soho

A former industrial wasteland, Tribeca (the Triangle Below Canal Street) is now one of the city's most expensive areas. Likewise, Soho (the area South of Houston Street) was once a hardscrabble manufacturing zone with the derisive nickname Hell's Hundred Acres. Earmarked for destruction in the 1960s by over-zealous urban planner Robert Moses, its signature cast-iron warehouses were saved by the artists who inhabited them as cheap live-work spaces. Although the chain stores and sidewalk-encroaching street vendors along Broadway create a crush at weekends, there are some fabulous shops, galleries and eateries in the locale.

Sights & museums

Drawing Center

35 Wooster Street, between Broome & Grand Streets (1-212 219 2166, www.drawingcenter.org). Subway A, C, E, 1 to Canal Street. **Open** noon-6pm Wed, Fri-Sun; noon-8pm Thur. **Admission** $5; free-$3 reductions; free 6-8pm Thur. **Map** p58 C4 ⑱

Established in 1977, this non-profit standout recently reopened after expanding its gallery space by 50%. Now comprising three galleries, the Center assembles shows of museum-calibre legends such as Philip Guston, James Ensor and Willem de Kooning, but also 'Selections' surveys of newcomers. Art stars such as Kara Walker, Chris Ofili and Julie Mehretu received some of their earliest NYC exposure here.

Museum

NEW *Cortlandt Alley, between Franklin & White Streets. Subway J, N, Q, R, Z, 6 to Canal Street (no phone, www.mmuseumm.com).* **Open** 11am-7pm Sat, Sun. **Admission** free. **Map** p56 C1 ⑲

See box p66.

Eating & drinking

Balthazar

80 Spring Street, between Broadway & Crosby Street (1-212 965 1414, www.balthazarny.com). Subway N, R

Small wonder

NYC's tiniest museum occupies a Tribeca elevator shaft.

Institutions like the Metropolitan Museum of Art and the American Museum of Natural History are home to thousands of treasures – more than you can possibly see in one outing. On the other, much smaller end of the spectrum, there's **Museum** (see p65), a 60-square-foot repository located in an abandoned Tribeca freight elevator. (Finding it feels like an adventure in itself – it's on Cortlandt Alley, a narrow throughway located between Broadway and Lafayette Streets.)

The walk-in-closet-size space, which debuted in May 2012, showcases a mishmash of found objects and artefacts donated by hobbyists; its permanent holdings include an index card detailing a pot dealer's pricing scale, and – allegedly – the shoe that was infamously thrown at President George W Bush in Iraq in 2008. (The museum's founders, indie filmmakers Alex Kalman, Josh Safdie and Benny Safdie, say they're not legally allowed to reveal the anonymous donor of this particular piece of history.)

Temporary exhibits, which change roughly twice a year, have included such varied displays as a collection of fake vomit from around the world, objects made in US prisons and a selection of *Screw* magazine founder Al Goldstein's personal belongings. Reflecting the founders' deadpan commitment to offering all the accoutrements of a bona fide cultural institution, there is even a gift shop (selling postcards, tote bags, pins and items that tie in to each exhibition) and café (an espresso machine in one corner).

Although Museum is only open at weekends, curious viewers can also get a peek at the space when it's closed (look for the small peepholes in a metal door between Franklin and White Streets).

to Prince Street; 6 to Spring Street.
Open 7.30-11.30am, noon-5pm, 6pm-midnight Mon-Thur; 7.30-11.30am, noon-5pm, 6pm-1am Fri; 9am-4pm, 6pm-1am Sat; 9am-4pm, 5.30pm-midnight Sun. **$$**. **French.**
Map p58 C4 ⑳
At dinner, this iconic eaterie is perennially packed with rail-thin lookers dressed to the nines. But it's more than simply fashionable – the kitchen rarely makes a false step and the service is surprisingly friendly. The $155 three-tiered seafood platter casts an impressive shadow, and the roast chicken on mashed potatoes for two is *délicieux.*

Brushstroke

30 Hudson Street, at Duane Street (1-212 791 3771, www.davidbouley.com). Subway 1, 2, 3 to Chambers Street.
Open 5.30-10pm Mon-Sat. **$$$.**
Japanese. Map p56 B2 ㉑
Prominent local chef David Bouley's name may be behind this venture, but he's not in the kitchen. Instead, he has handed the reins to talented import Isao Yamada, who turns out some of the most accomplished Japanese food in the city. The ever-changing seasonal menu is best experienced as an intricate multicourse feast inspired by the Japanese *kaiseki.* (A small à la carte selection is also available.) A meal might start with muted petals of raw *kombu*-wrapped sea bass, before building slowly towards a subtle climax. In keeping with the basic tenets of this culinary art form, the savoury procession concludes with a rice dish – such as seafood and rice cooked in a clay casserole – and delicate sweets such as creamy soy-milk panna cotta. The sushi bar is run by Tokyo-trained chef Eiji Ichimura, who serves a traditional Edomae-style *omakase.*

Corton

239 West Broadway, between Walker & White Streets (1-212 219 2777, www.cortonnyc.com). Subway A, C, E to Canal Street; 1 to Franklin Street.
Open 5.30-10.30pm Tue-Sat. **$$$.**
French. Map p56 B1 ㉒
When it opened in 2008, Corton was given the highest possible star rating by *Time Out New York* magazine's critics. A meal here is still an extraordinary experience. Veteran restaurateur Drew Nieporent's white-on-white sanctuary focuses all attention on chef Paul Liebrandt's finely wrought food. The presentations, in the style of the most esteemed modern kitchens of Europe, are Photoshop flawless: sweet bay scallops, for example, anchor a visual masterpiece featuring wisps of radish, marcona almonds and sea urchin.

The Dutch

131 Sullivan Street, at Prince Street (1-212 677 6200, www.thedutchnyc.com). Subway C, E to Spring Street. **Open** 11.30am-3pm, 5.30-11pm Mon-Wed; 11.30am-3pm, 5.30pm-1am Thur, Fri; 10am-3pm, 5.30pm-1am Sat; 10am-3pm, 5.30-11pm Sun. **$$. American. Map** p58 C4 ㉓
Andrew Carmellini, Josh Pickard and Luke Ostrom – the white-hot team behind Italian hit Locanda Verde in the Greenwich Hotel (see p172) – turned to American eats for their sophomore effort. The Dutch boasts late-night hours and a freewheeling menu, completing Carmellini's progression from haute golden boy (Café Boulud, Lespinasse) to champion of lusty plates and raucous settings. Carmellini plays off the country's diverse influences with a broad spectrum of dishes. Mini fried-oyster sandwiches, dry-aged steaks and peel 'n' eat prawns all get their due. Drop by the airy oak bar or adjacent oyster room to order from the full menu or sip cocktails such as the Dutch Manhattan, a twist on the classic with house-made vanilla bitters.

Jack's Wife Freda

224 Lafayette Street, between Kenmare & Spring Streets (1-212 510 8550, jackswifefreda.com). Subway 6 to

Spring Street. **Open** 10am-midnight
Mon-Sat; 10am-10pm Sun. **$$**. **Café**.
Map p59 D4 ㉔

Keith McNally protégé Dean Jankelowitz
is behind this café. The 40-seat spot –
sporting dark-green leather banquettes,
brass railings and marble counters –
serves homey fare, like Jankelowitz's
grandmother's matzo ball soup made
with duck fat or a skirt steak sandwich
accompanied by hand-cut fries.

Osteria Morini

*218 Lafayette Street, between
Kenmare & Spring Streets (1-212
965 8777, www.osteriamorini.com).
Subway 6 to Spring Street.* **Open**
11.30am-11pm daily. **$$**. **Italian**.
Map p59 D4 ㉕

Michael White (Alto, Marea) is one of
New York's most prolific and successful Italian-American chefs, and this
terrific downtown homage to a classic
Bolognese tavern is the most accessible restaurant in his stable. The toque
spent seven years cooking in Italy's
Emilia-Romagna region, and his connection to the area surfaces in the
rustic food. Handmade pastas are fantastic across the board. Superb s,
meanwhile, include porchetta with
crisp, crackling skin and potatoes
bathed in pan drippings.

Pegu Club

*2nd Floor, 77 W Houston Street,
between West Broadway & Wooster
Street (1-212 473 7348, www.pegu
club.com). Subway B, D, F, M to
Broadway-Lafayette Street; N, R
to Prince Street.* **Open** 5pm-2am
Mon-Thur, Sun; 5pm-4am Fri, Sat.
Bar. **Map** p58 C4 ㉖

Audrey Saunders, the drinks maven
who turned Bemelmans Bar (see p140)
into one of the city's most respected
cocktail lounges, is behind this sleek liq-
uid destination. Tucked away on the second floor, the sophisticated spot was
inspired by a British officers' club in
Burma. The cocktail list features classics
culled from decades-old booze bibles,

and gin is the key ingredient – these are
serious drinks for grown-up tastes.

Silver Lining

*75 Murray Street, between West
Broadway & Greenwich Street (1-212
513 1234, www.silverliningbar.com).
Subway A, C, 1, 2, 3 to Chambers
Street.* **Open** 5pm-1am Mon-Thur;
5pm-2am Fri; 7pm-2am Sat. **Bar**.
Map p56 B2 ㉗

New York is packed with venues
offering craft cocktails and ones that
spotlight live jazz. But enjoying these
two noble pursuits in the same place
has been nigh impossible. At this well-
heeled Tribeca drinkery, the sound of
piano keys and shaking jiggers find a
common stage inside a majestic 19th-
century townhouse. Little Branch vets
Joseph Schwartz and Vito Dieterle,
along with bar guru Sasha Petraske,
have transported their studied classic
cocktails to Tribeca, and Dieterle –
who moonlights on the tenor sax –
curates the talent.

Shopping

(3x1)

*15 Mercer Street, between Howard
& Grand Streets (1-212 391 6969,
www.3x1.us). Subway A, C, E, J, N,
Q, R, Z, 1, 6 to Canal Street.* **Open**
11am-7pm Mon-Sat; noon-6pm Sun.
Map p58 C5 ㉘

Denim obsessives who are always
looking for the next It jeans have
another place to splurge: (3x1) creates
entirely limited-edition styles sewn in
the store. Designer Scott Morrison, who
previously launched Paper Denim &
Cloth and Earnest Sewn, fills the large,
gallery-like space with a variety of
jeans for men and women (prices start
at $195) and other denim pieces such
as shorts or miniskirts. Watch the construction process take place in a glass-
walled design studio, positioned in the
middle of the boutique. You can even
go bespoke and design your own jeans
from scratch (starting at $1,200).

Chinatown p71

Housing Works Bookstore Café

126 Crosby Street, between Houston & Prince Streets, Soho (1-212 334 3324, www.housingworksbookstore.org). Subway B, D, F, M to Broadway-Lafayette Street; N, R to Prince Street; 6 to Bleecker Street. **Open** 10am-9pm Mon-Fri; 10am-5pm Sat, Sun. **Map** p58 C4 ㉙

This endearing two-level space – which stocks literary fiction, non-fiction, rare books and collectibles – is a peaceful spot to relax over coffee or wine. All proceeds go to providing support services for people living with HIV/AIDS.

In God We Trust

265 Lafayette Street, between Prince & Spring Streets (1-212 966 9010, www.ingodwetrustnyc.com). Subway N, R to Prince Street; 6 to Spring Street. **Open** noon-8pm Mon-Sat; noon-7pm Sun. **Map** p59 D4 ㉚

Designer Shana Tabor's cosy antique-furnished store caters to that ever-appealing vintage-intellectual aesthetic, offering locally crafted collections for men and women. The line of well-priced, cheeky accessories is a highlight – for example, gold heart-shaped pendants engraved with blunt sayings like 'Boring' or 'Blah, blah, blah', rifle-shaped tie bars, and a wide selection of retro sunglasses for only $20 a pair.

Kiki de Montparnasse

79 Greene Street, between Broome & Spring Streets (1-212 965 8150, www.kikidm.com). Subway N, R to Prince Street; 6 to Spring Street. **Open** 11am-7pm Mon, Sun; 11am-8pm Tue-Sat. **Map** p58 C4 ㉛

This luxury lingerie boutique channels the spirit of its namesake, a 1920s sexual icon and Man Ray muse, with a posh array of tastefully provocative contemporary underwear and ensembles in satin and French lace. Look out for novelties such as cotton tank tops with built-in garters, and panties embroidered with saucy legends.

Kiosk

2nd floor, 95 Spring Street, between Broadway & Mercer Street (1-212 226 8601, www.kioskkiosk.com). Subway 6 to Spring Street. **Open** noon-7pm Mon-Sat. **Map** p58 C4 ㉜

Don't be deterred by the graffiti-covered stairwell that leads up to this gem of a shop. Alisa Grifo has collected an array of inexpensive items – mostly simple and functional but with a strong design aesthetic – from around the world, such as cool Japanese can openers, colourful net bags from Germany and Shaker onion baskets handmade in New Hampshire.

Opening Ceremony

33 & 35 Howard Street, between Broadway & Lafayette Street (1-212 219 2688, www.openingceremony.us). Subway J, N, Q, R, Z, 6 to Canal Street. **Open** 11am-8pm Mon-Sat; noon-7pm Sun. **Map** p58 C5 ㉝

The name references the Olympic Games; each year Opening Ceremony assembles wares from hip US designers (the likes of Band of Outsiders, Alexander Wang, Patrik Ervell and Rodarte) and pits them against the competition from abroad. The store has been so popular that it recently expanded, adding a book and music section upstairs and a men's shop next door. There's also an outpost in the hip Ace Hotel (see p176).

What Goes Around Comes Around

351 West Broadway, between Broome & Grand Streets (1-212 343 1225, www.whatgoesaroundnyc.com). Subway A, C, E, 1 to Canal Street. **Open** 11am-8pm Mon-Sat; noon-7pm Sun. **Map** p58 C4 ㉞

A favourite among the New York fashion cognoscenti, this vintage destination sells highly curated stock alongside its own retro label. Style mavens particularly recommend it for 1960s, '70s and '80s rock T-shirts, pristine Alaïa clothing and vintage furs.

Nightlife

Santos Party House

96 Lafayette Street, between Walker & White Streets (1-212 584 5492, www.santospartyhouse.com). Subway J, N, Q, R, Z, 6 to Canal Street. **Open** varies (see website for schedule). **Map** p56 C1 ③⑤

Launched by a team that includes rocker Andrew WK, Santos Party House – two black, square rooms done out in a bare-bones, generic club style – was initially hailed as a scene game-changer. While those high expectations didn't exactly pan out, it's still a solid choice, featuring everything from hip hop to underground house.

SOB's

204 Varick Street, at Houston Street (1-212 243 4940, www.sobs.com). Subway 1 to Houston Street. **Map** p58 B4 ③⑥

The titular Sounds of Brazil (SOB, geddit?) are just some of the many global genres that keep this spot hopping. Hip hop, soul, reggae and Latin beats all figure in the mix, with Raphael Saadiq, Maceo Parker and Eddie Palmieri each appearing of late. The drinks are expensive, but the sharp-looking clientele doesn't seem to mind.

Arts & leisure

HERE

145 Sixth Avenue, between Broome & Spring Streets (1-212 647 0202, Theatremania 1-212 352 3101, http://here.org). Subway C, E to Spring Street. **Map** p58 C4 ③⑦

Dedicated to not-for-profit arts enterprises, this complex has been the launch pad for such well-known shows as Eve Ensler's *The Vagina Monologues*. More recently, HERE has showcased the talents of the brilliantly freaky playwright-performer Taylor Mac.

Soho Rep

46 Walker Street, between Broadway & Church Street (1-212 941 8632, www.sohorep.org). Subway A, C, E, J, N, Q, R, Z, 6 to Canal Street; 1 to Franklin Street. **Map** p56 C1/p58 C5 ③⑧

A couple of years ago, this Off-Off mainstay moved to an Off Broadway contract, but tickets for most shows have remained cheap for Off Broadway. Artistic director Sarah Benson's programming is diverse and audacious: recent productions include works by Young Jean Lee, Sarah Kane and the Nature Theater of Oklahoma.

Chinatown, Little Italy & Nolita

Take a walk around the area south of Broome Street and east of Broadway, and you'll feel as though you've entered a different continent. New York's Chinatown is one of the largest Chinese communities outside Asia. Here, crowded Mott and Grand Streets are lined with fish-, fruit- and vegetable-stocked stands, and Canal Street glitters with cheap jewellery and gift shops, but beware furtive vendors of (undoubtedly fake) designer goods. The main attraction is the food: Mott Street, between Kenmare and Worth Streets, is packed with restaurants.

Little Italy once stretched from Canal to Houston Streets, between Lafayette Street and the Bowery, but these days a strong Italian presence can only truly be observed on the blocks immediately surrounding Mulberry Street. Ethnic pride remains, though: Italian-Americans flood in from across the city during the 11-day Feast of San Gennaro (see p40).

Nolita (North of Little Italy) became a magnet for pricey boutiques and trendy eateries in the 1990s. Elizabeth, Mott and Mulberry Streets, between Houston and Spring Streets, in particular, are home to hip designer shops.

NEW YORK BY AREA

Sights & museums

Museum of Chinese in America

215 Centre Street, between Grand & Howard Streets (1-212 619 4785, www.mocanyc.org). Subway J, N, Q, R, Z, 6 to Canal Street. **Open** 11am-6pm Tue, Wed, Fri-Sun; 11am-9pm Thur. **Admission** $10; free-$5 reductions; free Thur. **Map** p57 D1/p59 D5 ㉟

Designed by prominent Chinese-American architect Maya Lin, MoCA reopened in an airy former machine shop in 2009. Its interior is loosely inspired by a traditional Chinese house, with rooms radiating off a central courtyard and areas defined by screens. The core exhibition traces the development of Chinese communities in the US from the 1850s to the present through objects, images and video. Innovative displays cover the development of industries such as laundries and restaurants in New York, Chinese stereotypes in pop culture, and the suspicion and humiliation Chinese-Americans endured during World War II and the McCarthy era. A mocked-up Chinese general store evokes the feel of the multi-purpose spaces that served as vital community lifelines for men severed from their families under the 1882 Exclusion Act, which restricted immigration. A gallery is devoted to temporary exhibitions, such as *New York Times* photographer Annie Ling's images of Chinatown, on view winter 2013-14.

Eating & drinking

Café Habana

17 Prince Street, at Elizabeth Street (1-212 625 2001, www.ecoeatery.com). Subway N, R to Prince Street; 6 to Spring Street. **Open** 9am-midnight daily. **$. Cuban. Map** p59 D4 ㊵

Trendy Nolita types storm this chrome corner fixture for the addictive grilled corn: golden ears doused in fresh mayo, chargrilled, and generously sprinkled with chilli powder and grated *cotija* cheese. Staples include a Cuban sandwich of roasted pork, ham, melted swiss and pickles, and beer-battered catfish with spicy mayo. At the takeout annexe next door, you can get that corn-on-a-stick to go.

Ed's Lobster Bar

222 Lafayette Street, between Kenmare & Spring Streets (1-212 343 3236, www.lobsterbarnyc.com). Subway B, D, F, M to Broadway-Lafayette Street. **Open** noon-3pm, 5-11pm Mon-Thur; noon-3pm, 5pm-midnight Fri; noon-midnight Sat; noon-9pm Sun. **$$. Seafood. Map** p59 D4 ㊶

Chef Ed McFarland (formerly of Pearl Oyster Bar) is behind this tiny seafood joint. If you secure a place at the 25-seat marble bar or one of the few tables in the whitewashed eaterie, expect superlative raw-bar eats, delicately fried clams and lobster served every which way: steamed, grilled, broiled, chilled, stuffed into a pie and – the crowd favourite – the lobster roll. Here, it's a buttered bun stuffed with premium chunks of meat and just a light coating of mayo.

Nom Wah Tea Parlor

13 Doyers Street, between Bowery & Pell Street (1-212 962 6047, www.nomwah.com). Subway J, N, Q, R, Z, 6 to Canal Street; J, Z to Chambers Street. **Open** 10.30am-9pm Mon-Thur, Sun; 10.30am-10pm Fri, Sat. **$. Chinese. Map** p57 D1 ㊷

New York's first dim sum house, Nom Wah opened in 1920 and was owned by the same family for more than three decades. The current owner, Wilson Tang, has revamped it in a vintage style true to the restaurant's archival photographs. The most important tweaks, though, were behind the scenes: Tang updated the kitchen and did away with the procedure of cooking dim sum en masse. Now, each plate (ultra-fluffy oversize roasted-pork buns, flaky fried crêpe egg rolls) is cooked to order.

Parm & Torrisi Italian Specialties

Parm *248 Mulberry Street, between Prince and Spring Streets (1-212 993 7189, www.parmnyc.com).* **Open** 11am-11pm Mon-Wed, Sun; 11am-midnight Thur-Sat. **$**.

Torrisi Italian Specialties *250 Mulberry Street, between Prince & Spring Streets (1-212 965 0955, www.torrisinyc.com).* **Open** 5.30-11pm Mon-Thur; noon-1.45pm, 5.30-11pm Fri-Sun. **$$**.

Both *Subway N, R to Prince Street; 6 to Spring Street.* **Italian**. **Map** p59 D4 ㊸

Young guns Mario Carbone and Rich Torrisi, two fine-dining vets, brought a cool-kid sheen to red-sauce plates in 2010, when they debuted Torrisi Italian Specialties, a deli by day and haute eaterie by night. People lined up for their buzzworthy sandwiches (outstanding herb-rubbed roasted turkey, classic cold cuts or chicken parmesan) and hard-to-score dinner seats, packing the joint until it outgrew the space. The pair smartly split the operations, devoting their original flagship to tasting menus and transplanting the sandwich offerings to fetching diner digs next door.

Xi'an Famous Foods

67 Bayard Street, between Elizabeth & Mott Streets (no phone, www.xianfoods. com). Subway J, N, Q, R, Z, 6 to Canal Street. **Open** 11.30am-9pm Mon-Thur, Sun; 11.30am-9.30pm Fri, Sat. No credit cards. **$**. **Chinese**. **Map** p57 D1 ㊹

This cheap Chinese chainlet, which got the seal of approval from celebrity chef Anthony Bourdain, highlights the mouth-tingling cuisine of Xi'an, an ancient capital along China's Silk Road. Claim one of the 35 stools and nosh on spicy noodles or a cumin-spiced burger for less than $5.

Shopping

Creatures of Comfort

205 Mulberry Street, between Kenmare & Spring Streets (1-212 925 1005, www.creaturesofcomfort.us). Subway 6 to Spring Street; N, R to Prince Street. **Open** 11am-7pm Mon-Sat; noon-7pm Sun. **Map** p59 D4 ㊺

Jade Lai opened Creatures of Comfort in Los Angeles in 2005 and brought her cool-girl aesthetic east five years later. Occupying the former home of the 12th police precinct, the New York offshoot offers a similar mix of pricey but oh-so-cool pieces from various avant-garde lines, such as MM6 Maison Martin Margiela, Acne and Isabel Marant's Etoile, plus the store's own-label bohemian basics and shoes and accessories.

Downtown Music Gallery

13 Monroe Street, between Catherine & Market Streets (1-212 473 0043, www.downtownmusicgallery.com). Subway J, Z to Chambers Street; 4, 5, 6 to Brooklyn Bridge-City Hall. **Open** noon-6pm Mon-Wed; noon-7pm Thur-Sun. **Map** p57 D2 ㊻

Many landmarks of the so-called downtown music scene have closed, but as long as DMG exists, the community will have a sturdy anchor. The shop stocks the city's finest selection of avant-garde jazz, contemporary classical, progressive rock and related styles.

Erica Weiner

173 Elizabeth Street, between Kenmare & Spring Streets (1-212 334 6383, www.ericaweiner.com). Subway 6 to Spring Street. **Open** noon-8pm daily. **Map** p59 D4 ㊼

Seamstress-turned-jewellery-designer Erica Weiner sells her own bronze, brass, silver and gold creations – many priced at under $100 – alongside vintage and reworked baubles. Old wooden cabinets and stacked crates showcase rings and charm-laden necklaces, the latter laden with the likes of tiny dangling harmonicas and steel penknives. Other favourites include brass ginkgo-leaf earrings, and moveable-type-letter necklaces for your favourite wordsmith.

Warm

NEW *181 Mott Street, between Broome & Kenmare Streets (1-212 925 200, www.warmny.com). Subway J, Z to Bowery; 6 to Spring Street.* **Open** noon-7pm Mon-Sat; noon-6pm Sun. **Map** p59 D4 ⑬

The husband-and-wife owners, Rob Magnotta and Winnie Beattie, curate an eclectic selection of women's threads, accessories and vintage books, influenced by their globe-trotting surfer lifestyle. The laid-back looks include urban boho-chic clothing from Vanessa Bruno, Giada Forte and Maison Olga, and handcrafted jewellery by artist Suzannah Wainhouse.

Lower East Side

Once better known for bagels and bargains, this area – formerly an immigrant enclave – is now brimming with vintage and indie-designer boutiques, fashionable bars and, since the New Museum of Contemporary Art opened a $50 million building on the Bowery in late 2007, dozens of storefront galleries.

Sights & museums

Lower East Side Tenement Museum

Visitors' centre, 103 Orchard Street, at Delancey Street (1-212 982 8420, www.tenement.org). Subway F to Delancey Street; J, Z to Delancey-Essex Streets. **Open** Museum shop & ticketing 10am-6pm Mon-Wed, Fri-Sun; 10am-8.30pm Thur. *Tours* 10.30am-5pm Mon-Wed, Fri-Sun; 10.30am-8pm Thur (see website for schedule). **Admission** $22-$25; $17-$20 reductions. **Map** p59 E4 ⑬

This fascinating museum – actually a series of restored tenement apartments at 97 Orchard Street – is accessible only by guided tour, which start at the visitors' centre at 103 Orchard Street. Tours often sell out, so it's wise to book ahead.

'Hard Times' visits the homes of an Italian and a German-Jewish clan; 'Sweatshop Workers' explores the apartments of two Eastern European Jewish families as well as a garment shop where many of the locals would have found employment; and 'Irish Outsiders' unfurls the life of the Moore family, who are coping with the loss of their child. Families may want to stop by quarters once occupied by a Sephardic Jewish Greek family and speak to an interpreter in period costume channelling the 14-year-old daughter of the house, Victoria Confino. A new tour, 'Shop Life', explores the diverse retailers that occupied the building's storefronts, including a 19th-century German saloon. From mid March through December, the museum also conducts themed daily walking tours of the Lower East Side ($22-$45, $17-$40 reductions).

Museum at Eldridge Street (Eldridge Street Synagogue)

12 Eldridge Street, between Canal & Division Streets (1-212 219 0302, www.eldridgestreet.org). Subway F to East Broadway. **Open** 10am-5pm Mon-Thur, Sun; 10am-3pm Fri. **Admission** $10; free-$8 reductions; free Mon. **Map** p57 D1/61 E5 ⑳

With an impressive façade that combines Romanesque, Moorish and elements, the first grand synagogue on the Lower East Side is now surrounded by dumpling shops and Chinese herb stores. As Jews left the area the building fell into disrepair. However, a 20-year, $18.5 million facelift has restored its splendour; the soaring main sanctuary features hand-stencilled walls and a resplendent stained-glass rose window incorporating Star of David motifs. The renovations were completed in 2010, with the installation of a new stained-glass window designed by artist Kiki Smith and architect Deborah Gans. The admission price includes a guided tour (see website for schedule). In the new orientation centre, opening in December 2013, touch-screens highlight the synagogue's architecture, aspects of worship and local history, including other Jewish landmarks.

New Museum of Contemporary Art

235 Bowery, at Prince Street (1-212 219 1222, www.newmuseum.org). Subway F to Lower East Side-Second Avenue; J, Z to Bowery; N, R to Prince Street; 6 to Spring Street. **Open** 11am-6pm Wed, Fri-Sun; 11am-9pm Thur. **Admission** $14; free-$12 reductions; free 7-9pm Thur. **Map** p59 D4 ⑤

Having occupied various sites for 30 years, New York City's only contemporary art museum finally got its own purpose-built space in late 2007. Dedicated to emerging media and under-recognised artists, the seven-floor space is worth a look for the architecture alone – a striking, off-centre stack of aluminium-mesh-clad boxes designed by the cutting-edge Tokyo architectural firm Sejima + Nishizawa/SANAA. At weekends, don't miss the fabulous views from the minimalist seventh-floor Sky Room, and be sure to stop into the adjacent Studio 231, which features projects by emerging artists from around the world.

Event highlights 'Chris Burden: Extreme Measures' (through 12 Jan 2014).

Eating & drinking

Attaboy

NEW *134 Eldridge Street, between Broome & Delancey Streets (no phone). Subway F to Delancey Street; J, Z to Delancey-Essex Streets.* **Open** 6.45pm-3am daily. **Bar**. **Map** p59 D4 ⑤

Occupying the original Milk and Honey (see p112) digs and run by alums Sam Ross and Michael McIlroy, Attaboy has a livelier, lighter air than Sasha Petraske's big-league cocktail den. The tucked-away haunt has kept

the same bespoke protocol as its forebear: at the brushed-steel bar, suspender-clad drinks slingers stir off-the-cuff riffs to suit each customer's preference. Wistful boozers can seek solace in Petraske-era standard-bearers, like Ross's signature Penicillin, a still-inspiring blend of Laphroaig ten-year, honey-ginger syrup and lemon.

Clinton Street Baking Company & Restaurant

4 Clinton Street, between Houston & Stanton Streets (1-646 602 6263, www.clintonstreetbaking.com). Subway F to Delancey Street; J, Z to Delancey-Essex Streets. **Open** 8am-4pm, 6-11pm Mon-Sat; 8am-6pm Sun. **$**. **American**. **Map** p59 E4 ⑤

The warm buttermilk biscuits and fluffy pancakes at this pioneering little eatery give you reason enough to face the guaranteed brunch-time crowds. If you want to avoid the onslaught, however, the homely spot is just as reliable at both lunch and dinner; drop in for the $15 beer-and-burger special (6-8pm Mon-Thur).

Freemans

2 Freeman Alley, off Rivington Street, between Bowery & Chrystie Street (1-212 420 0012, www.freemans restaurant.com). Subway F to Lower East Side-Second Avenue; J, Z to Bowery. **Open** 11am-4pm, 6-11.30pm Mon-Fri; 10am-4pm, 6-11.30pm Sat, Sun. **$$**. **American**. **Map** p59 D4 ⑤

Up at the end of a graffiti-marked alley, Freemans' appealing colonial-tavern-meets-hunting-lodge style is still a hit with retro-loving New Yorkers. Garage-sale oil paintings and moose antlers serve as backdrops to a curved zinc bar, while the menu recalls a simpler time – devils on horseback (prunes stuffed with stilton and wrapped in bacon); rum-soaked ribs, the meat falling off the bone with a gentle nudge of the fork; and stiff cocktails that'll get you good and sauced.

Lower East Side Tenement
Museum p74

Katz's Delicatessen

205 E Houston Street, at Ludlow Street (1-212 254 2246, www.katzs delicatessen.com). Subway F to Lower East Side-Second Avenue. **Open** 8am-10.45pm Mon-Wed; 8am-2.45am Thur; 24hrs Fri (from 8am), Sat; closes 10.45pm Sun. **$-$$. Delicatessen.** **Map** p59 E4 ⑤

A visit to Gotham isn't complete without a stop at a quintessential New York deli, and this Lower East Side survivor is the real deal. You might get a kick out of the famous faces (from Bill Clinton to Ben Stiller) plastered to the panelled walls, or the spot where Meg Ryan faked it in *When Harry Met Sally…*, but the real stars of this cafeteria are the thick-cut pastrami sandwiches and the crisp-skinned all-beef hot dogs – the latter are a mere $3.45.

Mission Chinese Food

NEW *154 Orchard Street, between Rivington & Stanton Streets (1-212 529 8800, www.missionchinesefood.com). Subway F to Lower East Side-Second Avenue.* **Open** noon-3pm, 5.30pm-midnight daily. **$$. Chinese.** **Map** p59 E4 ⑤

Anthony Myint and Daniel Bowien shook up the San Francisco dining scene with their eclectic Asian soul food before Bowien opened this Lower East Side outpost, masquerading as a cheap takeout joint. His cooking features intensely personal spins on a host of Szechuan and Chinese-American classics. The *ma po* tofu spotlights pork shoulder slow-cooked for six hours under seaweed sheets to ramp up the umami, along with new dimensions of tongue-numbing heat. Rather than the usual chicken, the *kung pao* comes with excellent house-smoked pastrami.

Spitzer's Corner

101 Rivington Street, at Ludlow Street (1-212 228 0027, www.spitzerscorner. com). Subway F to Delancey Street; J, Z to Delancey-Essex Streets. **Open** noon-4am Mon-Fri; 10am-4am Sat, Sun. **Bar.** **Map** p59 E4 ⑤

Referencing the Lower East Side's pickle-making heritage, the walls at this rustic gastropub are made from salvaged wooden barrels. The formidable beer list – 40 rotating draughts – includes Bear Republic's fragrant Racer 5 IPA. Mull over your selection, with the help of appetising tasting notes, at one of the wide communal tables. The gastro end of things is manifest in the menu of quality pub grub – truffle mac and cheese, for example – or a lamb burger.

Shopping

Alife Rivington Club

158 Rivington Street, between Clinton & Suffolk Streets (1-212 432 7200, www.alifenewyork.com). Subway F to Delancey Street; J, Z to Delancey-Essex Streets. **Open** noon-7pm Mon-Sat; noon-6pm Sun. **Map** p59 E4 ⑤

Whether you're looking for a simple white trainer or a trendy graphic style, you'll want to gain entry to this 'club', which stocks a wide range of major brands such as Nike (including sought-after re-issues like Air Jordan), Adidas and New Balance. You'll also find lesser-known names including the shop's own label.

The Cast

71 Orchard Street, between Broome & Grand Streets (1-212 228 2020, www.thecast.com). Subway F to Lower East Side-Second Avenue. **Open** noon-8pm Mon-Sat; noon-7pm Sun. **Map** p59 E4 ⑤

At the core of Chuck Guarino's rock 'n' roll-inspired collection is the trinity of well-cut denim, superior leather jackets based on classic motorcycle styles, and the artful T-shirts that launched the label in 2004. The ladies have their own line, Bitch Club, covering similar ground.

Dear: Rivington

95 Rivington Street, between Ludlow & Orchard Streets (1-212 673 3494, www.dearrivington.com). Subway F to Delancey Street; J, Z to Delancey-Essex Streets. **Open** noon-7pm daily. **Map** p59 E4 ⑥⓪

The glass storefront is a stage for Moon Rhee and Hey Ja Do's art installation-like displays; inside the white bi-level space, head downstairs for their own Victorian-inspired line and select pieces by avant-garde Japanese labels such as Comme des Garçons and Yohji Yamamoto. Upstairs is a fascinating archive of vintage homewares, objects and contemporary art, including framed antique silhouettes, old globes and tins.

Doyle & Doyle

189 Orchard Street, between E Houston & Stanton Streets (1-212 677 9991, www.doyledoyle.com). Subway F to Lower East Side-Second Avenue. **Open** 1-7pm Tue, Wed, Fri; 1-8pm Thur; noon-7pm Sat, Sun. **Map** p59 D4 ⑥①

Whether your taste is art deco or nouveau, Victorian or Edwardian, gemologist sisters Pam and Elizabeth Doyle, who specialise in estate and antique jewellery, will have that one-of-a-kind item you're looking for, including engagement and eternity rings. The artfully displayed pieces within wall-mounted wood-frame cases are just a fraction of what they have in stock.

The Dressing Room

75A Orchard Street, between Broome & Grand Streets (1-212 966 7330, www.thedressingroomnyc.com). Subway B, D to Grand Street; F to Delancey Street; J, Z to Delancey-Essex Streets. **Open** 1pm-midnight Tue, Wed; 1pm-2am Thur-Sat; 1-8pm Sun. **Map** p59 E4 ⑥②

At first glance, the Dressing Room may look like any Lower East Side lounge, thanks to a handsome wood bar, but this quirky co-op cum watering hole rewards the curious. The adjoining room displays lines by indie designers alongside select vintage pieces, and there's also a second-hand clothing exchange downstairs.

Honey in the Rough

161 Rivington Street, between Clinton & Suffolk Streets (1-212 228 6415, www.honeyintherough.com). Subway F to Delancey Street; J, Z to Delancey-Essex Streets. **Open** noon-8pm Mon-Sat; noon-7pm Sun. **Map** p59 E4 ⑥③

Looking for something sweet and charming? Hit this cosy, ultra-femme boutique. Owner Ashley Hanosh fills the well-worn spot with an excellent line-up of local indie labels, including Samantha Pleet, Whit and Nomia, alongside carefully selected accessories, some of which are exclusive to the shop.

The Hoodie Shop

181 Orchard Street, between E Houston & Stanton Streets (1-646 559 2716, www.thehoodieshop.com). Subway 1 to Houston Street. **Open** noon-9pm Mon-Sat; 11am-7pm Sun. **Map** p59 D4 ⑥④

Up to 50 different brands of hooded apparel for men and women are showcased in this '70s-inspired boutique, from retro zip-ups to army-print utility jackets. The shop has a DJ booth and movie screen for late-night shopping parties and other in-store events.

Obsessive Compulsive Cosmetics

174 Ludlow Street, between E Houston & Stanton Streets (1-212 675 2404, www.occmakeup.com). Subway F to Lower East Side-Second Avenue. **Open** 11am-7pm Mon-Sat; noon-6pm Sun. **Map** p59 E4 ⑥⑤

Creator David Klasfeld founded OCC in the kitchen of his Lower East Side apartment in 2004. The make-up artist has since expanded his 100% vegan and cruelty-free cosmetics line from just two shades of lip balm to an extensive assortment of bang-for-your-buck beauty products. In his flagship, you can browse more than 30 shades of nail polish and nearly 40 loose eye-shadow powders, among other products, but we especially like the Lip Tars, which glide on like a gloss but have the matte finish and saturated pigmentation of a lipstick.

Reed Space

151 Orchard Street, between Rivington & Stanton Streets (1-212 253 0588, www.thereedspace.com). Subway F to Delancey Street; J, Z to Delancey-Essex Streets. **Open** 1-7pm Mon-Fri; noon-7pm Sat, Sun. **Map** p59 D4 66

Reed Space is the brainchild of Jeff Ng (AKA Jeff Staple), who has worked on product design and branding with the likes of Nike and Timberland. It stocks local and international urban menswear brands (10.Deep, Undefeated) and footwear, including exclusive Staple collaborations. Art books and culture mags are shelved on an eye-popping installation of four stacked rows of white chairs fixed to one wall.

Russ & Daughters

179 E Houston Street, between Allen & Orchard Streets (1-212 475 4880, www.russanddaughters.com). Subway F to Lower East Side-Second Avenue. **Open** 8am-8pm Mon-Fri; 8am-7pm Sat; 8am-5.30pm Sun. **Map** p59 D4 67

The daughters in the name have given way to great-grandchildren, but this Lower East Side survivor, established in 1914, is still run by the same family. Specialising in smoked and cured fish and caviar, it sells about ten varieties of smoked salmon, eight types of herring and many other Jewish-inflected Eastern European delectables. Filled bagels are available to take away.

Nightlife

Bowery Ballroom

6 Delancey Street, between Bowery & Chrystie Street (1-212 533 2111, www.boweryballroom.com). Subway B, D to Grand Street; J, Z to Bowery; 6 to Spring Street. **Map** p59 D4 68

It's probably the best venue in the city for seeing indie bands, either on the way up or holding their own. Still, the Bowery also manages to bring in a diverse range of artists from home and abroad. Expect a clear view and bright sound from any spot. The spacious downstairs lounge is a great place to hang out between sets.

Cake Shop

152 Ludlow Street, between Rivington & Stanton Streets (1-212 253 0036, www.cake-shop.com). Subway F to Lower East Side-Second Avenue. **Open** 5pm-2am Mon-Thur; 5pm-4am Fri-Sat. **Map** p59 E4 69

It can be hard to see the stage in this narrow, stuffy basement, but Cake Shop gets big points for its keen indie and underground-rock bookings, among the most adventurous in town. True to its name, the venue sells vegan pastries and coffee upstairs, and record-store ephemera in the street-level back room.

Mercury Lounge

217 E Houston Street, between Essex & Ludlow Streets (1-212 260 4700, www.mercuryloungenyc.com). Subway F to Lower East Side-Second Avenue. **Map** p59 E4 70

The unassuming, boxy Mercury Lounge is an old standby, with solid sound and sight lines (and a cramped bar in the front room). There are four-band bills most nights, though they can seem stylistically haphazard and set times are often later than advertised. It's a good idea to book bigger shows in advance.

The Slipper Room

NEW 167 Orchard Street, at Stanton Street, Lower East Side (1-212 253 7246, www.slipperroom.com). Subway F to Lower East Side-Second Avenue. **Open** varies Mon, Sun; 8.30pm-2am Tue; 7pm-2am Wed, Thur; 8.30pm-4am Fri, Sat. **Map** p59 D4 71

This venue was the epicentre of the neoburlesque and vaudeville scenes in

NYC and helped launch the careers of many a burly-Q star (Dirty Martini, Julie Atlas Muz, Murray Hill and boylesquer Tigger!, to name a few). After 11 years of debauchery, co-owner and creative director James Habacker – better known as his borscht belt alter ego, Mel Frye – shuttered the space in 2010 to rebuild it from the ground up. The refurbished club now has state-of-the-art lighting and sound systems, plus a fly-rig for aerial acts.

Arts & leisure

Abrons Arts Center

466 Grand Street, at Pitt Street (1-212 598 0400, www.henrystreet.org/arts). Subway B, D to Grand Street; F to Delancey Street; J, Z to Delancey-Essex Streets. **Map** p59 E4 **72**
This multidisciplinary arts venue, which features a beautiful proscenium theatre, focuses on a wealth of contemporary dance, courtesy of artistic director Jay Wegman. It's worth a look, especially in January when the American Realness festival fills the space's three theatres with experimental work.

East Village

The area east of Broadway between Houston and 14th Streets has a long history as a countercultural hotbed. From the 1950s to the '70s, St Marks Place (8th Street, between Lafayette Street & Avenue A) was a hangout for artists, writers, radicals and musicians. It's still packed until the wee hours, but these days it's with crowds of college students and tourists browsing for bargain T-shirts, used CDs and pot paraphernalia. While legendary music venues such as CBGB are no more, a few bohemian hangouts endure, and the East Village has also evolved into a superior cheap-eats hotspot. In the neighbourhood's renovated green space, Tompkins

Square Park, bongo beaters, guitarists, yuppies and the homeless all mingle.

Sights & museums

Museum of Reclaimed Urban Space

NEW *155 Avenue C, between 9th & 10th Streets (1-646 833 7764, www.morusnyc.org). Subway L to First Avenue.* **Open** 11am-7pm Tue, Thur-Sun. **Admission** free (donations appreciated). **Map** p59 E2 **73**
Co-founded by Bill Di Paola, director of advocacy group Time's Up!, this monument to local activism is housed in C-Squat, a five-floor walk-up that has sheltered activists, down-on-their-luck artists and members of several punk bands (including Leftover Crack, Old Skull and Nausea) from the 1970s through the present. Artefacts from Occupy Wall Street (including an energy bike that helped power Zuccotti Park during its occupation in 2011) and earlier causes show how city residents, both past and present, created, protected and took back community spaces.

Eating & drinking

Back Forty

190 Avenue B, between 11th & 12th Streets (1-212 388 1990, www.back fortynyc.com). Subway L to First Avenue. **Open** 6-11pm Mon-Thur; 6pm-midnight Fri; 11am-3.30pm, 6pm-midnight Sat; 11am-3.30pm, 6-10pm Sun. **$$. American. Map** p59 E2 **74**
Peter Hoffman (the pioneering chef who launched the now-defunct, market-driven restaurant Savoy) is behind this East Village seasonal-eats tavern, where pared-down farmhouse chic prevails in the decor and on the menu. House specialities include juicy grass-fed burgers and ice-cream floats made with small-batch root beer. The spacious back garden is a bonus during the warmer months.

Big Gay Ice Cream Shop

125 E 7th Street, between First Avenue & Avenue A (1-212 533 9333, www. biggayicecream.com). Subway L to First Avenue. **Open** 1pm-midnight Mon, Wed-Sun; 4-11pm Tue (see website for reduced winter hours). **$. Ice-cream**. **Map** p59 E3 ⑦⑤

Ice-cream truckers Doug Quint and Bryan Petroff now have two brick-and-mortar shops dispensing their quirky soft-serve creations (the second is in the West Village). Toppings run the gamut from cayenne pepper to bourbon-butterscotch sauce, or opt for one of the signature combos like the Salty Pimp (vanilla ice-cream, dulce de leche, sea salt and chocolate dip) or the Bea Arthur (vanilla ice-cream, dulce de leche and crushed Nilla wafers).

Caracas Arepa Bar

93½ E 7th Street, between First Avenue & Avenue A (1-212 228 5062, www.caracasarepabar.com). Subway F to Lower East Side-Second Avenue; 6 to Astor Place. **Open** noon-11pm daily. **$. Venezuelan**. **Map** p59 D3 ⑦⑥

This endearing spot, with floral vinyl-covered tables and bare-brick walls, zaps you straight from New York to Caracas. Each *arepa* is made from scratch daily; the pitta-like pockets are stuffed with a choice of a dozen fillings, such as the classic beef with black beans, cheese and plaintain, or chicken and avocado. Top off your snack with a *cocada*, a thick and creamy milkshake made with freshly grated coconut and cinnamon.

Crif Dogs

113 St Marks Place, between First Avenue & Avenue A (1-212 614 2728, www.crifdogs.com). Subway L to First Avenue; 6 to Astor Place. **Open** noon-2am Mon-Thur; noon-4am Fri, Sat; noon-1am Sun. **$. Hot dogs**. **Map** p59 D3 ⑦⑦

You'll recognise this place by the giant hot dog outside, bearing the come-on 'Eat me'. Crif offers the best New Jersey-style dogs this side of the Hudson: handmade smoked-pork tube-steaks that are deep-fried until they're bursting out of their skins. While they're served in various guises, among them the Spicy Redneck (wrapped in bacon and covered in chilli, coleslaw and jalapeños), we're partial to the classic with mustard and kraut. If you're wondering why there are so many people hanging around near the public phone booth at night, it's because there's a trendy cocktail bar, PDT (see p85), concealed behind it.

DBGB Kitchen & Bar

299 Bowery, at Houston Street (1-212 933 5300, www.danielnyc.com). Subway B, D, F, M to Broadway-Lafayette Street; 6 to Bleecker Street. **Open** noon-11pm Mon; noon-midnight Tue-Thur; noon-1am Fri; 11am-1am Sat; 11am-11pm Sun. **$$. French**. **Map** p59 D3 ⑦⑧

This big, buzzy brasserie – chef Daniel Boulud's most populist venture – stands out for its kitchen-sink scope. Around nine kinds of sausage, from Thai-accented to Tunisienne, are served alongside burgers, offal and haute bistro fare. The best way to get your head around the schizophrenic enterprise is to bring a large group and try to sample as much of the range as possible, including ice-cream sundaes or sumptuous cakes for dessert.

Death & Company

433 E 6th Street, between First Avenue & Avenue A (1-212 388 0882, www.deathandcompany.com). Subway F to Lower East Side-Second Avenue; 6 to Astor Place. **Open** 6pm-2am Mon-Thur, Sun; 6pm-3am Fri, Sat. **Bar**. **Map** p59 E3 ⑦⑨

The nattily attired mixologists are deadly serious about drinks at this pseudo speakeasy with Gothic flair (don't be intimidated by the imposing wooden door). Black walls and cushy booths combine with chandeliers to set the luxuriously sombre mood. The inventive cocktails are matched by top-notch nibbles, such as Welsh rarebit.

Dirt Candy

430 E 9th Street, between First Avenue & Avenue A (1-212 228 7732, www.dirtcandynyc.com). Subway L to First Avenue; 6 to Astor Place. **Open** 5.30-11pm Tue-Sat. $$. **Vegetarian.** **Map** p59 E2 ❹

The shiny, futuristic surroundings here look more like a chic nail salon than a restaurant. Chef-owner Amanda Cohen has created an unlikely space to execute her less-likely ambition: to make people crave vegetables. She mostly succeeds. Elaborate dishes might include a a pungent portobello mousse accompanied by shiitake mushrooms and fennel-peach compote, or stone-ground grits served with corn cream, pickled shiitake mushrooms, *huitlacoche* (Mexican truffle) and a tempura poached egg.

Dos Toros

137 Fourth Avenue, between 13th & 14th Streets (1-212 677 7300, www.dostoros.com). Subway L to Third Avenue; L, N, Q, R, 4, 5, 6 to 14th Street-Union Square. **Open** 11.30am-10.30pm Mon; 11.30am-11pm Tue-Fri; noon-11pm Sat; noon-10.30pm Sun. $. **Mexican.** **Map** p58 C2 ❸

When it hit NYC a few years ago, this bright little Cal-Mex taqueria was lauded by *Time Out New York* critics for its bangin' burritos, and it hasn't lost a step since. The fillings – juicy flap steak, moist grilled chicken, smooth guacamole – are among the best in town.

Il Buco Alimentari & Vineria

53 Great Jones Street, between Bowery and Lafayette Street (1-212 837 2622, www.ilbucovineria.com). Subway B, D, F, M to Broadway-Lafayette Street; 6 to Bleecker Street. **Open** 7am-midnight Mon-Thur; 7am-1am Fri; 9am-1am Sat; 9am-11pm Sun. $$. **Italian.** **Map** p59 D3 ❷

Il Buco has been a mainstay of the downtown dining scene since the '90s and a pioneer in the sort of rustic Italian food now consuming the city. Owner Donna Leonard took her sweet time (18 years, to be exact) to unveil her first offshoot, Il Buco Alimentari & Vineria. It was worth the wait: the new hybrid bakery, food shop, café and trattoria is as confident as its decades-old sibling with sure-footed service, the familial bustle of a neighbourhood pillar, and heady aromas of wood-fired short ribs and salt-crusted fish drifting from an open kitchen.

Other location Il Buco, 47 Bond Street, between Bowery & Lafayette Street (1-212 533 1932).

International Bar

120½ First Avenue, between St Marks Place & E 7th Street (1-212 777 1643). Subway F to Lower East Side-Second Avenue; L to First Avenue. **Open** 8am-4am Mon-Sat; noon-4am Sun. **Bar.** **Map** p59 D3 ❸

The walls have been cleared of graffiti, but the second coming of this legendary saloon stays true to its dive bar roots (the original closed in 2005 after more than 40 years of business). A scuffed mahogany bar and vintage film posters make up the decor, and the jukebox is still killer (Black Flag, Nina Simone). The cheap booze and grimy vibe foster the feeling that I-Bar never left.

Ippudo New York

65 Fourth Avenue, between 9th & 10th Streets (1-212 388 0088, www.ippudony.com). Subway 6 to Astor Place. **Open** 11am-3.30pm, 5-11.30pm Mon-Thur; 11am-3.30pm, 5pm-12.30am Fri-Sat; 11am-10.30pm Sun. $-$$. **Japanese.** **Map** p59 D2 ❸

This sleek outpost of a Japanese ramen chain is packed mostly with Nippon natives who queue up for a taste of 'Ramen King' Shigemi Kawahara's

proletariat_rare new and unusual beer

wandering star_red oktober 5   perfect crime_hollow point 10
midnight sun_panty peeler 8   nogne o_india saison 10
fishermans_pumpkin stout 5   yeastie boys_rex attitude 12
great divide_fresh hop 6   hofstettner_granit ice bock 12
oud beersel_framboise 12   local option_american muscle 8
nogne o_sunturnbrew 8   bear republic_late harvest 8
                    cash only

Proletariat p85

tonkotsu – a pork-based broth. About half a dozen varieties include the Akamaru Modern, a smooth, buttery soup topped with scallions (spring onions), cabbage, a slice of roasted pork and pleasantly elastic noodles.

Jimmy's No. 43

43 E 7th Street, between Second & Third Avenues (1-212 982 3006, www. jimmysno43.com). Subway F to Lower East Side-Second Avenue; 6 to Astor Place. **Open** noon-2am Mon-Thur; noon-4am Fri, Sat; 11.30am-2am Sun. **No credit cards. Bar**. Map p59 D3 ⑳
You could easily miss this worthy subterranean spot if it weren't for the sign painted on a doorway over an inconspicuous set of stairs. Descend them and you'll encounter burnt-yellow walls displaying taxidermy, mismatched wood tables and medieval-mistyle arched passageways that lead to different rooms. Beer is a star here, with 12 quality selections on tap (40 in the bottle), many of which also make it into the slow-food dishes filled with organic ingredients.

McSorley's Old Ale House

15 E 7th Street, between Second & Third Avenues (1-212 473 9148). Subway F to Lower East Side-Second Avenue. **Open** 11am-1am Mon-Sat; 1pm-1am Sun. No credit cards. **Bar**.
Map p59 D3 ⑳
Ladies should probably leave the Manolos at home. In traditional Irish-pub fashion, McSorley's floor has been thoroughly scattered with sawdust to take care of the spills and other messes that often accompany large quantities of cheap beer. Established in 1854, McSorley's became an institution by remaining steadfastly authentic and providing only two choices to its customers: McSorley's Dark Ale and McSorley's Light Ale.

Mighty Quinn's

NEW *103 Second Avenue, at E 6th Street (1-212 677 3733, www.mighty quinnsbbq.com). Subway 6 to Astor*
Place. **Open** 11.30am-11pm Mon-Thur, Sun; 11.30am-midnight Fri, Sat.
Barbecue. Map p59 D3 ⑳
Drummer-turned-chef Hugh Mangum first hawked his Texalina (Texas spice meets Carolina vinegar) specialities at his immensely popular stand at Smorgasburg (see p41). When the operation went brick-and-mortar, the hungry throngs followed. Lines of customers snake through the steel-tinged East Village joint, watching as black-gloved carvers give glistening meat porn a dash of Maldon salt before slinging it down the assembly line. Paprika-rubbed brisket is slow-cooked for 22 hours, and the Jurassic-sized beef rib is so impossibly tender, one bite will quiet the pickiest barbecue connoisseur.

Momofuku Ssäm Bar

207 Second Avenue, at 13th Street (1-212 254 3500, www.momofuku.com). Subway L to First or Third Avenue; L, N, Q, R, 4, 5, 6 to 14th Street-Union Square. **Open** 11.30am-3.30pm, 5pm-midnight Mon-Thur, Sun; 11.30am-3.30pm, 5pm-1am Fri, Sat. **$$**.
Korean. Map p59 D2 ⑳
At chef David Chang's second restaurant, waiters hustle to noisy rock music in the 72-seat space, which feels expansive compared with its Noodle Bar predecessor's crowded counter dining. Try the wonderfully fatty pork-belly steamed bun with hoisin sauce and cucumbers or one of the ham platters, but you'll need to come with a crowd to sample the house speciality, *bo ssäm* (a slow-roasted hog butt that is consumed wrapped in lettuce leaves, with a dozen oysters and other accompaniments); it serves six to ten people and must be ordered in advance. Chang has further expanded his E Vill empire with a bar at this location and a sweet spin-off, Milk Bar (one of several in the city), across the street (251 E 13th Street, at Second Avenue). Other Momofuku branches are at 163 First Avenue, at 10th Street; and 171 First Avenue, between 10th and 11th Streets.

Northern Spy Food Co

511 E 12th Street, between Avenues A & B (1-212 228 5100, www.northern spyfoodco.com). Subway L to First Avenue. **Open** 10am-4pm, 5.30-11pm Mon-Fri; 10am-3.30pm, 5.30-11pm Sat, Sun. **$. American.** Map p59 E2 ⑥⑨
Named after an apple indigenous to the Northeast, Northern Spy serves locally sourced meals at reasonable prices. The frequently changing menu is based almost entirely on what's in season. The food isn't fancy, but it satisfies: a recent dish paired toothsome pastured pork loin in a rich pork jus with sautéed leeks, green cabbage and brussels-sprout leaves.

PDT

113 St Marks Place, between First Avenue & Avenue A (1-212 614 0386). Subway L to First Avenue; 6 to Astor Place. **Open** 6pm-2am Mon-Thur, Sun; 6pm-4am Fri, Sat. **Bar.** Map p59 D3 ⑨⓪
Word has got out about 'Please Don't Tell', the faux speakeasy inside gourmet hot dog joint Crif Dogs (see p81), so it's a good idea to reserve a booth in advance. Once you arrive, you'll notice people lingering outside an old wooden phone booth near the front. Slip inside, pick up the receiver and the host opens a secret panel to the dark, narrow space. The cocktails surpass the gimmicky entry: try the house old-fashioned, made with bacon-infused bourbon, which leaves a smoky aftertaste.

Porchetta

110 E 7th Street, between First Avenue & Avenue A (1-212 777 2151, www.porchettanyc.com). Subway F to Lower East Side-Second Avenue; L to First Avenue; 6 to Astor Place. **Open** 11.30am-10pm Mon-Thur, Sun; 11.30am-11pm Fri, Sat.
Sandwiches. Map p59 E3 ⑨①
This small, subway-tiled space has a narrow focus: central Italy's classic boneless roasted pork. The meat – available as a sandwich or a platter – is amazingly moist and tender, having been slowly roasted with rendered pork fat, seasoned with fennel pollen, herbs and spices, and flecked with brittle shards of skin. The other menu items (a mozzarella sandwich, humdrum sides) seem incidental; the pig is the point.

Proletariat

NEW *102 St Marks Place, between First Avenue & Avenue A (1-212 777 6707, www.proletariatny.com). Subway 6 to Astor Place.* **Open** 5pm-2am daily.
Bar. Map p59 D3 ⑨②
Proletariat is a much-deserved look into no-holds-barred beer geekdom, blissfully free of TVs and generic pub grub. With just 12 stools and a space so tight that clunky menus have been replaced with a QR code (scan it with your smartphone), brewhounds get the type of intimacy usually afforded only to the cocktail and wine crowds. The expert servers have a story for every keg they tap, from the newest local brews to obscure New Zealand ales and deep cuts from the Belgian canon. Sure, the name out front may feel ironic when you're sipping a $10 pour of a Norwegian saison you can't pronounce, but Gotham's beer scene is ready for a place that doesn't compromise.

Terroir

413 E 12th Street, between First Avenue & Avenue A (1-646 602 1300, www.wineisterroir.com). Subway L to First Avenue; L, N, Q, R, 4, 5, 6 to 14th Street-Union Square. **Open** 5pm-2am Mon-Sat; 5pm-midnight Sun. **Wine bar.** Map p59 D2 ⑨③
The surroundings are stripped-back basic at this wine-bar offspring of nearby restaurant Hearth – the focus is squarely on the drinks. Co-owner and oenoevangelist Paul Grieco preaches the powers of *terroir* – grapes that express a sense of place – and the knowledgeable waitstaff deftly help patrons to navigate about 45 by-the-glass options. Pair the stellar sips with their restaurant-calibre small plates.

Shopping

Bond No.9

*9 Bond Street, between Broadway
& Lafayette Street (1-212 228 1732,
www.bondno9.com). Subway B, D, F,
M to Broadway-Lafayette Street; 6 to
Bleecker Street.* **Open** 11am-8pm Mon-
Fri; 10am-7pm Sat; noon-6pm Sun.
Map p59 D3 ❾❹

The collection of scents here pays olfac-
tory homage to New York City. Choose
from 60 'neighbourhoods' and 'sensibil-
ities', including Wall Street, Park
Avenue, Eau de Noho, the High Line,
even Chinatown (but don't worry, it
smells of peach blossom, gardenia and
patchouli, not fish stands). The arty
bottles and the neat, colourful packaging are highly gift-friendly.

Bond Street Chocolate

*63 E 4th Street, between Bowery &
Second Avenue (1-212 677 5103,
www.bondstchocolate.com). Subway
6 to Bleecker Street.* **Open** noon-8pm
Tue-Sat; 2-6pm Sun. **Map** p59 D3 ❾❺

Former pastry chef Lynda Stern's East
Village spot is a grown-up's candy
store, with quirky chocolate confections in shapes ranging from gilded
Buddhas (and other religious figures)
to skulls, and flavours from elderflower
to bourbon and absinthe.

Fabulous Fanny's

*335 E 9th Street, between First &
Second Avenues (1-212 533 0637,
www.fabulousfannys.com). Subway
L to First Avenue; 6 to Astor Place.*
Open noon-8pm daily. **Map** p59 D2 ❾❻

Formerly a Chelsea flea market booth,
this two-room shop is the city's best
source of period glasses, stocking more
than 30,000 pairs of spectacles, from
Jules Verne-esque wire rims to 1970s
rhinestone-encrusted Versace shades.

The Future Perfect

*55 Great Jones Street, between Bowery
& Lafayette Street (1-212 473 2500,
www.thefutureperfect.com). Subway 6*

to Bleecker Street. **Open** 10am-7pm
Mon-Fri; noon-7pm Sat. **Map** p59 D3 ❾❼

Championing avant-garde interior
design, this innovative store showcases international and local talent –
it's the exclusive US stockist of Dutch
designer Piet Hein Eek's furniture
and pottery. Look out for Kiel Mead's
quirky gold and silver jewellery and
colourful driftwood wall hooks,
crafted from wood found on New
York State beaches.

INA

*15 Bleecker Street, between Bowery
& Lafayette Street (1-212 228 8511,
www.inanyc.com). Subway B, D, F,
M to Broadway-Lafayette Street; 6 to
Bleecker Street.* **Open** noon-8pm Mon-
Sat; noon-7pm Sun. **Map** p59 D3 ❾❽

For more than 20 years, INA has been
a leading light of the designer-resale
scene. A string of five consignment
shops offers immaculate, bang-on-
trend items (Christian Louboutin and
Manolo Blahnik shoes, Louis Vuitton
and Marc Jacobs bags, clothing by
Alexander McQueen and Marni) at a
fraction of their original prices. This
branch caters to both sexes.

Kiehl's

*109 Third Avenue, between 13th
& 14th Streets (1-212 677 3171,
www.kiehls.com). Subway L to Third
Avenue; L, N, Q, R, 4, 5, 6 to 14th
Street-Union Square.* **Open** 10am-
8pm Mon-Sat; 11am-6pm Sun.
Map p59 D2 ❾❾

The apothecary founded on this East
Village site in 1851 has morphed into a
major skincare brand, but the products,
in their minimal packaging, are still
good value and effective. Lip balms
and the thick-as-custard Creme de
Corps have become cult classics.

Obscura Antiques
& Oddities

*207 Avenue A, between 12th &
13th Streets (1-212 505 9251, www.
obscuraantiques.com). Subway L to*

Poetry and pasties

A burlesque club and a literary venue are unlikely partners.

Duane Park

For a city that thrives on its subcultures and scenes, New York has surprisingly few poetry-dedicated spots. So when verse-slinger and event organiser Bob Holman opened the Bowery Poetry Club in 2002, it was with the gambit that, as he puts it, 'Poetry would be able to sustain itself seven nights a week, from the coffee shop in the morning to the end of the slam at night.'

Though that business model didn't ultimately shake out, a decade down the line Holman has found a canny compromise. The rechristened **Bowery Poetry** has joined forces with Southern-inflected supper club **Duane Park** (see p88) to share the space at 308 Bowery. The location operates as Duane Park from Tuesday to Saturday, with poetry on Sundays and Mondays. This mash-up of spoken word with burlesque and variety aims to ensure the ongoing survival of both in the neighbourhood.

At Duane Park's previous location in Tribeca, the landlords were raising the rent beyond the club's means. Owner Marisa Ferrarin and Holman, who are old friends, made the decision to fuse the two ventures.

'It's a perfect match,' explains Ferrarin. 'Tribeca was the totally wrong area for us – it's a very sleepy neighbourhood. Here, we'll actually get people walking in off the street.' The relocation involved a complete overhaul of the old BPC space, courtesy of British artist Paul Etienne Lincoln, to recreate the glamorous New Orleans-style aesthetic of Duane Park's previous digs.

The new venture fits firmly in the continuum for the neighbourhood, whose history as a downtown arts hub dates back to the early 19th century. 'It's really the birthplace of the populist arts in New York,' says Holman. 'Up and down the Bowery, you'll find the birthplace of vaudeville, tap dance, burlesque, Yiddish theatre, the punk scene, free jazz…. I see the programming that's going on at Duane Park as a continuation of that.'

First Avenue. **Open** noon-8pm Mon-Sat; noon-7pm Sun. **Map** p59 E2 ⓿

Housed inside a former funeral home, this eccentric shop specialises in items like medical and scientific antiques, human skulls and taxidermied animals dating from the 19th century. Business partners Evan Michelson and Mike Zohn scour flea markets, auctions and even museums for rare artefacts; recently, we found plaster anatomical models and a bottle of snake wine imported from Vietnam.

Other Music

15 E 4th Street, between Broadway & Lafayette Street (1-212 477 8150, www.othermusic.com). Subway B, D, F, M to Broadway-Lafayette Street; 6 to Bleecker Street. **Open** 11am-9pm Mon-Fri; noon-8pm Sat; noon-7pm Sun. **Map** p58 C3 ⓫

Other Music opened in the shadow of Tower Records in the mid '90s, a pocket of resistance to chain-store tedium. All these years later, the Goliath across the street is gone, but tiny Other Music carries on. Whereas the shop's mishmash of indie rock, experimental music and stray slabs of rock's past once seemed adventurous, the curatorial foundation has proved prescient, amid the emergence of mixed-genre venues in the city.

Strand Book Store

828 Broadway, at 12th Street (1-212 473 1452, www.strandbooks.com). Subway L, N, Q, R, 4, 5, 6 to 14th Street-Union Square. **Open** 9.30am-10.30pm Mon-Sat; 11am-10.30pm Sun. Rare book room closes at 6.15 daily. **Map** p58 C2 ⓬

Boasting 18 miles of books, the Strand has a mammoth collection of more than two million discount volumes, and the store is made all the more daunting by its chaotic, towering shelves and some-times crotchety staff. Reviewer discounts are in the basement, while rare volumes lurk upstairs. If you spend enough time here you can find just

about anything, from that out-of-print Victorian book on manners to the kitschiest of sci-fi pulp.

Nightlife

Duane Park & Bowery Poetry

NEW *308 Bowery, between Bleecker & E Houston Streets (Duane Park 1-212 732 5555, duaneparknyc.com; Bowery Poetry 1-212 334 2216, www.bowery poetry.com). Subway F to Lower East Side-Second Avenue; 6 to Astor Place.* **Map** p59 D3 ⓭

See box p87.

Joe's Pub

Public Theater, 425 Lafayette Street, between Astor Place & E 4th Street (1-212 967 7555, www.joespub.com). Subway N, R to 8th Street-NYU; 6 to Astor Place. **Map** p59 D3 ⓮

One of the city's premier small spots for sit-down audiences, Joe's Pub brings in impeccable talent of all genres and origins. While some well-established names play here (Steve Martin's bluegrass crew, the Steep Canyon Rangers, for example), Joe's also lends its stage to up-and-comers (this is where Amy Winehouse made her debut in the United States), drag acts and comedy and cabaret per-formers (Justin Vivian Bond is a mainstay). A small but solid menu and deep bar selections seal the deal to make this a place for a great night out – but keep an eye on those drinks prices.

Nowhere

322 E 14th Street, between First & Second Avenues (1-212 477 4744, www.nowherebarnyc.com). Subway L to First Avenue. **Open** 3pm-4am daily. **Map** p59 D2 ⓯

Low ceilings and dim lighting help to create a speakeasy vibe at this subter-ranean gay bar. The place attracts everyone from cross-dressers to bears, thanks to an entertaining line-up of theme nights. Tuesday nights are especially fun, when DJ Damian Cote's long-running Buddies party takes over. The pool table is also a big draw.

Webster Hall

125 E 11th Street, between Third & Fourth Avenues (1-212 353 1600, www.websterhall.com). Subway L to Third Avenue; L, N, Q, R, 4, 5, 6 to 14th Street-Union Square.
Map p59 D2 ⑩⑥

Dinosaur venue Webster Hall is booked by Bowery Presents, the folks who run Bowery Ballroom and Mercury Lounge. Expect to find high-calibre indie acts (the likes of Animal Collective, Battles and Gossip), but be sure to show up early if you want a decent view. Friday night's Girls & Boys bash attracts music makers of the stature of Grandmaster Flash and dubstep duo Nero.

Arts & leisure

Anthology Film Archives

32 Second Avenue, at E 2nd Street (1-212 505 5181, www.anthologyfilm archives.org). Subway F to Lower East Side-Second Avenue; 6 to Bleecker Street. No credit cards.
Map p59 D3 ⑩⑦

This red-brick building feels a little like a fortress – and in a sense, it is one, protecting the legacy of NYC's fiercest experimenters. Anthology is committed to screening the world's most adventurous fare, from 16mm found-footage works to digital video dreams. Dedicated to the preservation, study and exhibition of independent and avant-garde films, it houses a gallery and film museum, in addition to its two screens.

Great Jones Spa

29 Great Jones Street, at Lafayette Street (1-212 505 3185, www.great jonesspa.com). Subway 6 to Astor Place. **Open** 9.30am-10.30pm daily.
Map p59 D3 ⑩⑧

Based on the theory that water brings health, Great Jones is outfitted with a popular water lounge complete with subterranean pools, saunas, steam rooms and a three-and-a-half-storey waterfall. Access is complimentary with services over $100 – treat yourself to a facial, massage or one of the many indulgent packages. Alternatively, a three-hour pass to the 15,000sq ft paradise costs $50.

New York Theatre Workshop

79 E 4th Street, between Bowery & Second Avenue (1-212 460 5475, www.nytw.org). Subway F to Lower East Side-Second Avenue; 6 to Astor Place. **Map** p59 D3 ⑩⑨

Founded in 1979, the New York Theatre Workshop works with emerging directors eager to take on challenging pieces. Besides presenting plays by world-class artists such as Caryl Churchill and Tony Kushner, this company also premièred *Rent*, Jonathan Larson's seminal 1990s musical. The iconoclastic Flemish director Ivo van Hove has made the NYTW his New York pied-à-terre.

Public Theater

425 Lafayette Street, between Astor Place & E 4th Street (1-212 539 8500, tickets 1-212 967 7555, www.public theater.org). Subway N, R to 8th Street-NYU; 6 to Astor Place.
Map p59 D3 ⑪⑩

Under the guidance of civic-minded artistic director Oskar Eustis, this local institution – dedicated to producing the work of new American playwrights, but also known for its Shakespeare productions (Shakespeare in the Park) – has retaken its place at the forefront of the Off Broadway world. The ambitious, multicultural programming ranges from new works by major playwrights to the annual Under the Radar festival for emerging artists. The company's home building, an Astor Place landmark, has five stages, plus cabaret venue Joe's Pub (see p88), and has recently been extensively renovated.

The Stone

Avenue C, at E 2nd Street (no phone, www.thestonenyc.com). Subway F to Lower East Side-Second Avenue. No credit cards. **Map** p59 E3 ⓫

Don't call sax star John Zorn's not-for-profit venture a 'club'. You'll find no food or drinks here, and there's no nonsense, either: the Stone is an art space dedicated to 'the experimental and the avant-garde'. And if you're down for some rigorously adventurous sounds (with intense improvisers such as Tim Berne and Okkyung Lee, or moonlighting rock mavericks like Thurston Moore), Zorn has made it easy: there are no advance sales, and all ages are admitted. The bookings for each month are left to a different artist-curator.

Greenwich Village

Stretching from Houston Street to 14th Street, between Broadway and Sixth Avenue, the Village has been inspiring bohemians for almost a century. Now that it's one of the most expensive neighbourhoods in the city, you need a lot more than a struggling artist's income to inhabit its leafy streets, but it's still a fine place for idle wandering, candlelit dining and hopping between bars and cabaret venues.

Sights & museums

Washington Square Park

Subway A, B, C, D, E, F, M to W 4th Street. **Map** p58 C3 ⓬

The city's main burial ground until 1825, Washington Square Park has served ever since as the spiritual home, playground and meeting place for Greenwich Village. The Washington Square Arch at the northern end was designed by Stanford White and dedicated in 1895. It marks the southern end of Fifth Avenue. The central fountain, completed in 1872, was recently shifted to align it with the arch, as part of extensive park renovations.

In the 1960s, the park was a frequent gathering spot for the Beat poets – with Allen Ginsberg giving several impromptu readings here – and it retains its vitality, thanks to the numerous street performers, NYU students, chess players, political agitators and hustlers who congregate when the weather is fine.

Eating & drinking

Blue Hill

75 Washington Place, between Sixth Avenue & Washington Square West (1-212 539 1776, www.bluehill nyc.com). Subway A, B, C, D, E, F, M to W 4th Street. **Open** 5-11pm Mon-Sat; 5-10pm Sun. **$$$**. **American**. **Map** p58 C3 ⓭

More than a mere crusader for sustainability, Dan Barber is also one of the most talented cooks in town, building his menu around whatever's at its peak on his family farm in Great Barrington, Massachusetts, and the not-for-profit Stone Barns Center for Food and Agriculture in Westchester, NY (home to a sibling restaurant), among other suppliers. The evening may begin with a sophisticated seasonal spin on a pig-liver terrine and move on to a sweet slow-roasted parsnip 'steak' with creamed spinach and beet ketchup.

Carbone

NEW *181 Thompson Street, between Bleecker & W Houston Streets (1-212 254 3000, www.carbonenewyork.com). Subway C, E to Spring Street.* **Open** 5.30pm-midnight daily. **$$$**. **Italian**. **Map** p58 C3 ⓮

Nostalgia specialists Rich Torrisi and Mario Carbone honour Gotham's legendary red-sauce relics (Rao's, Bamonte's) with their high-profile revamp of historic Rocco's Ristorante.

Suave, tuxedo-clad waiters – Bronx accents intact, but their burgundy threads designed by Zac Posen – tote an avalanche of complimentary extras: chunks of chianti-infused Parm, olive-oil-soaked 'Grandma Bread' and slivers of smoky prosciutto. Follow updated renditions of classic pasta like a spicy, über-rich rigatoni alla vodka with mains such as sticky cherry-pepper ribs and lavish takes on tiramisu for dessert.

Corkbuzz Wine Studio

NEW *13 E 13th Street, between Fifth Avenue & University Place (1-646 873 6071, www.corkbuzz.com). Subway L, N, Q, R, 4, 5, 6 to 14th Street-Union Square.* **Open** 5pm-midnight Mon-Wed; 5pm-1am Thur, Fri; 4pm-1am Sat; 4pm-midnight Sun (call or see website for summer hours). **Wine bar**. Map p58 C2 ⓯

This intriguing and elegant hybrid, owned by the world's youngest master sommelier, Laura Maniec, comprises a restaurant, a wine bar and an educational centre. Before you drink anything, chat with one of the staffers, who preach the Maniec gospel to patrons as they navigate 35 by-the-glass options and around 250 bottles.

Kin Shop

469 Sixth Avenue, between 11th & 12th Streets (1-212 675 4295, www.kinshopnyc.com). Subway F, M to 14th Street; L to Sixth Avenue. **Open** 11.30am-3pm, 5.30-10pm Mon-Wed; 11.30am-3pm, 5.30-11pm Thur-Sat; 11.30am-3pm, 5-10pm Sun. **$$**. **Thai**. Map p58 B2 ⓰

Top Chef champ Harold Dieterle channels his South-east Asian travels into the menu at this eaterie, which serves classic Thai street food alongside more upmarket Thai-inspired dishes. The traditional fare seems extraneous, but Dieterle's auteur creations are often inspired. A salad of fried oysters, slivered celery and crispy pork belly was bright and refreshing, while a chefly riff on massaman curry featured long-braised goat neck with a silky sauce infused with coconut milk, duck fat and pineapple juice.

Minetta Tavern

113 MacDougal Street, between Bleecker & W 3rd Streets (1-212 475 3850, www.minettatavernny.com). Subway A, B, C, D, E, F, M to W 4th Street. **Open** 5.30pm-midnight Mon, Tue; noon-2.45pm, 5.30pm-midnight Wed-Fri; 11am-2.45pm, 5.30pm-midnight Sat, Sun. **$$**. **Eclectic**. Map p58 C3 ⓱

Thanks to restaurateur extraordinaire Keith McNally's spot-on restoration, this former literati hangout, which was once frequented by Hemingway and Fitzgerald, is as buzzy now as it must have been in its mid-20th-century heyday. The big-flavoured bistro fare includes classics such as roasted bone marrow, trout meunière topped with crabmeat, and an airy Grand Marnier soufflé for dessert. But the most illustrious thing on the menu is the Black Label burger. You might find the $26 price tag a little hard to swallow, but the superbly tender sandwich – essentially chopped steak in a bun smothered with caramelised onions – is worth every penny.

Num Pang Sandwich Shop

21 E 12th Street, between Fifth Avenue & University Place (1-212 255 3271, www.numpangnyc.com). Subway L, N, Q, R, 4, 5, 6 to 14th Street-Union Square. **Open** 11am-10pm Mon-Sat; noon-9pm Sun. **$**. **Cambodian**. Map p58 C2 ⓲

At this small shop, the rotating varieties of *num pang* (Cambodia's answer to the Vietnamese *banh mi*) include pulled duroc pork with spiced honey, peppercorn catfish, and hoisin veal meatballs, each stuffed into a crusty baguette. There's counter seating upstairs, or get it to go and eat in nearby Washington Square Park.

Vol de Nuit Bar (aka Belgian Beer Lounge)

148 W 4th Street, between Sixth Avenue & MacDougal Street (1-212 982 3388, www.voldenuitbar.com). Subway A, B, C, D, E, F, M to W 4th Street. **Open** 4pm-midnight daily.
Bar. Map p58 C3 **119**

Duck through an unmarked doorway on a busy stretch of West 4th Street and find yourself in a red-walled Belgian bar that serves brews exclusively from the motherland. Clusters of European grad students knock back glasses of Palm and La Chouffe – just two of 13 beers on tap and 22 by the bottle. Moules and frites, fittingly, are the only eats available (Mon-Sat).

Shopping

CO Bigelow Chemists

414 Sixth Avenue, between 8th & 9th Streets (1-212 473 7324, www.bigelowchemists.com). Subway A, B, C, D, F, M to W 4th Street; 1 to Christopher Street. **Open** 7.30am-9pm Mon-Fri; 9am-7pm Sat; 8.30am-5.30pm Sun.
Map p58 C3 **120**

Established in 1838, Bigelow is the oldest apothecary in America. Its simply packaged and appealingly old-school line of toiletries include such tried-and-trusted favourites as Mentha Lip Shine, Barber Cologne Elixirs and Lemon Body Cream. The spacious, chandelier-lit store is packed with natural and homeopathic remedies, organic skin-care products and drugstore essentials – and they still fill prescriptions.

Nightlife

Blue Note

131 W 3rd Street, between MacDougal Street & Sixth Avenue (1-212 475 8592, www.bluenote.net). Subway A, B, C, D, E, F, M to W 4th Street.
Map p58 C3 **121**

The Blue Note prides itself on being 'the jazz capital of the world'. Bona fide musical titans (Jimmy Heath, Lee Konitz) rub against contemporary heavyweights (The Bad Plus), while the close-set tables in the club get patrons rubbing up against each other. The Sunday brunch is the best bargain bet.

Comedy Cellar

117 MacDougal Street, between Bleecker & W 3rd Streets (1-212 254 3480, www.comedycellar.com). Subway A, B, C, D, E, F, M to W 4th Street.
Map p58 C3 **122**

Despite being named one of NYC's best stand-up clubs year after year, the Cellar maintains a hip, underground feel. It gets packed, but no-nonsense comics such as Dave Chapelle, Jim Norton and Marina Franklin will distract you from your bachelorette-party neighbours.

Le Poisson Rouge

158 Bleecker Street, at Thompson Street (1-212 505 3474, www.lepoissonrouge.com). Subway A, B, C, D, E, F, M to W 4th Street.
Map p58 C3 **123**

Tucked into the basement of the long-gone Village Gate – a legendary performance space that hosted everyone from Miles Davis to Jimi Hendrix – Le Poisson Rouge was opened in 2008 by a group of young music enthusiasts with ties to both the classical and indie rock worlds. The cabaret space's booking policy reflects both camps, often on a single bill. No other joint in town books such a wide range of great music, whether from a feverish Malian band (Toumani Diabaté's Symmetric Orchestra), rising indie talent (Zola Jesus) or young classical stars (pianist Simone Dinnerstein).

Sullivan Room

218 Sullivan Street, between Bleecker & W 3rd Streets (1-212 252 2151, www.sullivanroom.com). Subway A, B, C, D, E, F, M to W 4th Street. **Open** 10pm-5am Tue-Sun. **Map** p58 C3 **124**

This unmarked subterranean space hosts some of the best deep-house, tech-house and breaks bashes the city has to offer. It's an utterly unpretentious place, but all you really need are some thumpin' beats and a place to move your feet, right? Keep a special lookout for the nights hosted by local stalwarts Sleepy and Boo, featuring top house music stars such as Derrick Carter and Mark Farina.

Arts & leisure

IFC Center

323 Sixth Avenue, at W 3rd Street (1-212 924 7771, www.ifccenter.com). Subway A, B, C, D, E, F, M to W 4th Street. **Map** p58 B3 (125)

The long-darkened 1930s Waverly cinema was reborn in 2005 as the modern three-screen arthouse IFC Center, showing the latest indie hits, choice midnight cult items and foreign classics. You may even see the directors or the actors on the screen in the flesh, as many introduce their work on opening nights.

West Village & Meatpacking District

The area west of Sixth Avenue to the Hudson River, from 14th Street to Houston Street, has held on to much of its picturesque charm. Bistros abound along Seventh Avenue and Hudson Street and high-rent shops proliferate on this stretch of Bleecker Street, including no fewer than three Marc Jacobs boutiques. The West Village is also a long-standing gay mecca, although the scene has largely moved north to Chelsea and Hell's Kitchen. The north-west corner of the West Village is known as the Meatpacking District, dating from its origins as a wholesale meat market in the 1930s. In recent years designer stores, trendy eateries and nightclubs have moved in, and the area is the starting point for the High Line.

Sights & museums

High Line

1-212 500-6035, www.thehighline.org. **Open** usually 7am-10pm daily (hours vary seasonally; see website for updates). **Map** p58 A2 (126)

Running from Gansevoort Street in the Meatpacking District through Chelsea's gallery district to 30th Street, this slender, sinuous green strip – formerly an elevated freight train track – has been designed by landscape architects James Corner Field Operations and architects Diller Scofidio + Renfro. In autumn 2012, construction began on the final section, which will open in three phases, starting in 2014. Stretching from 30th to 34th Streets, it skirts the West Side Rail Yards, which are being developed into a long-planned residential and commercial complex, Hudson Yards. See also p44-46.

Eating & drinking

Blind Tiger Ale House

281 Bleecker Street, at Jones Street (1-212 462 4682, www.blindtigeralehouse.com). Subway A, B, C, D, E, F, M to W 4th Street; 1 to Christopher Street-Sheridan Square. **Open** 11.30am-4am daily. **Bar. Map** p58 B3 (127)

Brew geeks descend upon this hops heaven for boutique ales and 28 daily rotating, hard-to-find draughts (like Dale's Pale Ale and Allagash barrel-aged Curieux). The clubby room features windows that open on to bustling Bleecker Street. Late afternoons and early evenings are ideal for serious sippers enjoying plates of Murray's Cheese, while the after-dark set veers dangerously close to Phi Kappa territory.

Buvette

42 Grove Street, between Bedford & Bleecker Streets (1-212 255 3590, www.ilovebuvette.com). Subway 1 to Christopher Street-Sheridan Square. **Open** 8am-2am Mon-Fri; 10am-2am Sat, Sun. **$$. French.** **Map** p58 B3 ❶❷❽

Chef Jody Williams has filled every nook of tiny, Gallic-themed Buvette with old picnic baskets, teapots and silver trays, among other vintage ephemera. The food is just as thoughtfully curated – Williams's immaculate renditions of coq au vin, goose-fat rillettes or intense, lacquered wedges of tarte Tatin arrive on tiny plates, in petite jars or in miniature casseroles, her time-warp flavours recalling an era when there were classic bistros on every corner.

Chez Sardine

NEW *183 W 10th Street, at W 4th Street (1-646 360 3705, www.chez sardine.com). Subway A, B, C, D, E, F, M to W 4th Street; 1 to Christopher Street-Sheridan Square.* **Open** 5.30-11pm Mon-Wed; 5.30pm-1am Thur, Fri; 11am-2.45pm, 5.30pm-1am Sat; 11am-2.45pm, 5.30-11pm Sun. **$$. Eclectic/Japanese.** **Map** p58 B3 ❶❷❾

Prolific restaurateur Gabriel Stulman's fifth Village venture is a cross-cultural *izakaya*. The slim restaurant's sardine-can-size kitchen, run by Fedora's (see right) creatively hard-charging Mehdi Brunet-Benkritly, sends out wild riffs on sushi, like pork belly or chopped beef with uni. The inspiration and compact dimensions are steeped in Japan. The execution, though, is pure Quebecois gluttony, with a grilled cheese sandwich oozing melted foie gras; and pancakes stacked with briny roe, fish tartare and cool, tangy yoghurt.

Corner Bistro

331 W 4th Street, at Jane Street (1-212 242 9502). Subway A, C, E to 14th Street; L to Eighth Avenue.

Open 11.30am-4am Mon-Sat; noon-4am Sun. No credit cards. **Bar.** **Map** p58 B2 ❶❸❶

There's only one reason to come to this legendary pub: it serves what many believe are the city's best burgers – and beer is just $3 a mug (well, that makes two reasons). The prime patties here are no frills and served on a paper plate. To get one, you may have to wait for a good hour, especially on weekend nights; if the wait is too long for a table, try to slip into a space at the bar.

Employees Only

510 Hudson Street, between Christopher & W 10th Streets (1-212 242 3021, www.employeesonlynyc. com). Subway 1 to Christopher Street-Sheridan Square. **Open** 6pm-4am daily. **Bar.** **Map** p58 B3 ❶❸❶

This Prohibition-themed bar cultivates an exclusive vibe, but there's no cover and no trouble at the door. Pass by the palm reader in the window (it's a front) and you'll find an amber-lit art deco interior where formality continues to flourish: servers wear custom-designed frocks and bartenders don waitstaff whites. The real stars are cocktails such as the West Side, a lethal mix of lemon vodka, lemon juice, mint and club soda:

Fedora

239 W 4th Street, between Charles & W 10th Streets (1-646 449 9336, www.fedoranyc.com). Subway A, B, C, D, E, F, M to W 4th Street; 1 to Christopher Street-Sheridan Square. **Open** 5.30-11pm Mon, Sun; 5.30pm-2am Tue-Sat. **$$. Canadian.** **Map** p58 B3 ❶❸❷

This clubby French-Canadian knock-out is part of restaurateur Gabriel Stulman's expanding Village mini-empire, which also includes nearby Joseph Leonard, Perla and Chez Sardine (see left). Chef Mehdi Brunet-Benkritly produces some of the most exciting toe-to-tongue cooking in town, plying epicurean hipsters with

Quebecois party food that's eccentric, excessive and fun – crisp duck breast with hazelnuts, for example, or scallops with bacon, tomatoes and polenta.

Kesté Pizza & Vino

271 Bleecker Street, between Cornelia & Jones Streets (1-212 243 1500, www.kestepizzeria.com). Subway 1 to Christopher Street-Sheridan Square. **Open** noon-3.30pm, 5-11pm Mon-Thur; noon-11.30pm Fri, Sat; noon-10.30pm Sun. **$**. **Pizza**. Map p58 B3 ⓭
If anyone can claim to be an expert on Neapolitan pizza, it's Kesté's Roberto Caporuscio: as president of the US branch of the Associazione Pizzaiuoli Napoletani, he's top dog for the training and certification of *pizzaioli*. At his intimate, 46-seat space, it's all about the crust – blistered, salty and elastic, it could easily be eaten plain. Add fantastic toppings such as sweet-tart San Marzano tomato sauce, milky mozzarella and fresh basil, and you have one of New York's finest pies.

Pearl Oyster Bar

18 Cornelia Street, between Bleecker & W 4th Streets (1-212 691 8211, www.pearloysterbar.com). Subway A, B, C, D, E, F, M to W 4th Street. **Open** noon-2.30pm, 6-11pm Mon-Fri; 6-11pm Sat. **$$**. **Seafood**. Map p58 B3 ⓭
There's a good reason this convivial, no-reservations, New England-style fish joint always has a queue – the food is outstanding. Signature dishes include the lobster roll – sweet lemon-scented meat laced with mayonnaise on a butter-enriched bun – and a contemporary take on bouillabaisse: a briny lobster broth packed with mussels, cod, scallops and clams, topped with an aïoli-smothered croûton.

RedFarm

529 Hudson Street, between Charles & W 10th Streets (1-212 792 9700, www.redfarmnyc.com). Subway 1 to Christopher Street-Sheridan Square.
Open 5-11.45pm Mon-Fri; 11am-2.30pm, 5-11.45pm Sat; 11am-2.30pm, 5-11pm Sun. **$$**. **Chinese**. Map p58 B3 ⓭
The high-end ingredients and whimsical plating at Ed Schoenfeld's interpretive Chinese restaurant have helped pack the narrow contemporary dining room since opening night. Chef Joe Ng is known for his dim sum artistry: scallop and squid shumai come skewered over shot glasses of warm carrot soup – designed to be eaten and gulped in rapid succession; other nouveau creations include pastrami-stuffed egg rolls and miso-glazed filet mignon in crispy tartlet shells.

The Spotted Pig

314 W 11th Street, at Greenwich Street (1-212 620 0393, www.the spottedpig.com). Subway A, C, E to 14th Street; L to Eighth Avenue. **Open** noon-2am Mon-Fri; 11am-2pm, 5.30pm-2am Sat, Sun. **$$**. **Eclectic**. Map p58 B3 ⓭
With a creaky interior that recalls an ancient pub, this Anglo-Italian hybrid from Ken Friedman and chef April Bloomfield (formerly of London's River Café) is still hopping a decade after opening. The gastropub doesn't take reservations and a wait can always be expected. The burger is a must-order: a top-secret blend of ground beef, covered with gobs of pungent roquefort and served with a tower of rosemary-spiked shoestring fries. The indulgent desserts, like the flourless chocolate cake and banoffee pie, are worth loosening your belt for.

Sweet Revenge

62 Carmine Street, between Bedford Street & Seventh Avenue (1-212 242 2240, www.sweetrevengenyc.com). Subway A, B, C, D, E, F, M to W 4th Street; 1 to Christopher Street-Sheridan Square. **Open** 7am-11pm Mon-Thur; 7am-12.30am Fri; 10.30am-12.30am Sat; 10.30am-10pm Sun. **$**. **Café/Bar**. Map p58 B3 ⓭

Baker Marlo Scott steamrollered over the Magnolia Bakery-model cupcake's innocent charms: at her café/bar, she pairs her confections with wine or beer; where there were pastel swirls of frosting, there are now anarchic spikes of peanut butter, cream cheese and milk-chocolate icing. In the process, she saved the ubiquitous treat from becoming a cloying cliché. Gourmet sandwiches and other plates cater to non-sweet-tooths.

Shopping

Castor & Pollux

238 W 10th Street, between Bleecker & Hudson Streets (1-212 645 6572, www.castorandpolluxstore.com). Subway A, B, C, D, E, F, M to W 4th Street; 1 to Christopher Street-Sheridan Square. **Open** noon-7pm Tue-Sat; 1-6pm Sun (closed June-Aug). **Map** p58 B3 **138**

This small Brooklyn-born boutique showcases a diverse cross-section of clothing and accessories in a stylish yet relaxed setting. Owner Kerrilynn Pamer mixes European labels such as Ter et Bantine with New York names like Gary Graham, Apiece Apart and Alasdair, former stylist April Johnson's easy-to-wear staples in elegant fabrics. Pamer's own jewellery line, launched with simple brass bracelets and since expanded, has become a cult hit.

Jeffrey New York

449 W 14th Street, between Ninth & Tenth Avenues (1-212 206 1272, www.jeffreynewyork.com). Subway A, C, E to 14th Street; L to Eighth Avenue. **Open** 10am-8pm Mon-Wed, Fri; 10am-9pm Thur; 10am-7pm Sat; 12.30-6pm Sun. **Map** p58 A2 **139**

Jeffrey Kalinsky, a former Barneys shoe buyer, was a Meatpacking District pioneer when he opened his store in 1999. Designer clothing abounds here – by Yves Saint Laurent, Céline, L'Wren Scott and young British star Christopher Kane, among others.

But the centrepiece is the shoe salon, featuring Manolo Blahnik, Prada and Christian Louboutin, as well as newer names to watch.

Owen

NEW *809 Washington Street, between Gansevoort & Horatio Streets (1-212 524 9770, www.owennyc.com). Subway A, C, E to 14th Street; L to Eighth Avenue.* **Open** 11am-7pm Mon-Wed, Sun; 11am-8pm Thur-Sat. **Map** p58 A2 **140**

FIT grad Phillip Salem founded this upscale boutique featuring more than 30 emerging and already-established brands. Look out for Phillip Lim's cool, urban menswear, feminine frocks by Lover and soft, silk-lined leather T-shirts and jackets by New York designer Jonathan Simkhai. The modern threads for both genders are displayed atop quartz slab tables and hung on blackened steel bars.

Rag & Bone

100 & 104 Christopher Street, between Bedford & Bleecker Streets (1-212 727 2990 women, 2999 men, www.rag-bone.com). Subway 1 to Christopher Street-Sheridan Square. **Open** 11am-8pm Mon-Sat; noon-7pm Sun. **Map** p58 B3 **141**

Born out of its founders' frustration with mass-produced jeans, what began as a denim line back in 2002 has since expanded to cover clothing and accessories for both men and women, all put together with an emphasis on craftsmanship. The designs, in substantial, luxurious fabrics such as cashmere and tweed, make a nod towards tradition (riding jackets, granddad cardigans), while exuding an utterly contemporary vibe. This aesthetic is reflected in the brand's elegant, industrial-edged his 'n' hers stores.

Nightlife

Cielo

18 Little West 12th Street, between Ninth Avenue & Washington Street (1-212 645 5700, www.cieloclub.com).

Chez Sardine p94

Subway A, C, E to 14th Street; L to Eighth Avenue. **Open** 10pm-4am Mon, Wed-Sat. **Map** p58 A2 **142**

You'd never guess from all the Kardashian wannabes hanging out in the neighbourhood that the attitude inside this exclusive club is close to zero – at least once you get past the bouncers. On the sunken dancefloor, hip-to-hip crowds gyrate to deep beats from top DJs, including NYC old-schoolers François K, Tedd Patterson and Louie Vega. Cielo, which features a crystal-clear sound system, has won a bevy of 'best club' awards – and it deserves them all.

Henrietta Hudson

438 Hudson Street, at Morton Street (1-212 924 3347, www.henrietta hudson.com). Subway 1 to Christopher Street-Sheridan Square. **Open** 5pm-2am Mon, Tue; 4pm-4am Wed-Fri; 2pm-4am Sat; 2pm-2am Sun. **Map** p58 B3 **143**

A much-loved lesbian nightspot, this glam lounge attracts young hottie girls from all over the New York area. Every night's a different party, with hip hop, pop and rock music and live shows among the musical pulls.

Smalls Jazz Club

183 W 10th Street, at W 4th Street (no phone, www.smallsjazzclub.com). Subway A, B, C, D, E, F, M to W 4th Street; 1 to Christopher Street-Sheridan Square. **Open** 7.30pm-3.30am Mon, Tue; 6pm-3.30am Wed, Thur; 4pm-4am Fri, Sat; 1pm-3.30am Sun. No credit cards. **Map** p58 B3 **144**

This cosy basement venue feels like one of those hole-in-the-wall New York jazz haunts of yore over which fans routinely obsess. The line-up is solid and there's a fully stocked bar. Night owls should stop by for the fun 'after hours' jam session most nights at 12.30am (1am weekends), when admission drops to $10. It's a great place to catch the best and brightest up-and-comers as well as the occasional moonlighting star.

Stonewall Inn

53 Christopher Street, between Seventh Avenue South & Waverly Place (1-212 488 2705, www.the stonewallinnnyc.com). Subway 1 to Christopher Street-Sheridan Square. **Open** 2pm-4am daily. **Map** p58 B3 **145**

This gay landmark is the site of the famous 1969 rebellion against police harassment (though back then it also included the building next door). Is it hip? Not really. But you have to give the Stonewall credit for its history, and for being one of the few queer bars that cater equally to males and females. Special nights range from dance soirées and drag shows to bingo gatherings.

Village Vanguard

178 Seventh Avenue South, at Perry Street (1-212 255 4037, www.village vanguard.com). Subway A, C, E, 1, 2, 3 to 14th Street; L to Eighth Avenue. **Map** p58 B2 **146**

Still going strong after more than three-quarters of a century, the Village Vanguard is one of New York's legendary jazz centres. History surrounds you: John Coltrane, Miles Davis and Bill Evans have all grooved in this hallowed hall. Big names both old and new still fill the schedule, and the Grammy Award-winning Vanguard Jazz Orchestra has been the Monday-night regular for almost 50 years.

Arts & leisure

Film Forum

209 W Houston Street, between Sixth Avenue & Varick Street (1-212 727 8110, www.filmforum.org). Subway 1 to Houston Street. **Map** p58 B4 **147**

The city's leading revival and repertory cinema is programmed by fest-scouring staff who take their duties as seriously as a Kurosawa samurai. The print qualities are invariably excellent, and a recent renovation included comfy new seats.

Grand Central Terminal p129

Midtown

Soaring office towers, crowded pavements and taxi-choked streets – that's the image most people have of midtown, the area roughly between 14th Street and 59th Street, from river to river. This part of town draws visitors to some of the city's best-known landmarks, including the electronic spectacle that is Times Square, the Empire State Building, the Chrysler Building and Rockefeller Center. But there's more to midtown than iconic architecture and commerce. It contains the city's most concentrated contemporary gallery district (Chelsea), its hottest gay enclave (Hell's Kitchen), some of its swankiest shops (Fifth Avenue) and most of its big theatres on Broadway.

Chelsea

The corridor between 14th and 29th Streets west of Sixth Avenue emerged as the nexus of New York's queer life in the 1990s. While it's slowly being eclipsed by Hell's Kitchen to the north as a gay hotspot, it's still home to numerous bars, restaurants and shops catering to 'Chelsea boys'. The western edge of the neighbourhood is the city's major contemporary art gallery zone.

Sights & museums

Museum at FIT

Building E, Seventh Avenue, at 27th Street (1-212 217 4558, www.fitnyc.edu/museum). Subway 1 to 28th Street. **Open** noon-8pm Tue-Fri; 10am-5pm Sat. **Admission** free. **Map** p100 C3 ❶

The Fashion Institute of Technology owns one of the largest and most impressive collections of clothing, textiles and accessories in the world, including some 50,000 costumes and fabrics dating from the fifth century to the present. Under the directorship of

Midtown 1

D

E

F

See p103

E 48TH ST

E 46TH ST

Japan Society

Grand Central Terminal

101
104

Chrysler Building

100

102

United Nations Headquarters

1

M 7

M S,4,5,6,7

E 44TH ST

106

E 42ND ST

TUDOR CITY PL

QUEENS-MIDTOWN TUNNEL

NY Public Library

47

50

E 40TH ST

Scandinavia House: The Nordic Center in America

East River

E 38TH ST

43

Morgan Library

E 36TH ST

2

Empire State Building

M 6

E 34TH ST

26

49

E 32ND ST

MADISON AVE

PARK AVE SOUTH

E 30TH ST

45

E 28TH ST

E 28TH ST

0   300 m

Museum of Sex

M 6

LEXINGTON AVE

THIRD AVE

SECOND AVE

MT CARMEL PL

FIRST AVE

0   300 yds

22

21 **Museum of Mathematics (MoMath)**

E 26TH ST

© Copyright Time Out Group 2013

3

20

Madison Square

28

E 24TH ST

Manhattan Marina

70

M

19

31

M 6

51

E 23RD ST

ASSER LEVY PL

FRANKLIN D ROOSEVELT DR

GRAMERCY PARK

Peter Cooper Village

69

4

Iron ding

BROADWAY

38

Theodore Roosevelt Birthplace

48

Gramercy Park

E 22ND ST

E 20TH ST

24

National Arts Club

PARK AVE SOUTH

IRVING PL

34 25

E 18TH ST

RUTHERFORD PL

NATHAN D PERLMAN PL

Stuyvesant Town

40

46

52

E 16TH ST

Stuyvesant Square

FIFTH AVE

Union Square

1 Sights & museums

1 Eating & drinking

L,N,Q,R, M 4,5,6

M

L

M

L

1 Shopping

1 Nightlife

DOWNTOWN (pp54-98)

FOURTH AVE

E 12TH ST

1 Arts & leisure

UNIVERSITY PL

ST

ST

Grace Church

St Mark's Church in-the-Bowery

AVE

E 11TH ST

E 10TH ST

AVE

E 9TH ST

Midtown 2

W 72ND ST

A **B** **C** Strawberry Fields

1,2,3 Ⓜ

W 70TH ST

Sheep Meadow

1

W 68TH ST

W 66TH ST

CENTRAL PARK WEST

COLUMBUS AVE

AMSTERDAM AVE

WEST END AVE

HENRY HUDSON PKWY

MPL

Ⓜ 1

W 64TH ST

65TH ST TRANS

Lincoln Center

W 62ND ST

Heckscher Playground

RIVERSIDE BLVD

2

W 60TH ST

A,B,C,D Ⓜ

99

Columbus Circle

98

Time Warner Center

94

W 58TH ST

Hearst Tower ■ ■ Museum of Arts & Design Ⓜ N,

97

W 57TH ST

80

96

W 56TH ST

Carnegie Hall

95

67

94

W 54TH ST

HELL'S KITCHEN

72

B,D,E Ⓜ Officia Inform Ce

3

De Witt Clinton Park

76

SEVENTH AVE

92

W 52ND ST

64

90

W 50TH ST

71

66

78

C,E Ⓜ

79

74

Ⓜ Ⓜ N,

TWELFTH AVE

ELEVENTH AVE

TENTH AVE

NINTH AVE

W 48TH ST

75

1 Ⓜ

88

THEATER DISTRICT

Times Squ Visitor Ce

Intrepid Sea, Air & Space Museum

W 46TH ST

69

65

63

86 61

77

68

TKTS

84

W 44TH ST

70

73

83

EIGHTH AVE

83 60

Times Square

81

82

A,C,E Ⓜ

LINCOLN TUNNEL

Port Authority Bus Terminal

W 42ND ST

84

85

N,C, 1,

W 40TH ST

Madame Tussaud's New York

82

5

78

GARMENT DISTRICT

W 38TH ST

SEVENTH AVE

76

Javits Center

W 36TH ST

Macy's

See p100 ▼

A,C,E Ⓜ

1,2,3 Ⓜ

W 34TH ST

fashion historian Valerie Steele, the museum showcases a selection from the permanent collection, as well as temporary exhibitions focusing on individual designers or the role fashion plays in society.

Rubin Museum of Art

150 W 17th Street, at Seventh Avenue (1-212 620 5000, www.rmanyc.org). Subway A, C, E to 14th Street; L to Eighth Avenue; 1 to 18th Street. **Open** *11am-5pm Mon, Thur; 11am-7pm Wed; 11am-10pm Fri; 11am-6pm Sat, Sun.* **Admission** *$10; free-$5 reductions; free 6-10pm Fri.* **Map** p100 C4 ❷

Dedicated to Himalayan art, the Rubin is a very stylish museum – a fact that falls into place when you learn that the six-storey space was once occupied by famed fashion store Barneys. Rich-toned walls are classy foils for the serene statuary and intricate, multicoloured painted textiles. The second level is dedicated to 'Gateway to Himalayan Art', a yearly rotating display of selections from the permanent collection of more than 2,000 pieces dating from the second century to the present day. The upper floors are devoted to temporary themed exhibitions.

Event highlights The All-Knowing Buddha: A Secret Guide (through 11 Feb 2014).

Eating & drinking

Cookshop

156 Tenth Avenue, at 20th Street (1-212 924 4440, www.cookshop ny.com). Subway C, E to 23rd Street. **Open** *8.30-11am, 11.30am-4pm, 5.30-11.30pm Mon-Fri; 10.30am-4pm, 5.30-11.30pm Sat, Sun.* **$$**. **American**. **Map** p100 B4 ❸

Chef Marc Meyer and his wife/co-owner Vicki Freeman want Cookshop to be a platform for sustainable ingredients from independent farmers. True to the restaurant's mission, the ingredients

are consistently top-notch, and the menu changes daily. While organic ingredients alone don't guarantee a great meal, Meyer knows how to let the natural flavours speak for themselves, and Cookshop scores points for getting the house-made ice-cream to taste as good as Ben & Jerry's.

Half King

505 W 23rd Street, between Tenth & Eleventh Avenues (1-212 462 4300, www.thehalfking.com). Subway C, E to 23rd Street. **Open** *11am-4am Mon-Fri; 9am-4am Sat, Sun.* **Bar**. **Map** p100 B4 ❹

Don't let their blasé appearance fool you – the creative types gathered at the Half King's yellow pine bar are probably as excited as you are to catch a glimpse of the part-owner, author Sebastian Junger. While you're waiting, order one of the 16 draught beers – including several local brews – or a seasonal cocktail.

Shopping

Antiques Garage

112 W 25th Street, between Sixth & Seventh Avenues (1-212 243 5343, www.annexmarkets.com). Subway F, M to 23rd Street. **Open** *9am-5pm Sat, Sun. No credit cards.* **Map** p100 C3 ❺

Designers (along with the occasional celebrity) hunt regularly at this flea market held in a vacant parking garage. Specialities include old prints, vintage clothing and household paraphernalia. The weekend outdoor Hell's Kitchen Flea Market (39th Street, between Ninth & Tenth Avenues), run by the same people, features a mix of vintage clothing and textiles, as well as furniture and miscellaneous bric-a-brac.

Billy's Bakery

184 Ninth Avenue, between 21st & 22nd Streets (1-212 647 9956, www.billysbakerynyc.com). Subway

C, E to 23rd Street. **Open** 8.30am-11pm Mon-Thur; 8.30am-12.30am Fri; 9am-12.30am Sat; 9am-11pm Sun. **Map** p100 B4 ⑥

Amid super-sweet retro delights such as coconut cream pie, cupcakes and Famous Chocolate Icebox Cake, you'll find friendly service in a setting that will remind you of grandma's kitchen – or at least, it will if your grandmother was Betty Crocker.

Loehmann's

101 Seventh Avenue, at 16th Street (1-212 352 0856, www.loehmanns.com). Subway A, C, E to 14th Street; L to Eighth Avenue; 1 to 18th Street. **Open** 9am-10pm Mon-Sat; 11am-8pm Sun. **Map** p100 C5 ⑦

You'll find five floors of major markdowns on current and off-season clothes at this venerable discount emporium. Make a beeline upstairs to the 'Back Room' for big names such as Prada and Armani.

Mantiques Modern

146 W 22nd Street, between Sixth & Seventh Avenues (1-212 206 1494, www.mantiquesmodern.com). Subway 1 to 23rd Street. **Open** 10.30am-6.30pm Mon-Fri; 11am-7pm Sat, Sun. **Map** p100 C4 ⑧

Specialising in industrial and modernist furnishings and art from the 1880s to the 1980s, Mantiques Modern is a fantastic repository of beautiful and bizarre items, from kinetic sculptures and early-20th-century wooden artists' mannequins to a Russian World War II telescope and a rattlesnake frozen in a slab of Lucite. Pieces by famous designers such as Hermès sit side by side with natural curiosities, and skulls (in metal or Lucite), crabs, animal horns and robots are all recurring themes.

Printed Matter

195 Tenth Avenue, between 21st & 22nd Streets (1-212 925 0325, www.printedmatter.org). Subway C,

E to 23rd Street. **Open** 11am-7pm Mon-Wed, Sat; 11am-8pm Thur, Fri. **Map** p100 B4 ⑨

This non-profit organisation is devoted to artists' books – ranging from David Shrigley's deceptively naive illustrations to provocative photographic self-portraits by Matthias Herrmann – and operates a public reading room as well as a shop. Works by unknown and emerging artists share shelf space with those by veterans such as Yoko Ono and Edward Ruscha.

Nightlife

Eagle

554 W 28th Street, between Tenth & Eleventh Avenues (1-646 473 1866, www.eaglenyc.com). Subway C, E to 23rd Street. **Open** 10pm-4am Mon-Sat; 5pm-4am Sun. No credit cards. **Map** p100 A3 ⑩

You don't have to be a kinky leather daddy to enjoy this manly outpost, but it definitely doesn't hurt. The gay fetish bar is home to an array of beer blasts, foot-worship fêtes and leather soirées, plus simple pool playing and cruising nights. In summer, the rooftop is a surprising oasis.

G Lounge

225 W 19th Street, between Seventh & Eighth Avenues (1-212 929 1085, www.glounge.com). Subway 1 to 18th Street. **Open** 4pm-4am daily. No credit cards. **Map** p100 C4 ⑪

The neighbourhood's original slick boy lounge – a rather moodily lit cave with a cool brick-and-glass arched entrance – wouldn't look out of place in an upscale boutique hotel. An excellent roster of DJs stays on top of the mood at this popular gay after-work cocktail spot.

Highline Ballroom

431 W 16th Street, between Ninth & Tenth Avenues (1-212 414 5994, www.highlineballroom.com). Subway A, C, E to 14th Street; L to Eighth Avenue. **Map** p100 B5 ⑫

This West Side club is LA-slick and bland, in a corporate sense. But it still has a lot to recommend it: the acoustics are first class and sightlines are pretty good too. The bookings are also impressive, ranging from hip hop heat-seekers such as Yelawolf and Wiz Khalifa, to singer-songwriter pop, world music and burlesque.

Upright Citizens Brigade Theatre

307 W 26th Street, between Eighth & Ninth Avenues (1-212 366 9176, www.ucbtheatre.com). Subway C, E to 23rd Street; 1 to 28th Street. No credit cards. **Map** p100 B3 ⑬

The Upright Citizens Brigade, which migrated from Chicago in the 1990s, has been the most visible catalyst in New York's current alternative comedy boom. The improv troupes and sketch groups here are some of the best in the city. Stars of *Saturday Night Live* and writers for late-night talk shows gather on Sunday nights to wow crowds in the long-running *ASSSSCAT 3000*. Other premier teams include the Stepfathers (Fridays) and Death by Roo Roo (Saturdays). Arrive early so you can choose a good seat – the venue has challenging sightlines.

Event highlights *ASSSSCAT 3000* (7.30pm, 9.30pm Sun).

Arts & leisure

Atlantic Theater Company

336 W 20th Street, between Eighth & Ninth Avenues (1-212 691 5919, Ticket Central 1-212 279 4200, www.atlantictheater.org). Subway C, E to 23rd Street. **Map** p100 B4 ⑭

Created in 1985 as an offshoot of acting workshops led by playwright David Mamet and actor William H Macy, the dynamic Atlantic Theater Company has presented dozens of new plays, including Steven Sater and Duncan Sheik's rock musical *Spring Awakening*, and John Guare's *3 Kinds of Exile*. The Atlantic Theater Company also has a smaller second stage deep underground at 330 W 16th Street.

Chelsea Piers

Piers 59-62, W 17th to 23rd Streets, at Eleventh Avenue (1-212 336 6666, www.chelseapiers.com). Subway C, E to 23rd Street. **Open** times vary; phone or check website for details. **Map** p100 A4 ⑮

Chelsea Piers is still the most impressive all-in-one athletic facility in New York. Between the ice rink (Pier 61, 1-212 336 6100), the bowling alley (between Piers 59 & 60, 1-212 835 2695), the driving range (Pier 59, 1-212 336 6400) and scads of other choices, there's definitely something here for everyone. The Field House (between Piers 61 & 62, 1-212 336 6500) has a climbing wall, a gymnastics centre, batting cages and basketball courts. At the Sports Center Health Club (Pier 60, 1-212 336 6000), you'll find a gym complete with comprehensive weight deck and cardiovascular machines, plus classes covering everything from boxing to triathlon training in the pool.

Joyce Theater

175 Eighth Avenue, at 19th Street (1-212 242 0800, www.joyce.org). Subway A, C, E to 14th Street; 1 to 18th Street; L to Eighth Avenue. **Map** p100 B4 ⑯

This intimate space houses one of the finest theatres – we're talking about sightlines – in town. Companies and choreographers that present work here, among them Ballet Hispanico, Pilobolus Dance Theater and Doug Varone, tend to be somewhat traditional. The Joyce hosts dance throughout much of the year – Pilobolus is a summer staple.

The Kitchen

512 W 19th Street, between Tenth & Eleventh Avenues (1-212 255 5793, www.thekitchen.org). Subway A, C, E to 14th Street; L to Eighth Avenue. **Map** p100 B4 ⑰

The Kitchen offers some of the best experimental dance around – inventive, provocative and rigorous. Some of New York's finest artists have performed here: Sarah Michelson (who also curates artists), Dean Moss, Ann Liv Young and Jodi Melnick.

Sleep No More

McKittrick Hotel, 530 W 27th Street, between Tenth & Eleventh Avenues (Ovationtix 1-866 811 4111, www. sleepnomorenyc.com). Subway 1 to 28th Street; C, E to 23rd Street. **Map** p100 A3 ⑱
A multitude of searing sights await at this bedazzling and uncanny installation by British company Punchdrunk. Your sense of space is blurred as you wend your way through more than 90 discrete spaces, from a cloistral chapel to a ballroom floor. A Shakespearean can check off allusions to *Macbeth*; others can just revel in the haunted-house vibe.

Flatiron District & Union Square

Taking its name from the distinctive wedge-shaped **Flatiron Building**, this district extends from 14th to 30th Streets, between Sixth and Park Avenues. The former commercial area became more residential in the 1980s as buyers were drawn to its early 20th-century industrial architecture and 19th-century brownstones; clusters of restaurants and shops followed.

Sights & museums

Flatiron Building

175 Fifth Avenue, between 22nd & 23rd Streets. Subway N, R, 6 to 23rd Street. **Map** p101 D4 ⑲
One of New York's most celebrated structures, the Flatiron Building was the world's first steel-frame skyscraper when it was completed in 1902. The 22-storey Beaux Arts edifice is clad in white limestone and terracotta, but it's the unique triangular shape as well as its singular position at the crossing of Fifth Avenue and Broadway that draws admiration from sightseers and natives alike.

Madison Square Park

23rd to 26th Streets, between Fifth & Madison Avenues (www.madison squarepark.org). Subway N, R, 6 to 23rd Street. **Map** p101 D3/D4 ⑳
Madison Square Park, which first opened in 1847, is one of the most elegant spaces in New York, surrounded by some of the city's most fabled buildings. The world's tallest skyscraper from 1909 to 1913, the Metropolitan Life Tower at 1 Madison Avenue was designed to resemble the Campanile in Venice's Piazza San Marco, whose reconstruction (after a collapse in 1902) Met Life had funded. The Appellate Division Courthouse at 27 Madison Avenue is one of the finest Beaux Arts buildings in New York. The park itself hosts summer concerts, literary readings and kids' events. The undoubted star of the initiative is Mad Sq Art, a year-round 'gallery without walls', featuring changing installations by big-name artists such as Antony Gormley and Jaume Plensa.

Museum of Mathematics (MoMath)

NEW *11 E 26th Street, between Fifth & Madison Avenues (1-212 542 0566, www.momath.org). Subway N, R, 6 to 23rd Street.* **Open** 10am-5pm daily (10am-2.30pm 1st Wed of each mth). **Admission** $16; free-$10 reductions. **Map** p101 D3 ㉑
See box p126.

Museum of Sex

233 Fifth Avenue, at 27th Street (1-212 689 6337, www.museumof sex.com). Subway N, R, 6 to 28th Street. **Open** 10am-8pm Mon-Thur,

Sun; 10am-9pm Fri, Sat. **Admission** $17.50; $15.25 reductions. Under-18s not admitted. Map p101 D3 ㉒

Situated in the former Tenderloin district, which bumped and ground with dance halls and brothels in the 1800s, MoSex explores its subject within a cultural context. Highlights of the permanent collection range from the tastefully erotic to the outlandish: an 1890s anti-onanism device looks as uncomfortable as the BDSM gear donated by a local dominatrix; there is kinky art courtesy of Picasso and Keith Haring, and a lifesize silicone Real Doll. Rotating exhibitions in the three-level space include the likes of 'The Sex Lives of Animals'. The gift shop stocks books and arty sex toys, while the museum's bar dispenses aphrodisiac cockails, stimulating soft drinks and light bites.

Eating & drinking

230 Fifth

230 Fifth Avenue, between 26th & 27th Streets (1-212 725 4300, www. 230-fifth.com). Subway N, R to 28th Street. **Open** 4pm-4am Mon-Fri; 10am-4am Sat, Sun. **Bar**. Map p101 D3 ㉓

The 14,000sq ft roof garden dazzles with truly spectacular views, including a close-up of the Empire State Building, but the glitzy indoor lounge – with its floor-to-ceiling windows, wraparound sofas and bold lighting – shouldn't be overlooked. While the sprawling outdoor space gets mobbed on sultry nights, it's less crowded in the cooler months when heaters, fleece robes and hot ciders make it a winter hotspot.

ABC Cocina

NEW *38 E 19th Street, between Broadway & Park Avenue South (1-212 677 2233, www.abccocina nyc.com). Subway N, R, 6 to 23rd Street.* **Open** 5.30-10.30pm Mon-Wed; 5.30-11pm Thur; 5.30-11.30pm Fri, Sat; 5.30-10pm Sun. **$$**. **Latin American**. Map p101 D4 ㉔

Jean-Georges Vongerichten gives Latin America a bump with this highly anticipated sibling to ABC Kitchen (see below) within the ABC Carpet & Home store. Chef Dan Kluger oversees a market-driven menu, highlighting sustainable seafood and heritage meats cooked over a wood-fired grill. Chilli and citrus pervade fare like chipotle chicken tacos topped with a jalapeño salsa, and beef tenderloin smothered in chimichurri. Tropical cocktails (rhubarb banana daiquiri, passion-fruit white sangria) are served at a 28-seat marble bar.

ABC Kitchen

35 E 18th Street, between Broadway and Park Avenue South (1-212 475 5829, www.abckitchennyc.com). Subway L, N, Q, R, 4, 5, 6 to 14th Street-Union Square. **Open** noon-3pm, 5.30-10.30pm Mon-Wed; noon-3pm, 5.30-11.30pm Thur, Fri; 11am-3pm, 5.30-11.30pm Sat; 11am-3pm, 5.30-10pm Sun. **$$**. **Eclectic**. Map p101 D4 ㉕

The haute green cooking at Jean-Georges Vongerichten's artfully decorated restaurant inside a landmark Flatiron furniture store is based on the most gorgeous ingredients from up and down the East Coast. Local, seasonal bounty finds its way into such dishes as a salad of cumin-and-citrus-laced roasted carrots with avocado and crunchy sunflower, pumpkin and sesame seeds, or kasha and bowtie pasta with veal meatballs. A sundae of salted caramel ice-cream, candied peanuts and popcorn with chocolate sauce reworks the kids' treat to thrill a grown-up palate. ABC delivers one message overall: food that's good for the planet needn't be any less opulent, flavourful or stunning to look at.

Artisanal

2 Park Avenue, at E 32nd Street (1-212 725 8585, www.artisanalbistro.com). Subway 6 to 33rd Street. **Open** 11.30am-10pm Mon-Wed; 10.30am-10.45pm Thur-Sat; 10.30am-3.45pm, 5-8.45pm Sun. **$$**. **French**. Map p101 D3 ㉖

Murray Hill makeover

An influx of upscale spots is transforming frat-boy territory.

Milk and Honey

Once a run-down corner of the Flatiron District, NoMad (North of Madison Square Park) has been gathering steam as a dining and drinking destination, largely thanks to the opening of two hipster hubs, the **Ace Hotel New York** (see p176) and the **NoMad** (see p178). And, more recently, food-and-drink-scene movers and shakers have been migrating further east to Murray Hill, for years dominated by the hard-partying post-frat set.

In spring 2012, visionary barman Sasha Petraske, who paved the way for the modern cocktail bar with Milk and Honey in 2000, planted a flag here for artisanal tipples with **Middle Branch** (see p115). No sly speakeasy for the cognoscenti, the bi-level drinkery has open french windows to welcome an after-work crowd to its crimson banquettes. A year later, Petraske relocated his original cocktail den nearby to the sports-bar-saturated Flatiron District. The new **Milk and Honey** (see p112) may be more accessible than the reservations-only original – walk-ins are

welcome – but cocktail menus are still absent. Ask for one of the bar's contemporary classics like the ginger-and-Scotch Penicillin.

The decor of **Salvation Taco** (see p115) – coloured Christmas lights, fake fruit – may evoke that Cancun vacation, but the fiesta fare doled out at this Murray Hill cantina has an upscale bent, thanks to the duo of April Bloomfield and Ken Friedman (of the Spotted Pig, see p95, and the Ace Hotel's Breslin, see p111). Exotic fillings include Moroccan-spiced lamb and Korean-barbecue-style beef. Even a margarita gets a chefly update with a zippy *guajillo* chilli salt rim.

It's easy to find a cheap ramen joint in this postgrad mecca, but house-made soba crowned with shaved black truffles? That's only at **Kajitsu** (see p115). The minimalist, Michelin-starred den displays a devotion to produce, influenced by the monk-approved *shojin-ryori* (vegetarian) tradition. The sublime fare has made it a cult favourite among top-notch toques like Momofuku's David Chang.

ABC Cocina p108

As New York's bistros veer towards uniformity, Terrance Brennan's high-ceilinged deco gem makes its mark with an all-out homage to *fromage*. Skip the appetisers and open with fondue, which comes in three varieties. Familiar bistro fare awaits, with such dishes as steak frites, mussels, and chicken baked 'under a brick', but the curd gets the last word with the cheese and wine pairings. These selections of three cheeses – chosen by region, style or theme (for example, each one produced in a monastery) – are matched with three wines (or beers or even sakés) for a sumptuous and intriguing finale.

Breslin Bar & Dining Room

Ace Hotel New York, 16 W 29th Street, at Broadway (1-212 679 1939, www.thebreslin.com). Subway N, R to 28th Street. **Open** 7am-midnight daily. **$$$. Eclectic. Map** p101 D3 ㉗
The third project from restaurant savant Ken Friedman and Anglo chef April Bloomfield, the Breslin broke gluttonous new ground. Expect a wait at this no-reservations hotspot – you can quell your appetite at the bar with an order of scrumpets (fried strips of lamb belly). The overall ethos could best be described as late-period Henry VIII: groaning boards of house-made terrines feature thick slices of guinea hen, rabbit and pork. The pig's foot for two – half a leg, really – could feed the whole Tudor court. Desserts include amped-up childhood treats like ice-cream sundaes.

Eleven Madison Park

11 Madison Avenue, at E 24th Street (1-212 889 0905, www.elevenmadison park.com). Subway N, R, 6 to 23rd Street. **Open** 5.30-10pm Mon-Wed, Sun; noon-1pm, 5.30-10pm Thur-Sat. **$$$$. American. Map** p101 D4 ㉘
Chef Daniel Humm and impresario partner Will Guidara – who bought Eleven Madison Park from their old boss, legendary restaurateur Danny Meyer – are masters of reinvention. And once again, they've hit on a winning formula, this time for a 16-course Gotham-themed meal – marked by stagecraft and tricks – that departs from the city's upper echelons of Old World-dominated fine dining. On a recent meal, a glass cloche rose over a puff of smoke, unveiling smoked sturgeon above smouldering embers. Rib eye, aged an astonishing 140 days, was served with a side of oxtail jam with melted foie gras and whipped potato icing that's as rich as it sounds, and a waiter performed a card trick with a chocolate payoff – a nod to the city's old street-corner shysters.

Hanjan

NEW *36 W 26th Street, between Broadway & Sixth Avenue (1-212 206 7226, www.hanjan26.com). Subway N, R to 28th Street.* **Open** 5.30pm-1am Mon-Sat. **$$. Korean. Map** p100 C3 ㉙
Hanjan is a shining example of a *joomak*, the Korean equivalent of the English gastropub. Strap in for a barrage of deeply satisfying dishes: glutinous rice cakes licked with spicy pork fat; crispy scallion pancakes studded with squid; and skewers of fresh chicken thighs that you can swab with funky *ssamjang*. Each plate packs its own surprises, but the whole feast is tied together by a soulful bass note melding sweetness, spice and just the right amount of fishy funk.

John Dory Oyster Bar

Ace Hotel New York, 1196 Broadway, at W 29th Street (1-212 792 9000, www.thejohndory.com). Subway N, R to 28th Street. **Open** noon-midnight daily. **$$. American. Map** p101 D3 ㉚
April Bloomfield and Ken Friedman's original John Dory, in the Meatpacking District, was an ambitious, pricey endeavour, but its reincarnation in the Ace Hotel is an understated knockout. Tall stools face a raw bar stocked with East and West Coast oysters, all

expertly handled and impeccably sourced. True to form, the rest of Bloomfield's tapas-style seafood dishes are intensely flavoured – meaty lobster rolls in a pink dill and celery sauce, for example, or Mediterranean mussels stuffed with saffron aioli.

Milk and Honey

NEW *30 E 23rd Street, between Madison Avenue & Park Avenue South (no phone, www.mlkhny.com). Subway N, R, 6 to 23rd Street.* **Open** 6pm-4am daily. **Bar**. **Map** p101 D4 ③①
See box p109.

NoMad

1170 Broadway, at 28th Street (1-347 472 5660, www.thenomadhotel.com). N, R to 28th Street. **Open** 7am-10.30pm Mon-Thur; 7am-11pm Fri, Sat; 7am-10pm Sun. **$$$**. **American**. **Map** p101 D3 ③②
The sophomore effort from chef Daniel Humm and front-of-house partner Will Guidara, who've been in cahoots at Eleven Madison Park (see p111) since 2006, the NoMad features plush armchairs around well-spaced tables and a stylish return to three-course dining. The food, like the space, exudes unbuttoned decadence: a poached egg stars in one over-the-top starter, its barely contained yolk melting into a sweet, velvety soup of brown butter and Parmesan, with shaved white asparagus and toasted quinoa for crunch. And while there are plenty of rich-man roast chickens for two in New York, the amber-hued bird here – with a foie gras, brioche and black truffle stuffing under the skin – is surely the new gold standard, well worth its $79 price tag.

Rye House

11 W 17th Street, between Fifth & Sixth Avenues (1-212 255 7260, www.ryehousenyc.com). Subway F, M to 14th Street; L to Sixth Avenue. **Open** noon-2am Mon-Fri; 11am-2am Sat; 11am-midnight Sun. **Bar**. **Map** p101 D4 ③③

As the name suggests, American spirits are the emphasis at this dark, sultry bar. As well as bourbons and ryes, there are gins, vodkas and rums, most distilled in the States. Check out the jalapeño-infused Wake-up Call, one of the venue's most popular bourbon cocktails. While the focus is clearly on drinking, there's excellent upscale pub grub, such as truffle grilled cheese or potato pierogies.

Shopping

ABC Carpet & Home

888 Broadway, at 19th Street (1-212 473 3000, www.abchome.com). Subway L, N, Q, R, 4, 5, 6 to 14th Street-Union Square. **Open** 10am-7pm Mon-Wed, Fri, Sat; 10am-8pm Thur; 11am-6.30pm Sun. **Map** p101 D4 ③④
Most of ABC's 35,000-strong carpet range is housed in the store across the street at no.881 – except the rarest rugs, which reside on the sixth floor of the main store. Browse everything from organic soap to hand-beaded lampshades on the ground floor. Furniture, on the upper floors, spans every style, from European minimalism to antique oriental and mid-century modern.

Eataly

200 Fifth Avenue, between 23rd & 24th Streets (1-212 229 2560, www.eataly.com). Subway F, M, N, R to 23rd Street. **Open** 8am-11pm daily. **Map** p101 D4 ③⑤
This massive foodie destination, from Mario Batali and Joe and Lidia Bastianich, sprawls across 50,000sq ft. A spin-off of an operation by the same name just outside of Turin, the complex encompasses six restaurants and a rooftop beer garden. Adjacent retail areas offer gourmet provisions, including artisanal breads baked on the premises, fresh mozzarella, salumi and a vast array of olive oils.

Idlewild

12 W 19th Street, between Fifth & Sixth Avenues (1-212 414 8888, www.idlewildbooks.com). Subway F, M to 14th Street; L to Sixth Avenue. **Open** noon-7.30pm Mon-Thur; noon-6pm Fri, Sat; noon-5pm Sun. **Map** p101 D4 ❸❻

Opened by a former United Nations press officer, Idlewild stocks travel guides to more than 100 countries and all 50 states, which are grouped with related works of fiction and non-fiction. It also has a large selection of works in French, Spanish and Italian. Fun fact: Idlewild was the original name for JFK Airport before it was renamed to honour the assassinated president.

JJ Hat Center

310 Fifth Avenue, at W 32nd Street (1-212 239 4368, www.jjhatcenter.com). Subway B, D, F, M, N, Q, R to 34th Street-Herald Square. **Open** 9am-6pm Mon-Fri; 9.30am-5.30pm Sat; noon-5pm Sun (Oct-Dec). **Map** p101 D3 ❸❼

Trad hats may be back in fashion, but this venerable shop, in business since 1911, is oblivious to passing trends. Dapper gents sporting the shop's wares will help you choose from more than 4,000 fedoras, pork pies, caps and other styles on display in the splendid, chandelier-illuminated, wood-panelled showroom. Prices start at around $35 for a wool-blend cap.

LA Burdick

5 E 20th Street, between Fifth Avenue & Broadway (1-212 796 0143, www.burdickchocolate.com). Subway N, R to 23rd Street. **Open** 8am-9pm Mon-Wed; 8am-10pm Thur, Fri; 9am-10pm Sat; 9am-9pm Sun. **Map** p101 D4 ❸❽

Best known for its petite chocolate penguins and mice, the family-owned, New Hampshire-based chocolatier now has a shop and café in NYC. Assorted pastries share space in cases with pâtes de fruits, marzipan, dipped caramels and assorted truffles. Ponder the choices over a cup of dark, white or milk hot chocolate, or plump for dealer's choice with the assorted boxes.

Showplace Antique & Design Center

40 W 25th Street, between Fifth & Sixth Avenues (1-212 633 6063, www.nyshowplace.com). Subway F, M to 23rd Street. **Open** 10am-6pm Mon-Fri; 8.30am-5.30pm Sat, Sun. **Map** p100 C3 ❸❾

Set over four expansive floors, this indoor market houses more than 200 high-quality dealers selling everything from vintage designer wear to Greek and Roman antiquities. Among the highlights are Joe Sundlie's colourful, spot-on-trend vintage pieces from Lanvin and Alaïa, and Mood Indigo – arguably the best source in the city for collectible bar accessories and dinnerware. The array of Bakelite jewellery and table accessories and Fiestaware is dazzling.

Union Square Greenmarket

From 16th to 17th Streets, between Union Square East & Union Square West (1-212 788 7476, www.grownyc. org/unionsquaregreenmarket). Subway L, N, Q, R, 4, 5, 6 to 14th Street-Union Square. **Open** 8am-6pm Mon, Wed, Fri, Sat. **Map** p101 D4 ❹❶

There are more than 50 open-air Greenmarkets throughout the city run by the non-profit organisation GrowNYC. At this, the largest and best known, small producers of cheese, herbs, fruits and vegetables hawk their goods directly to the public.

Nightlife

Metropolitan Room

34 W 22nd Street, between Fifth & Sixth Avenues (1-212 206 0440, www.metropolitanroom.com). Subway F, M, N, R to 23rd Street. **Map** p100 C4 ❹❶

The Met Room occupies a comfortable middle zone on the city's cabaret spectrum, less expensive than the fancier supper clubs and more polished than the cheaper spots. Regular performers

NEW YORK BY AREA

range from rising jazz artists to established cabaret acts such as Baby Jane Dexter, plus legends like Tammy Grimes and Annie Ross.

Splash

50 W 17th Street, between Fifth & Sixth Avenues (1-212 691 0073, www.splashbar.com). Subway F, M to 14th Street; L to Sixth Avenue. **Open** 4pm-4am daily. No credit cards. **Map** p100 C4 ❷

This NYC queer institution has 10,000sq ft of dance and lounge space, staffed by super-muscular (and shirtless) bartenders. Nationally known DJs still rock the house, while local drag celebs give good face, and in-house VJs flash hypnotic snippets of classic musicals spliced with videos.

Gramercy Park & Murray Hill

A key to Gramercy Park, the gated square at the southern end of Lexington Avenue (between 20th & 21st Streets), is the preserve and privilege of residents of the surrounding homes (and members of a couple of venerable private clubs). Murray Hill spans 30th to 40th Streets, between Third and Fifth Avenues. Townhouses of the rich and powerful were once clustered around Madison and Park Avenues, but these days, only a few streets retain their former elegance and the area is largely populated by upwardly mobiles fresh out of university.

Sights & museums

Morgan Library & Museum

225 Madison Avenue, at E 36th Street (1-212 685 0008, www.themorgan.org). Subway 6 to 33rd Street. **Open** 10.30am-5pm Tue-Thur; 10.30am-9pm Fri; 10am-6pm Sat; 11am-6pm Sun. **Admission** $18; free-$12 reductions. **Map** p101 D2/p103 D5 ❸

This Madison Avenue institution began as the private library of financier J Pierpont Morgan. It houses first-rate works on paper, including drawings by Michelangelo, Rembrandt and Picasso; a copy of *Frankenstein* annotated by Mary Shelley; manuscripts by Steinbeck, Twain and Wilde; sheet music handwritten by Beethoven and Mozart; and an original edition of Dickens' *A Christmas Carol* that's displayed every Yuletide.

Event highlights Edgar Allan Poe: Terror of the Soul (through 26 Jan 2014); Leonardo da Vinci: Drawings from the Biblioteca Reale, Turin (25 Oct 2013-2 Feb 2014); The Little Prince (24 Jan-27 Apr 2014).

Eating & drinking

71 Irving Place Coffee & Tea Bar

71 Irving Place, between 18th & 19th Streets (1-212 995 5252, www.irvingfarm.com). Subway L, N, Q, R, 4, 5, 6 to 14th Street-Union Square. **Open** 7am-10pm Mon-Fri; 8am-10pm Sat. **$. Café. Map** p101 D4 ❹

Irving Farm's beans are roasted in a 100-year-old carriage house in the Hudson Valley; fittingly, its Gramercy Park café, in a stately brownstone, also has a quaint, rustic edge. Breakfast (granola, oatmeal, waffles, bagels), sandwiches and salads accompany the superior-quality java.

Cannibal

116 E 29th Street, between Park & Lexington Avenues (1-212 686 5480, www.thecannibalnyc.com). Subway 6 to 28th Street. **Open** 11am-11.30pm Mon-Sat; 11am-10.30pm Sun. **$-$$. Steakhouse. Map** p101 D3 ❺

Run by restaurateur Christian Pappanicholas and connected to his Belgian-American eatery, Resto, the Cannibal is an unusual retail-restaurant hybrid – a beer store and a butcher's shop but also a laid-back place to eat and drink. The meat counter supplies whole beasts for Resto's large-format feasts, but the carnivore's paradise is otherwise autonomous, with its own chef, Preston Clark (formerly of Jean Georges), and beer master, Julian Kurland. The food is best ordered in rounds, pairing beer and bites – wispy shavings of Kentucky ham, pâtés, sausages and tartares – as you work your way through some of the 400-plus selections on the drinks list.

Casa Mono

52 Irving Place, at E 17th Street (1-212 253 2773, www.casamononyc.com). Subway L to Third Avenue; L, N, Q, R, 4, 5, 6 to 14th Street-Union Square. **Open** noon-midnight daily. **$-$$.** **Spanish.** Map p101 E4 46

Offal-loving chef-partners Mario Batali and Andy Nusser broke new ground in NYC with their adventurous Spanish fare: oxtail-stuffed piquillo peppers, fried sweetbreads, foie gras with *cinco cebollas* (five types of onion), or the fried duck egg, a delicately flavoured breakfast-meets-dinner dish topping a mound of sautéed fingerling potatoes and salt-cured tuna loin. For a cheaper option, the attached Bar Jamón (125 E 17th Street; open 5pm-2am Mon-Fri; noon-2am Sat, Sun) offers tapas, treasured Ibérico hams and Spanish cheeses.

Kajitsu

NEW *125 E 39th Street, between Park & Lexington Avenues (1-212 228 4873, www.kajitsunyc.com). Subway S, 4, 5, 6, 7 to 42nd Street-Grand Central.* **Open** 11.45am-1.45pm, 5.30-10pm Mon-Sat (closed every 3rd Sat). **$$$.** **Japanese/ vegetarian.** Map p101 D2 47
See box p109.

Maialino

Gramercy Park Hotel, 2 Lexington Avenue, at E 21st Street (1-212 777 2410, www.maialinonyc.com). Subway 6 to 23rd Street. **Open** 7.30am-10.30pm Mon-Thur; 7.30am-11pm Fri; 10am-11pm Sat; 10am-10.30pm Sun. **$$.** **Italian.** Map p101 D4 48

Danny Meyer's first full-fledged foray into Italian cuisine is a dedicated homage to the Roman neighbourhood trattoria. Salumi and bakery stations between the front bar and the wood-beamed dining room – hog jowls and sausages dangling near shelves stacked with crusty loaves of bread – mimic a market off the Appian Way. Chef Nick Anderer's menu offers exceptional facsimiles of dishes specific to Rome: carbonara, braised tripe and suckling pig, among others.

Middle Branch

NEW *154 E 33rd Street, between Lexington & Third Avenues (1-212 213 1350). Subway 6 to 33rd Street.* **Open** 5pm-2am daily. **Bar.** Map p101 E2 49
See box p109.

Salvation Taco

NEW *145 E 39th Street, between Lexington & Third Avenues (1-212 865 5800, www.salvationtaco.com). Subway S, 4, 5, 6, 7 to 42nd Street-Grand Central.* **Open** 7am-5pm, 5.30pm-midnight daily. **$.** **Mexican.** Map p101 E2 50
See box p109.

Nightlife

Gramercy Theatre

127 E 23rd Street, between Park & Lexington Avenues (1-212 614 6932, www.thegramercytheatre.com). Subway N, R, 6 to 23rd Street. Map p101 D4 51

The Gramercy Theatre looks exactly like what it actually is, a run-down former movie theatre; yet it has a decent sound system and good sightlines. Concert-goers can lounge in raised seats on the top level or get closer to the stage lower down. Past bookings have included such Baby Boom underdogs as Todd Rundgren and Loudon Wainwright III, and the occasional comedy show, but tilt towards niche metal and emo bands.

Irving Plaza

*17 Irving Place, at E 15th Street
(1-212 777 6800, www.irvingplaza.
com). Subway L, N, Q, R, 4, 5, 6
to 14th Street-Union Square.*
Map p101 D5 ⑫
Lying just east of Union Square, this
mid-size rock venue has served as a
Democratic Party lecture hall (in the
19th century), a Yiddish theatre and
a burlesque house (Gypsy Rose Lee
made an appearance). Most importantly, it's a great place to see big
stars keeping a low profile (Jeff
Beck, Jane's Addiction and Lenny
Kravitz), along with medium heavies
on their way up.

Herald Square & Garment District

Seventh Avenue is the main drag
of the Garment District (roughly
from 34th to 40th Streets, between
Broadway & Eighth Avenue),
where designers feed America's
multibillion-dollar clothing
industry. The world's largest
store, Macy's, looms over
Herald Square (at the junction
of Broadway and Sixth Avenue).
To the east, the spas, restaurants
and karaoke bars of Koreatown
line 32nd Street, between Fifth
and Sixth Avenues.

Eating & drinking

Keens Steakhouse

*72 W 36th Street, between Fifth
& Sixth Avenues (1-212 947 3636,
www.keens.com). Subway B, D, F,
M, N, Q, R to 34th Street-Herald
Square.* **Open** 11.45am-10.30pm
Mon-Fri; 5-10.30pm Sat; 5-9.30pm
Sun. **$$. Steakhouse. Map**
p100 C2 ㊳
The ceiling and walls are hung with
pipes, some from such long-ago Keens
regulars as Babe Ruth, JP Morgan and
Teddy Roosevelt. Even in these non-

smoking days, you can catch a whiff
of the restaurant's 120-plus years of
history. Bevelled-glass doors, two
working fireplaces and a forest's
worth of dark wood suggest a time
when 'Diamond Jim' Brady piled his
table with bushels of oysters, slabs of
seared beef and troughs of ale. The
menu still lists a three-inch-thick mut-
ton chop (imagine a saddle of lamb but
with more punch), and the porter-
house (for two or three) holds its own
against any steak in the city.

Mandoo Bar

*2 W 32nd Street, between Fifth
Avenue & Broadway (1-212 279
3075). Subway B, D, F, M, N, Q,
R to 34th Street-Herald Square.*
Open 11am-10pm daily. **$. Korean.
Map** p101 D3 ㊴
If the staff painstakingly filling and
crimping dough squares in the front
window don't give it away, then we
will – this wood-wrapped industrial-
style spot elevates *mandoo* (Korean
dumplings) above mere appetiser sta-
tus. Six varieties of the tasty morsels
are filled with such delights as subtly
piquant kimchi, juicy pork, succulent
shrimp and vegetables. Try them
miniaturised, as in the 'baby mandoo',
swimming in a soothing beef broth or
atop springy, soupy ramen noodles.

Shopping

B&H

*420 Ninth Avenue, at W 34th Street
(1-212 444 5040, www.bhphoto
video.com). Subway A, C, E to 34th
Street-Penn Station.* **Open** 9am-7pm
Mon-Thur; 9am-2pm Fri; 10am-6pm
Sun. **Map** p100 B2 ㊵
B&H is the ultimate one-stop shop for
all your photographic, video and audio
needs. In this huge, busy store, goods
are transported from the stock room
via an overhead conveyor belt. Note
that, due to the largely Hasidic Jewish
staff, the store is closed on Saturdays
and other Jewish holidays.

Macy's

151 W 34th Street, between Broadway & Seventh Avenue (1-212 695 4400, www.macys.com). Subway B, D, F, M, N, Q, R to 34th Street-Herald Square; 1, 2, 3 to 34th Street-Penn Station. **Open** 9am-9.30pm Mon-Thur; 8am-11pm Fri; 7am-11pm Sat; 11am-8.30pm Sun. **Map** p100 C2/p102 C5 ⑤⑥

It may not be as glamorous as New York's other famous department stores, but for sheer breadth of stock, the 34th Street behemoth that is Macy's is hard to beat. The store recently unveiled a $400 million redesign of its ground floor, bringing new luxury accessories boutiques, including Gucci and Burberry, but mid-priced fashion for all ages and big beauty brands are its bread and butter. There's also a Ben & Jerry's outpost, should you need a post-shopping sugar fix.

Nepenthes New York

307 W 38th Street, between Eighth & Ninth Avenues (1-212 643 9540, www.nepenthesny.com). Subway A, C, E, 1, 2, 3 to 34th Street-Penn Station. **Open** noon-7pm Mon-Sat; noon-5pm Sun. **Map** p100 B2 ⑤⑦

Well-dressed dudes with an eye on the Japanese style scene will already be familiar with this Tokyo fashion retailer. The narrow, ground-floor Garment District shop – its first US location – showcases expertly crafted urban-rustic menswear from house label Engineered Garments, such as plaid flannel shirts and workwear-inspired jackets. There is also a small selection of its women's line, FWK.

Arts & leisure

Juvenex

5th Floor, 25 W 32nd Street, between Fifth Avenue & Broadway (1-646 733 1330, www.juvenexspa.com). Subway B, D, F, M, N, Q, R to 34th Street-Herald Square. **Open** 24hrs daily. **Map** p101 D3 ⑤⑧

This bustling Koreatown relaxation hub may be slightly rough around the edges (frayed towels, dingy sandals), but we embrace it for its bathhouse-meets-Epcot feel (igloo saunas, tiled 'soaking ponds' and a slatted bridge), and 24-hour availability (and it's women only between 8am and 5pm). A basic Purification Program – including soak and sauna, face, body and hair cleansing and a salt scrub – is great value at $115.

Madison Square Garden

Seventh Avenue, between 31st & 33rd Streets (1-212 465 6741, www.thegarden.com). Subway A, C, E, 1, 2, 3 to 34th Street-Penn Station. **Map** p100 C3 ⑤⑨

Some of music's biggest acts – Jay-Z, Lady Gaga, Rush – come out to play at the world's most famous basketball arena, home to the Knicks and also hockey's Rangers. Whether you'll actually be able to get a look at them depends on your seat number or the quality of your binoculars. While it is undoubtedly a part of the fabric of New York, the storied venue is too vast for a rich concert experience. However, it should be improved by a major renovation, which has already brought new seating and food from top NYC chefs and will restore the striking circular ceiling before wrapping up in autumn 2013.

Theater District & Hell's Kitchen

Times Square is the gateway to the Theater District, the zone roughly between 41st Street and 53rd Street, from Sixth Avenue to Ninth Avenue. Thirty-eight of the opulent show houses here – those with more than 500 seats – are designated as being part of Broadway (plus the Vivian Beaumont Theater, uptown at Lincoln Center; p149). Just west of Times Square is Hell's Kitchen, which maintained a crime-ridden, tough veneer well into the 1970s. Today, it's emerging as the city's new queer mecca. Pricey Restaurant Row (46th Street, between Eighth & Ninth Avenues) caters to theatregoers, but Ninth Avenue itself, with its cornucopia of cheap ethnic eateries, is a better bet.

Sights & museums

Circle Line Cruises

Pier 83, W 42nd Street, at the Hudson River (1-212 563 3200, www.circleline 42.com). Subway A, C, E to 42nd Street-Port Authority. **Tickets** $28-$39; $21-$34 reductions. **Map** p100 A1/p102 A4 ⑥⓪

Circle Line's famed three-hour guided circumnavigation of Manhattan Island is a fantastic way to get your bearings and see many of the city's sights as you pass under its iconic bridges. If you don't have time for the full round trip, try the semi-circle cruise of lower and midtown Manhattan, or the two-hour 'Liberty' tour that takes you around Downtown and back.

Intrepid Sea, Air & Space Museum

USS Intrepid, Pier 86, Twelfth Avenue & 46th Street (1-877 957 7447, www. intrepidmuseum.org). Subway A, C, E to 42nd Street-Port Authority, then M42 bus to Twelfth Avenue or 15min walk. **Open** *Apr-Oct* 10am-5pm Mon-Fri; 10am-6pm Sat, Sun. *Nov-Mar* 10am-5pm daily. **Admission** $24-$31; free-$27 reductions. **Map** p100 A1/p102 A4 ⑥①

Commissioned in 1943, this 27,000-ton, 898ft aircraft carrier survived torpedoes and kamikaze attacks in World War II, served during the Vietnam War and the Cuban Missile Crisis, and recovered two space capsules for NASA. It was decommissioned in 1974, then resurrected as an educational institution. On its flight deck and portside aircraft elevator are top-notch examples of American military might, including the US Navy F-14 Tomcat (as featured in *Top Gun*), an A-12 Blackbird spy plane and a fully restored Army AH-1G Cobra gunship helicopter. In summer 2011, the museum became home to the *Enterprise* (OV-101), the first Space Shuttle Orbiter, which was recently retired (entry to the new Space Shuttle Pavilion costs extra).

Times Square

From 42nd to 47th Streets, between Broadway & Seventh Avenue. Subway N, Q, R, S, 1, 2, 3, 7 to 42nd Street-Times Square; N, Q, R to 49th Street. **Map** p100 C1/p102 C4 ⑥②

Times Square's evolution from a traffic-choked fleshpot to a tourist-friendly theme park has accelerated in the past few years. Not only has the 'crossroads of the world' gained an elevated viewing platform atop the rebuilt TKTS discount booth, but in 2009 Mayor Bloomberg designated stretches of Broadway, including the area from 47th to 42nd Streets, as pedestrian zones.

Originally called Longacre Square, Times Square was renamed after the *New York Times* moved here in the early 1900s. The first electrified billboard graced the district in 1904. The same year, the inaugural New Year's Eve party in Times Square doubled as the *Times*' housewarming party in its new HQ. Today, around a million people gather here to watch a mirrorball descend every 31 December. The paper left the building only a decade after it arrived. However, it retained ownership of its old headquarters until the 1960s, and erected the world's first scrolling electric news 'zipper' in 1928. The readout, now sponsored by Dow Jones, has trumpeted breaking stories from the stock-market crash of 1929 to the death of Osama bin Laden in 2011.

Times Square

TKTS

*Father Duffy Square, Broadway &
47th Street (www.tdf.org). Subway
N, Q, R to 49th Street; N, Q, R, S, 1,
2, 3, 7 to 42nd Street-Times Square.*
Open *Evening tickets* 3-8pm Mon,
Wed-Sun; 2-8pm Tue. *Same-day
matinée tickets* 10am-2pm Wed,
Sat; 11am-3pm Sun. **Map** p100 C1/
p102 C4 ⑥③

At the architecturally striking TKTS
base, you can get tickets on the day of
the performance for as much as 50%
off face value. Although there's often
a queue when it opens for business,
this has usually dispersed one to two
hours later, so it's worth trying your
luck an hour or two before the show.
Never buy tickets from anyone who
approaches you in the queue as they
may have been obtained illegally.
While you're there, ascend the red
structural glass steps behind the
ticket windows for a great view of the
surrounding light show.

Eating & drinking

Ardesia

*510 W 52nd Street, between Tenth
& Eleventh Avenues (1-212 247 9191,
www.ardesia-ny.com). Subway C, E
to 50th Street.* **Open** 5pm-midnight
Mon-Wed; 5pm-2am Thur, Fri; 2pm-
2am Sat; 2-11pm Sun. **$. Wine bar.**
Map p102 B3 ⑥④

Le Bernardin vet Mandy Oser's iron-
and-marble gem offers superior wines
in an extremely relaxed setting. The 75-
strong collection of international bottles is a smart balance of Old and New
World options that pair beautifully
with the eclectic small plates. Our
grüner veltliner – a dry, oaky white
from the Knoll winery in Wachau,
Austria – had enough backbone to
stand up to a duck *banh mi* layered
with house-made pâté and duck prosciutto. A blended red from Spain's
Cellar Can Blau, meanwhile, was a
spicy, velvety match for coriander-rich
home-made mortadella.

Café Edison

*Hotel Edison, 228 W 47th Street,
between Broadway & Eighth Avenues
(1-212 354 0368). Subway N, Q, R to
49th Street; 1 to 50th Street.* **Open**
6am-9.30pm Mon-Sat; 6am-7.30pm
Sun. **$.** No credit cards. **American.**
Map p102 C4 ⑥⑤

This old-school no-frills eaterie draws
tourists, theatregoers, actors and just
about everyone else in search of
deli staples such as cheese blintzes
and giant open-faced Reubens. The
matzo ball soup is so restorative, you
can almost feel it bolstering your
immune system.

Don Antonio by Starita

*309 W 50th Street, between Eighth
& Ninth Avenues (1-646 719 1043,
www.donantoniopizza.com). Subway C,
E to 50th Street.* **Open** 11.30am-11pm
Mon-Thur; 11.30am-1am Fri, Sat;
11.30am-10.30pm Sun. **$$. Pizza.**
Map p102 C3 ⑥⑥

Pizza aficionados have been busy
colonising this collaboration between
Keste's (see p95) talented Roberto
Caporuscio and his Naples mentor,
Antonio Starita. Start with tasty
bites like the *frittatine* (a deep-fried
spaghetti cake oozing *prosciutto cotto*
and béchamel sauce). The main event
should be the habit-forming Montanara
Starita, which gets a quick dip in the
deep fryer before hitting the oven to
develop its puffy, golden crust. Topped
with tomato sauce, basil and intensely
smoky buffalo mozzarella, it's a wor-
thy addition to the pantheon of classic
New York pies.

Kashkaval

*856 Ninth Avenue, between 55th
& 56th Streets (1-212 581 8282,
www.kashkavalfoods.com). Subway
C, E to 50th Street.* **Open** 11am-
midnight Mon-Thur, Sun; 11am-1am
Fri, Sat. **$. Wine bar. Map** p102 B3 ⑥⑦
This charming cheese-shop-cum-wine-
bar evokes fondue's peasant origins,
with deep cast-iron pots and generous

baskets of crusty bread – steer clear of the bland and rubbery kashkaval (a Balkan sheep's-milk cheese) and order the gooey and surprisingly mild Gorgonzola. Or choose from the selection of tangy Mediterranean spreads – vinegary artichoke dip, hot-pink beet *skordalia* – and the impressive roster of charcuterie. End the meal with the bittersweet dark-chocolate fondue, a guaranteed crowd-pleaser served with fruit and mini marshmallows.

Pony Bar

637 Tenth Avenue, at W 45th Street (1-212 586 2707, www.theponybar. com). Subway C, E to 50th Street. **Open** 3pm-4am Mon-Fri; noon-4am Sat, Sun. **Bar**. **Map** p102 B4 ⑱
The Theater District isn't known for civilised, non-chain bars, but you need only walk a couple of blocks west to this convivial paean to American microbrews. Choose from a constantly changing selection of two cask ales and 20 beers on tap; daily selections are artfully listed on signboards according to provenance and potency. Despite the expert curation, the prices are kept low (all beers cost $6).

Shopping

Amy's Bread

672 Ninth Avenue, between 46th & 47th Streets (1-212 977 2670, www.amysbread.com). Subway C, E to 50th Street; N, Q, R to 49th Street. **Open** 7.30am-10pm Mon, Tue; 7.30am-11pm Wed-Fri; 8am-11pm Sat; 8am-10pm Sun. **Map** p100 B1/p102 B4 ⑲
Whether you want sweet (double chocolate pecan Chubbie cookies) or savoury (hefty French sourdough boules), Amy's never disappoints. Breakfast and snacks such as the grilled cheese sandwich (made with New York State cheddar) are served.

Domus

413 W 44th Street, between Ninth & Tenth Avenues (1-212 581 8099, www.domusnewyork.com). Subway A, C, E to 42nd Street-Port Authority. **Open** noon-8pm Tue-Sat; noon-6pm Sun. **Map** p102 B4 ⑳
Scouring the globe for unusual design products is nothing new, but owners Luisa Cerutti and Nicki Lindheimer take the concept a step further; each year they visit a far-flung part of the world to forge links with and support co-operatives and individual craftspeople. The beautiful results, such as vivid baskets woven from telephone wire by South African Zulu tribespeople, reflect a fine attention to detail and a sense of place. It's a great spot to find reasonably priced home goods and gifts, from Tunisian bath towels to Italian throws.

Fine and Dandy

NEW *445 W 49th Street, between Ninth & Tenth Avenues (1-212 247 4847, www.fineanddandyshop.com). Subway C, E to 50th Street.* **Open** noon-8pm Mon, Wed-Sat; 1-8pm Sun. **Map** p102 B4 ㉑
Following the success of several pop-ups around the city, owner Matt Fox opened his first permanent location. The accessories-only shop – decked out in flourishes such as collegiate trophies and ironing boards repurposed as tables – is a prime location for the modern gent to score of-the-moment retro accoutrements like bow ties, suspenders (braces) and spats. House-label printed ties are suspended inside propped-open vintage trunks, while patterned socks are displayed in old briefcases.

Nightlife

54 Below

254 W 54th Street, between Broadway & Eighth Avenues (Ticketweb 1-866 468 7619, 1-646-476 3551, www.54 below.com). Subway B, D, E to Seventh Avenue; C, E, 1 to 50th Street; R to 57th Street. **Map** p102 C3 ㉒
A team of top-drawer Broadway producers is behind this swank supper

club located in the bowels of the legendary Studio 54 space. The schedule is dominated by big Broadway talent – Patti LuPone and Ben Vereen had the first two major runs when it opened in 2012 – but there is also room for edgier talents such as Justin Vivian Bond and Jackie Hoffman, as well as weekly showcases for emerging Broadway songwriters.

Birdland
315 W 44th Street, between Eighth & Ninth Avenues (1-212 581 3080, www.birdlandjazz.com). Subway A, C, E to 42nd Street-Port Authority. **Open** 5pm-1am daily. **Map** p100 B1/p102 C4 ⑦

The flagship venue for Midtown's jazz resurgence, Birdland takes its place among the neon lights of Times Square seriously. That means it's a haven for great jazz musicians (Joe Lovano, Kurt Elling) as well as performers like John Pizzarelli and Aaron Neville. The club is also notable for its roster of bands-in-residence. Sundays belong to the Arturo O'Farrill Afro-Cuban Jazz Orchestra.

Carolines on Broadway
1626 Broadway, between 49th & 50th Streets (1-212 757 4100, www.carolines.com). Subway N, Q, R to 49th Street; 1 to 50th Street. **Map** p102 C3 ⑦

This New York City institution's long-term relationships with national comedy headliners, sitcom stars and cable-special pros ensure that its stage always features marquee names. Although a majority of the bookings skew towards mainstream appetites, the club also makes time for undisputedly darker fare such as Louis CK.

Fairytail Lounge
500 W 48th Street, between Tenth & Eleventh Avenues (1-646 684 3897, www.facebook.com/fairytaillounge). Subway C, E to 50th Street. **Open** 5pm-2am Mon, Tue; 5pm-3am Thur-Sun. **Map** p102 B4 ⑦

This Hell's Kitchen gay watering hole packs a lot of glittery, pseudo-Victorian personality into a small space. Patrons can sip cocktails off the backs of sexy centaur mannequins, or park at the bar while bobbing their heads to tunes from DJs during weekly theme nights.

Flaming Saddles
793 Ninth Avenue, at W 53rd Street (1-212 713 0481, www.flamingsaddles.com). Subway C, E to 50th Street. **Open** 4pm-4am Mon-Wed; 3pm-4am Thur, Fri; noon-4am Sat, Sun. No credit cards. **Map** p102 B3 ⑦

City boys can party honky-tonk-style at this country and western gay bar. The place is outfitted to look like a Wild West bordello, complete with red velvet drapes, antler sconces and rococo wallpaper. Performances by bartenders dancing in cowboy boots add to the raucous vibe.

Pacha
618 W 46th Street, between Eleventh & Twelfth Avenues (1-212 209 7500, www.pachanyc.com). Subway C, E to 50th Street. **Open** 10pm-6am Fri; 10pm-8am Sat. **Map** p100 A1/p102 A4 ⑦

The worldwide glam-club chain Pacha hit the US market in 2005 with this swanky joint helmed by superstar spinner Erick Morillo. The spot attracts heavyweights ranging from local hero Danny Tenaglia to international crowd-pleasers such as Fedde Le Grande and Benny Benassi. As with most big clubs, it pays to check the line-up in advance if you're into underground beats.

Arts & leisure

Avenue Q
New World Stages, 340 W 50th Street, between Eighth & Ninth Avenues (Telecharge 1-212 239 6200, www.avenueq.com). Subway C, E, 1 to 50th Street. **Map** p102 C3 ⑦

After many years, which have included a Broadway run followed by a return to its Off Broadway roots, the sassy and clever puppet musical doesn't show its age. The current cast is capable and likable, and Robert Lopez and Jeff Marx's deft *Sesame Street*-esque novelty tunes about porn and racism still earn their laughs. *Avenue Q* remains a sly and winning piece of metamusical tomfoolery.

The Book of Mormon

Eugene O'Neill Theatre, 230 W 49th Street, between Broadway & Eighth Avenue (Telecharge 1-212 239 6200, www.bookofmormon broadway.com). Subway C, E to 50th Street; N, Q, R, S, 1, 2, 3, 7 to 42nd Street-Times Square; N, R to 49th Street. **Map** p102 C4 ❼❾

If theatre is your religion, and the Broadway musical your particular sect, rejoice! This gleefully obscene and subversive satire is one of the funniest shows to grace the Great White Way since *The Producers* and *Urinetown*. Writers Trey Parker and Matt Stone of *South Park*, along with composer Robert Lopez (*Avenue Q*), find the perfect blend of sweet and nasty for this tale of mismatched Mormon proselytisers in Uganda.

Carnegie Hall

154 W 57th Street, at Seventh Avenue (1-212 247 7800, www.carnegie hall.org). Subway N, Q, R to 57th Street. **Map** p102 C3 ❽⓪

Artistic director Clive Gillinson continues to put his stamp on Carnegie Hall. The stars still shine the most brightly in the Isaac Stern Auditorium – but it's the upstart Zankel Hall that has generated the most buzz, offering an eclectic mix of classical, contemporary, jazz, pop and world music.

New York City Center

131 W 55th Street, between Sixth & Seventh Avenues (1-212 581 7907, www.nycitycenter.org). Subway B, D,

E to Seventh Avenue; F, N, Q, R to 57th Street. **Map** p102 C3 ❽❶

Before Lincoln Center changed the city's cultural geography, this was the home of American Ballet Theatre, the Joffrey Ballet and the New York City Ballet. City Center's lavish decor is golden – as are the companies that pass through here. Regular events include Alvin Ailey American Dance Theater in December and the popular Fall for Dance Festival, in autumn, which features mixed bills for just $15.

Newsies

Nederlander Theatre, 208 W 41st Street, between Broadway & Eighth Avenue (Ticketmaster 1-866 870 2717, www.newsiesthemusical.com). Subway A, C, E to 42nd Street-Port Authority; N, Q, R, S, 1, 2, 3, 7 to 42nd Street-Times Square. **Map** p102 C5 ❽❷

Not since *Wicked* has there been a big-tent, family-friendly Broadway musical that gets so much so right. Disney's barnstorming, four-alarm delight focuses on the newsboy strike of 1899, in which spunky (and high-kicking) newspaper hawkers stood up to media magnates. The Alan Menken tunes are pleasing, the book is sharp, and the dances are simply spectacular.

Once

Bernard B Jacobs Theatre, 242 W 45th Street, between Broadway & Eighth Avenue (Telecharge 1-212 239 6200, www.oncemusical.com). Subway A, C, E to 42nd Street-Port Authority; N, Q, R, S, 1, 2, 3, 7 to 42nd Street-Times Square. **Map** p102 C4 ❽❸

Known for big, splashy spectacles, Broadway also has room for more sincere and understated musicals. This touching hit, adapted from the 2006 indie flick about an Irish songwriter and the Czech immigrant who inspires and enchants him, has a brooding emo-folk score and a bittersweet sense of longing that make it an ideal choice for a romantic evening out.

Pershing Square Signature Center

NEW *480 W 42nd Street, at Tenth Avenue (1-212 244 7529, www. signaturetheatre.org). Subway A, C, E to 42nd Street-Port Authority.* **Map** p102 B4 ❸❹

The award-winning Signature Theatre Company, founded by James Houghton in 1991, focuses on exploring and celebrating playwrights in depth, with whole seasons devoted to works by individual living writers. Over the past years, the company has delved into the oeuvres of August Wilson, John Guare, Horton Foote and many more. Special programmes are designed to keep prices low. In 2012 the troupe expanded hugely into a new home – a theatre complex designed by Frank Gehry, with three major spaces and ambitious long-term commission programmes, cementing it as one of the city's key cultural institutions.

Playwrights Horizons

416 W 42nd Street, between Ninth & Tenth Avenues, Theater District (Ticket Central 1-212 279 4200, 1-212 564 1235, www.playwrights horizons.org). Subway A, C, E to 42nd Street-Port Authority. **Map** p102 B4 ❸❺

More than 300 important contemporary plays have been premièred here, among them well-known dramas such as *Driving Miss Daisy* and *The Heidi Chronicles* along with musicals such as Stephen Sondheim's *Assassins* and *Sunday in the Park with George*. Recent seasons have included works by Edward Albee, Craig Lucas and Annie Baker.

Fifth Avenue & around

The stretch of Fifth Avenue between Rockefeller Center and Central Park South showcases retail palaces bearing names that were famous long before the concept of branding was developed. Bracketed by Saks Fifth Avenue (49th to 50th Streets) and Bergdorf Goodman (57th to 58th Streets), tenants include Gucci, Prada and Tiffany & Co (and the parade of big names continues east along 57th Street). A number of landmarks and first-rate museums are on, or in the vicinity of, the strip.

Sights & museums

Empire State Building

350 Fifth Avenue, between 33rd & 34th Streets (1-212 736 3100, www.esbnyc.com). Subway B, D, F, M, N, Q, R to 34th Street-Herald Square. **Open** 8am-2am daily (last elevator at 1.15am). **Admission** *86th floor* $25; free-$22 reductions. *102nd floor* $17 extra (see website for express ticket options). **Map** p101 D2 ❽❻

Financed by General Motors executive John J Raskob at the height of New York's skyscraper race, the Empire State sprang up in a mere 14 months, weeks ahead of schedule and $5 million under budget. Since its opening in 1931, it's been immortalised in countless photos and films, from the original *King Kong* to *Sleepless in Seattle*. Following the destruction of the World Trade Center in 2001, the 1,250ft tower resumed its title as New York's tallest building but has since been overtaken by the new 1 World Trade Center. The nocturnal colour scheme of the tower lights – recently upgraded to flashy LEDs – often honours holidays, charities or special events.

The enclosed observatory on the 102nd floor is the city's highest lookout point, but the panoramic deck on the 86th floor, 1,050ft above the street, is roomier. From here, you can enjoy views of all five boroughs and five neighbouring states too (when the skies are clear).

International Center of Photography

1133 Sixth Avenue, at 43rd Street (1-212 857 0000, www.icp.org). Subway B, D, F, M to 42nd Street-Bryant Park; N, Q, R, S, 1, 2, 3 to 42nd Street-Times Square; 7 to Fifth Avenue. **Open** 10am-6pm Tue-Thur, Sat, Sun; 10am-8pm Fri. **Admission** $14; free-$10 reductions. Pay what you wish 5-8pm Fri. **Map** p103 D4 ⑥⑦

Since 1974, the ICP has served as a pre-eminent library, school and museum devoted to the photographic image. Photojournalism remains a vital facet of the centre's programming, which also includes contemporary photos and video. Recent shows in the two-floor exhibition space have focused on the work of Elliott Erwitt, Richard Avedon and Weegee.

Event highlights Lewis Hine (through 12 Jan 2014); JFK November 22, 1963: A Bystander's View of History (through 12 Jan 2014).

Museum of Modern Art (MoMA)

11 W 53rd Street, between Fifth & Sixth Avenues (1-212 708 9400, www.moma.org). Subway E, M to Fifth Avenue-53rd Street. **Open** 10.30am-5.30pm Mon-Thur, Sat, Sun; 10.30am-8pm Fri. 10.30am-8pm 1st Thur of the month & every Thur in July, Aug. **Admission** (incl admission to film programmes) $25; free-$18 reductions; free 4-8pm Fri. **Map** p103 D3 ⑥⑧

Following a two-year redesign by Japanese architect Yoshio Taniguchi, MoMA reopened in 2004 with almost double the space to display some of the world's most impressive artworks from the 19th to the 21st centuries. The museum's permanent collection is divided into seven curatorial departments: Architecture and Design; Drawings; Film; Media and Performance Art; Painting and Sculpture; Photography; and Prints and Illustrated Books. Among the collection's highlights are Picasso's *Les Demoiselles d'Avignon*, Dali's *The Persistence of Memory* and Van Gogh's *The Starry Night* as well as masterpieces by Giacometti, Hopper, Matisse, Monet, O'Keefe, Pollock, Rothko, Warhol and others. Outside the building, the Philip Johnson-designed Abby Aldrich Rockefeller Sculpture Garden contains works by Calder, Rodin and Moore. There's also a destination restaurant: the Modern, which overlooks the garden.

Event highlights Magritte: the Mystery of the Ordinary, 1926-1938 (28 Sept 2013-12 Jan 2014); Isa Genzken: Retrospective (23 Nov 2013-10 Mar 2014); Christopher Williams: the Production Line of Happiness (2 Aug-2 Nov 2014).

New York Public Library

455 Fifth Avenue, at 42nd Street (1-917 275 6975, www.nypl.org). Subway B, D, F, M to 42nd Street-Bryant Park; 7 to Fifth Avenue. **Open** 10am-6pm Mon, Thur-Sat; 10am-7.30pm Tue, Wed; 1-5pm Sun (closed Sun July, Aug). **Admission** free. **Map** p101 D1/p103 D5 ⑥⑨

Guarded by the marble lions Patience and Fortitude, this austere Beaux Arts edifice, designed by Carrère and Hastings, was completed in 1911. The building was renamed in honour of philanthropist Stephen A Schwarzman in 2008, but Gothamites still know it as the New York Public Library, although the citywide library system consists of 91 locations. Free hour-long tours (11am, 2pm Mon-Sat; 2pm Sun, except July & Aug) take in the Rose Main Reading Room on the third floor, which at 297ft long and 78ft wide is almost the size of a football field. Specialist departments include the Map Division, containing some 431,000 maps and 16,000 atlases, and the Rare Books Division boasting Walt Whitman's personal copies of the first (1855) and third (1860) editions of *Leaves of Grass*.

Go figure

Mathematics + high-tech interactive exhibits = fun.

NYC has museums dedicated to everything from tenement housing to copulation. So it's no surprise that the least-favourite subject of sixth-graders everywhere finally landed its very own tribute – the country's first **Museum of Mathematics** (see p107). MoMath replaces lectures and textbooks with more than 30 eclectic exhibits covering topics such as algebra and geometry.

Designed for visitors of all ages, the museum aims to eliminate the intimidation factor and 'show how everyone can experience and enjoy mathematical exploration at their own level,' according to hedge-funder-turned-executive director Glen Whitney.

There's plenty to intrigue and amaze. Think a ride on a square-wheeled trike could never be smooth? Find out just how bump-free it can be when you take said tricycle over a sunflower-shaped track, where the petals create strategically placed catenaries – curves used in geometry and physics – that make a level

ride possible. Elsewhere, you can pass 3-D objects (or even your own body) through the laser-light 'wall of fire', and the lasers will display the objects as two-dimensional cross-sections (a cone becomes a triangle and circle, for instance). Or collaborate with another two visitors to pan, zoom and rotate your own video cameras to create a single composite image, which can be manipulated into a bevy of interesting 'feedback fractals' (or fragmented shapes). If you like what you see on the live projection screen, click the snapshot button to save the image to your profile so that you can print a copy before you leave.

MoMath uses state-of-the-art technology to personalise each visit: Patrons' ticket stubs are wirelessly tracked as they traverse the two-floor space, and exhibits adapt based on user preferences from the first few electronic displays. For example, if you opt for more in-depth explanations, in Spanish, upcoming displays will default to those settings.

Paley Center for Media

25 W 52nd Street, between Fifth & Sixth Avenues (1-212 621 6600, www.paleycenter.org). Subway B, D, F, M to 47th-50th Streets-Rockefeller Center; E, M to Fifth Avenue-53rd Street. **Open** noon-6pm Wed, Fri-Sun; noon-8pm Thur. **Admission** $10; $5-$8 reductions. No credit cards. **Map** p103 D3 ❾⓿

A nirvana for TV addicts and pop-culture junkies, the Paley Center houses an immense archive of almost 150,000 radio and TV shows. Head to the fourth-floor library to search the system for your favourite episode of *Star Trek*, *Seinfeld*, or rarer fare, and watch it on your assigned console. Radio shows are also available. A theatre on the concourse level is the site of weekend screenings, premières and high-profile panel discussions.

Rockefeller Center

From 48th to 51st Streets, between Fifth & Sixth Avenues (tours & Top of the Rock 1-212 698 2000, NBC Studio Tours 1-212 664 3700, www.rockefellercenter.com). Subway B, D, F, M to 47th-50th Streets-Rockefeller Center. **Open** Tours vary. *Observation deck* 8am-midnight daily (last elevator 11pm). **Admission** *Rockefeller Center tours* $17 (under-6s not admitted). *NBC Studio tours* $24; $21 reductions (under-6s not admitted). *Observation deck* $27; free-$23 reductions. **Map** p103 D3/D4 ❾❶

Constructed under the aegis of industrialist John D Rockefeller in the 1930s, this art deco city-within-a-city is inhabited by NBC, Simon & Schuster, McGraw-Hill and other media giants, as well as Radio City Music Hall, Christie's auction house, and an underground shopping arcade. Guided tours of the entire complex are available daily, and there's a separate NBC Studio tour too.

The buildings and grounds are embellished with works by several well-known artists; look out for Isamu Noguchi's stainless-steel relief, *News*, above the entrance to 50 Rockefeller Plaza, and José Maria Sert's mural *American Progress* in the lobby of 30 Rockefeller Plaza. But the most breathtaking sights are those seen from the 70th-floor Top of the Rock observation deck. In winter, the Plaza's sunken courtyard transforms into an ice skating rink.

St Patrick's Cathedral

Fifth Avenue, between 50th & 51st Streets (1-212 753 2261, www.saint patrickscathedral.org). Subway B, D, F, M to 47th-50th Streets-Rockefeller Center; E, M to Fifth Avenue-53rd Street. **Open** 6.30am-8.45pm daily. **Admission** free. **Map** p103 D3 ❸❷

The largest Catholic church in the US, St Patrick's was built 1858-79. The Gothic-style façade features intricate white-marble spires, but just as impressive is the interior, including the Louis Tiffany-designed altar, solid bronze baldachin, and the rose window by stained-glass master Charles Connick. Note that due to crucial restoration work, part of the exterior may be under scaffolding until spring 2014.

Eating & drinking

Bar Room at the Modern

9 W 53rd Street, between Fifth & Sixth Avenues (1-212 333 1220, www.the modernnyc.com). Subway E, M to Fifth Avenue-53rd Street. **Open** 11.30am-3pm, 5-10.30pm Mon-Sat; 11.30am-3pm, 5-9.30pm Sun. **$$**. **American creative**. **Map** p103 D3 ❸❸

Those who can't afford to drop a pay cheque at award-winning chef Gabriel Kreuther's formal MoMA dining room, the Modern, can still dine in the equally stunning and less pricey bar at the front. The Alsatian-inspired menu is constructed of around 30 small and medium-sized plates that can be mixed and shared. Desserts come courtesy of pastry chef Marc Aumont, and the wine list is extensive to say the least.

Marea

*240 Central Park South, between
Seventh Avenue & Broadway (1-212
582 5100, www.marea-nyc.com).
Subway A, B, C, D, 1 to 59th Street-
Columbus Circle.* **Open** noon-2.30pm,
5.30-11pm Mon-Thur; noon-2.30pm,
5-11.30pm Fri; 5-11.30pm Sat;
5-10.30pm Sun. **$$$. Italian/
Seafood.** Map p102 C2 ❾❹
Chef Michael White's shrine to the
Italian coastline seems torn between its
high and low ambitions. You might
find lofty items such as an unorthodox
starter of cool lobster with creamy bur-
rata, while basic platters of raw oysters
seem better suited to a fish shack.
Seafood-focused pastas – fusilli with
braised octopus and bone marrow, or
tortelli filled with langoustine, dande-
lion and butternut squash, for example
– are the highlight.

Shopping

Bergdorf Goodman

*754 Fifth Avenue, between 57th
& 58th Streets (1-212 753 7300,
www.bergdorfgoodman.com).
Subway E to Fifth Avenue-53rd
Street; N, Q, R to Fifth Avenue-
59th Street.* **Open** 10am-8pm
Mon-Fri; 10am-7pm Sat; 11am-
6pm Sun. Map p103 D3 ❾❺
Synonymous with understated luxury,
Bergdorf's is known for its designer
clothes (the fifth floor is dedicated to
younger, trend-driven labels) and
accessories – seek out Kentshire's won-
derful vintage-jewellery cache on the
ground floor. The men's store is across
the street at 745 Fifth Avenue.

FAO Schwarz

*767 Fifth Avenue, at 58th Street (1-
212 644 9400, www.fao.com). Subway
N, Q, R to Fifth Avenue-59th Street; 4,
5, 6 to Lexington Avenue-59th Street.*
Open 10am-8pm Mon-Thur, Sun;
10am-9pm Fri, Sat. Map p103 D2 ❾❻
Although it's now owned by the ubiq-
uitous Toys 'R' Us company, this three-
storey emporium is still the ultimate
NYC toy box. Most people head straight
to the 22ft-long floor piano that Tom
Hanks famously tinkled in *Big*.
Children will marvel at the giant
stuffed animals, the detailed and imag-
inative Lego figures and the revolving
Barbie fashion catwalk.

Henri Bendel

*712 Fifth Avenue, at 56th Street
(1-212 247 1100, www.henribendel.com).
Subway E, M to Fifth Avenue-53rd
Street; N, Q, R to Fifth Avenue-59th
Street.* **Open** 10am-8pm Mon-Sat;
noon-7pm Sun. Map p103 D3 ❸❼
While Bendel's merchandise (a mix of
jewellery, fashion accessories, cosmet-
ics and fragrances) is comparable to
that of other upscale stores, it some-
how seems more desirable when
viewed in its opulent premises, a con-
glomeration of three 19th-century
townhouses – and those darling
brown-and-white striped shopping
bags don't hurt, either.

Nightlife

Radio City Music Hall

*1260 Sixth Avenue, at 50th Street
(1-212 247 4777, www.radiocity.
com). Subway B, D, F, M to 47th-
50th Streets-Rockefeller Center.*
Map p103 D3 ❸❽
Few rooms scream 'New York City!'
louder than this gilded hall, which has
recently drawn Leonard Cohen, Drake
and Bon Iver as headliners. The great-
est challenge for any performer is not
to be upstaged by the awe-inspiring
art deco surroundings. On the other
hand, those same surroundings lend
historic heft to even the flimsiest
showing. For more than 80 years, the
venue has been the home base of
high-kicking dance troupe the Radio
City Rockettes, stars of the annual
Christmas Spectacular.
Event highlights Radio City
Christmas Spectacular (8 Nov-
30 Dec 2013).

Arts & leisure

Caudalie Vinothérapie Spa
4th Floor, 1 W 58th Street, at Fifth Avenue (1-212 265 3182, www. caudalie-usa.com). Subway N, Q, R to Fifth Avenue-59th Street. **Open** 10am-7pm Tue-Sat; 10am-5pm Sun. **Map** p103 D2 ⓟ
The first Vinothérapie outpost in the US, this original spa harnesses the antioxidant power of grapes and vine leaves. The 8,000sq ft facility in the Plaza offers such treatments as a Red Vine bath ($75) in one of its cherry-wood 'barrel' tubs.

Midtown East

Shopping, dining and entertainment options wane east of Fifth Avenue in the 40s and 50s. However, this area is home to a number of landmarks. What the area lacks in street-level attractions it makes up for with an array of world-class architecture.

Sights & museums

Chrysler Building
405 Lexington Avenue, between 42nd & 43rd Streets. Subway S, 4, 5, 6, 7 to 42nd Street-Grand Central. **Map** p101 E1/p103 E4 ⓟ
Completed in 1930 by architect William Van Alen, the gleaming Chrysler Building is a pinnacle of art deco architecture, paying homage to the automobile with vast radiator-cap eagles in lieu of traditional gargoyles and a brickwork relief sculpture of racing cars complete with chrome hubcaps. During the famed three-way race for New York's tallest building, a needle-sharp stainless-steel spire was added to the blueprint to make it taller than 40 Wall Street, under construction at the same time – but the Chrysler Building was soon outdone by the Empire State Building.

Grand Central Terminal
From 42nd to 44th Streets, between Lexington & Vanderbilt Avenues (audio tours 1-917 566 0008, www.grandcentralterminal.com). Subway S, 4, 5, 6, 7 to 42nd Street-Grand Central. **Map** p101 D1/p103 D4 ⓟ
Each day, the world's rail largest terminal sees more than 750,000 people shuffle through its Beaux Arts threshold. Designed by Warren & Wetmore and Reed & Stern, the gorgeous transport hub opened in 1913 with lashings of Botticino marble and staircases modelled after those of the Paris opera house. After midcentury decline, the terminal underwent extensive restoration between 1996 and 1998 and is now a destination in itself, with shopping and dining options, including the Campbell Apartment (1-212 953 0409), the Grand Central Oyster Bar & Restaurant (see p130), and a sprawling Apple Store on the East Balcony. Check the website for information about self-guided audio tours ($8; $6-$7 reductions).

United Nations Headquarters
Temporary visitors' entrance: First Avenue, at 43rd Street (tours 1-212 963 8687, http://visit.un.org). Subway S, 4, 5, 6, 7 to 42nd Street-Grand Central. **Tours** 10.15am-4.15pm Mon-Fri. **Admission** $16; $9-$11 reductions (under-5s not admitted). **Map** p101 F1/p103 F4 ⓟ
The UN is undergoing extensive renovations that have left the Secretariat building, designed by Le Corbusier, gleaming – though that structure is off-limits to the public. The hour-long public tours discuss the history and role of the UN, and visit the Security Council Chamber (when not in session) in the newly renovated Conference Building. The General Assembly Hall is currently closed for building work until autumn 2014 or later. Although some artworks and objects given by member

nations are not on public display during this period, you can now see pieces such as Norman Rockwell's mosaic *The Golden Rule* for the first time in four years. Note that until the renovations are complete, tours must be booked in advance online.

Eating & drinking

Aretsky's Patroon Townhouse

160 E 46th Street, between Lexington & Third Avenues (1-212 883 7373, www.patroonrestaurant.com). Subway S, 4, 5, 6, 7 to 42nd Street-Grand Central. **Open** noon-2.30pm, 5.30-10pm Mon-Fri. **$$$. American.** **Map** p103 E4 103

Smokers at Patroon (which retains its in-house humidor) can ascend to the roof to puff in midtown bigwig-style. Down in the restaurant, the kitchen dishes out classic American fare in mover-shaker portions – the porterhouse is twice the thickness of a Delmonico steak. Sides, like creamed spinach, are just what you'd expect: heavy and delicious. And with a fine selection of brandies, Patroon offers a number of ways to get lit.

Grand Central Oyster Bar & Restaurant

Grand Central Terminal, Lower Concourse, 42nd Street, at Park Avenue (1-212 490 6650, www.oysterbarny.com). Subway S, 4, 5, 6, 7 to 42nd Street-Grand Central. **Open** 11.30am-9.30pm Mon-Fri. **$$. Seafood. Map** 105 D4 104

At the legendary 101-year-old Grand Central Oyster Bar, located in the epic and gorgeous hub that shares its name, the surly countermen at the mile-long bar (the best seats in the house) are part of the charm. Avoid the more complicated fish concoctions and play it safe with a reliably awe-inspiring platter of iced, just-shucked oysters – there can be a whopping 30 varieties to choose from at any given time.

Monkey Bar

Hotel Elysée, 60 E 54th Street, between Madison & Park Avenues (1-212 288 1010, www.monkeybarnewyork.com). Subway E, M to Lexington Avenue-53rd Street; 6 to 51st Street. **Open** 7am-9.45am, 11.30am-11pm Mon-Fri; 5.30-11pm Sat. **$$$. American.** **Map** p103 D3 105

After the repeal of Prohibition in 1933, this one-time piano bar in the swank Hotel Elysée became a boozy clubhouse for the glitzy artistic figures of the age, among them Tallulah Bankhead, Dorothy Parker and Tennessee Williams. Recently, publishing tycoon Graydon Carter assembled a dream team here, including cocktail doyenne Julie Reiner and downtown restaurateur Ken Friedman, to bring new buzz to the historic space. Perched at the bar with a pitch-perfect Vieux Carré or ensconced in a red leather booth with a plate of caviar-crowned smoked fettuccine, you'll find yourself seduced by that rare alchemy of old New York luxury and new-school flair. The only question that remains is just how long the star-power magic can last.

Sushi Yasuda

204 E 43rd Street, between Second & Third Avenues (212 972 1001, www.sushiyasuda.com). Subway S, 4, 5, 6, 7 to 42nd St-Grand Central. **Open** noon-2.15pm, 6-10.15pm Mon-Fri; 6-10.15pm Sat. **$$. Japanese.** **Map** p101 E1/p103 E4 106

Seeing the sushi master practise in this bamboo-embellished space is the culinary equivalent of observing Buddhist monks at prayer. Counter seating, where you can witness – and chat up – the chefs, is the only way to go. Prime your palate with a miso soup and segue into the raw stuff: petals of buttery fluke; rich eel; dessert-sweet egg custard; nearly translucent discs of sliced scallop over neat cubes of milky sushi rice. Still craving a California roll? Move along.

Central Park

Uptown

In the 19th century, the area above 59th Street was a bucolic getaway for locals living at the southern tip of the island. Today, much of this locale maintains an air of serenity, thanks largely to Central Park and the presence of a number of New York's premier cultural institutions.

Central Park

In 1858, the newly formed Central Park Commission chose landscape designer Frederick Law Olmsted and architect Calvert Vaux to turn a vast tract of rocky swampland into a rambling oasis of lush greenery. When their vision of an urban 'greensward' was realised in 1873, Central Park became the first man-made public park in the US.

As well as a wide variety of landscapes, from open meadows to woodland, the park offers numerous family-friendly attractions and activities,

from the **Central Park Zoo** (830 Fifth Avenue, between 63rd & 66th Streets, 1-212 439 6500, www.centralparkzoo.org; $12, free-$9 reductions) to marionette shows in the quaint **Swedish Cottage** (west side, at 81st Street). Stop by the visitor centre in the 1870 Gothic Revival **Dairy** (midpark at 65th Street, 1-212 794 6564, www.central parknyc.org) for information on activities and events. In winter, ice-skaters lace up at the picturesque **Trump Wollman Rink** (midpark at 62nd Street, 1-212 439 6900, www.wollmanskatingrink.com). A short stroll to about 64th Street brings you to the **Friedsam Memorial Carousel** (closed weekdays in winter), a bargain at $3 a ride.

Come summer, kites, Frisbees and soccer balls seem to fly every which way across **Sheep Meadow**, the designated quiet zone that begins at 66th Street.

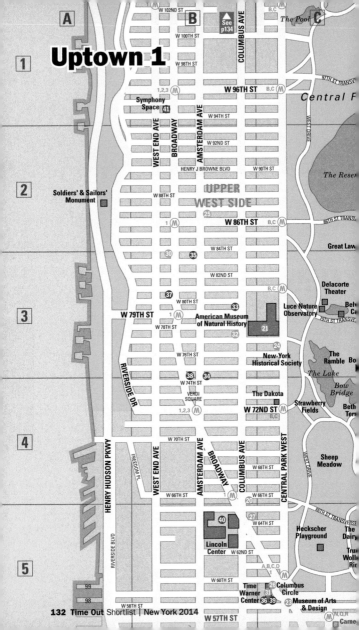

Uptown 1

W 102ND ST

COLUMBUS AVE

W 100TH ST

W 98TH ST

W 96TH ST

Central F

Symphony
Space 41

W 94TH ST

WEST END AVE

BROADWAY

AMSTERDAM AVE

W 92ND ST

HENRY J BROWNE BLVD

W 90TH ST

The Reser

Soldiers' &
Sailors'
Monument

UPPER
WEST SIDE

W 88TH ST

25

The Reser

W 86TH ST

86TH ST TRANSV

Great Law

30

W 84TH ST

35

W 82ND ST

37

W 80TH ST

33

W 79TH ST

American Museum
of Natural History

32

21

W 78TH ST

Delacorte
Theater

Luce Nature
Observatory

Belv
Ca

The
Ramble Bo

24

New-York
Historical Society

The Lake

Bow

38 34

W 74TH ST

VERDI
SQUARE

The Dakota

Strawberry
Fields

Bow
Bridge

Beth
Terr

1,2,3

W 72ND ST

RIVERSIDE DR

W 76TH ST

W 70TH ST

Sheep
Meadow

HENRY HUDSON PKWY

FREEDOM PL

WEST END AVE

AMSTERDAM AVE

BROADWAY

COLUMBUS AVE

CENTRAL PARK WEST

WEST DRIVE

W 68TH ST

W 66TH ST

20

27

Heckscher
Playground

The
Dairy

40

W 64TH ST

Lincoln
Center W 62ND ST

A,B,C,D
1

RIVERSIDE BLVD

W 60TH ST

Tru
Wolle
Ri

99

Time
Warner
Center 36 39

28 Columbus
Circle

23 Museum of Arts
& Design

98

W 58TH ST

31 29

W 57TH ST

N,Q,R

Carne

FIFTH AVE
MADISON AVE
PARK AVE
LEXINGTON AVE
THIRD AVE
SECOND AVE
FIRST AVE

E 102ND ST

D

E

See
p135

F

1

🔵 Sights & museums
🔵 Eating & drinking
🔵 Shopping
🔵 Nightlife
🔵 Arts & leisure

E 100TH ST

E 98TH ST
🔴 14

E 96TH ST Ⓜ 6

E 94TH ST

FRANKLIN D ROOSEVELT DR

E 92ND ST

🔴 3 Jewish
Museum
🔴 11 Cooper-Hewitt
National Design
Museum

E 90TH ST

2

🔴 8 Guggenheim
Museum
Neue Galerie

E 88TH ST

YORKVILLE

🔴 Gracie Mansion

EAST END AVE

🔴 7 12

E 86TH ST Ⓜ 4,5,6

Carl
Schutz
Park

E 84TH ST

🔴 16

UPPER
EAST SIDE

E 82ND ST

Metropolitan
Museum of Art

E 80TH ST

3

E 79TH ST

E 78TH ST

🔴 19 🔴 11

6 Ⓜ

E 76TH ST

John
Jay
Park

🔴 10

vatory
ter

🔴 9 Whitney Museum
of American Art

E 74TH ST

Roosevelt
Island

ourg
hell

E 72ND ST

4

🔴 2
The Frick
Collection

Asia Society
and Museum

E 70TH ST

E 68TH ST

FRANKLIN D ROOSEVELT DR

🔴 18

China
Institute

Ⓜ 6

Rockefeller
University

E 66TH ST

isch Children's
Zoo

🔴 13

E 64TH ST

0   300 m

Delacorte
Musical Clock

PARK AVE
LEXINGTON AVE
THIRD AVE
SECOND AVE
FIRST AVE

E 62ND ST

0   300 yds

© Copyright Time Out Group 2013

plars'
te
nd
 my
aza

FIFTH AVE
MADISON AVE

🔴 16

Ⓜ N,R

F Ⓜ

YORK AVE

🔴 17 Bloomingdale's

Ⓜ 4,5,6

Ⓜ N,R

E 60TH ST

TRAMWAY

E 58TH ST

ED KOCH
QUEENSBORO (59TH ST) BRIDGE

E 57TH ST

Time Out Shortlist | New York 2014 **133**

Trump Tower

PED BR

1 M

Riverside Park

HAMILTON HEIGHTS

W 143RD ST

W 143RD ST

BROADWAY

HENRY HUDSON PKWY

North River Water Pollution Control Plant & Riverbank State Park

W 141ST ST

HAMILTON PLACE

AMSTERDAM AVE

CONVENT AVE

W 141ST ST

EDGECOMBE AVE

CLAYTON POWELL JR BLVD

Abyssini Baptist Church

W 139TH ST

W 139TH ST

PED BR

W 137TH ST

M 1

W 137TH ST

Schombu Center

TWELFTH AVE

RIVERSIDE DR

W 135TH ST

City College of New York

St Nicholas Park

M B,C

ADAM

2

46

W 133RD ST

W 133RD ST

TWELFTH AVE

W 131ST ST

CONVENT AVE

ST NICHOLAS TER

ST CLAIR PL

MARTIN

W 129TH ST

HARLEM

RIVERSIDE DR EAST

Broadway

W 126TH ST

W 127TH ST

TIEMANN PL

LUTHER KING JR BLVD

Apollo Theater 48

RIVERSIDE DR WEST

LA SALLE ST

M A,B,C,D

W 125TH ST 42

3

W 123RD ST

FREDERICK DOUGLASS BLVD

Studio Mus in Harle

General Grant National Memorial

CLAREMONT AVE

Riverside Church

W 121ST ST

REINHOLD NIEBUHR PL

W 119TH ST

Columbia University

Morningside Park

ADAM CLAYTON POWELL JR BLVD

43

Barnard College

1 M

W 116TH ST

M B,C

4

W 115TH ST

MORNINGSIDE HEIGHTS

W 113TH ST

MORNINGSIDE DRIVE

MANHATTAN AVE

47

Cathedral of St John the Divine

22

W 111TH ST

29

Cathedral Close

ST NICHOLAS AVE

1

W 109TH ST

CATHEDRAL PARKWAY

M B,C

CENTRAL PARK NORTH

Riverside Park

W 107TH ST

WESTDRIVE

5

W 106TH ST

WEST END AVE

DUKE ELLINGTON BLVD

AMSTERDAM AVE

W 105TH ST

28

COLUMBUS AVE

Central P

W 103RD ST

1 M

See p132

M

The Pool

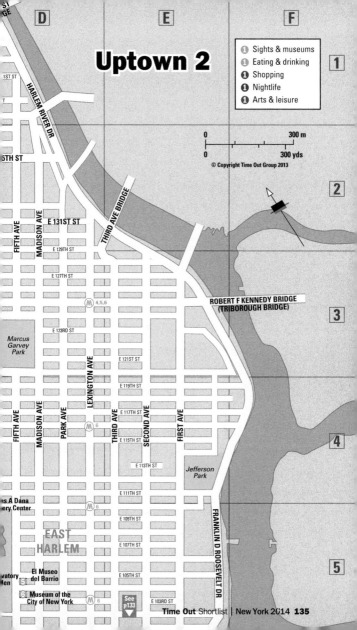

Uptown 2

❶	Sights & museums
❶	Eating & drinking
❶	Shopping
❶	Nightlife
❶	Arts & leisure

© Copyright Time Out Group 2013

D **E** **F**

1ST ST

HARLEM RIVER DR

5TH ST

E 131ST ST

E 129TH ST

E 127TH ST

THIRD AVE BRIDGE

Ⓜ 4,5,6

E 123RD ST

ROBERT F KENNEDY BRIDGE
(TRIBOROUGH BRIDGE)

*Marcus
Garvey
Park*

E 121ST ST

E 119TH ST

FIFTH AVE

MADISON AVE

PARK AVE

LEXINGTON AVE

THIRD AVE

SECOND AVE

FIRST AVE

Ⓜ

E 117TH ST

E 115TH ST

E 113TH ST

E 111TH ST

*Jefferson
Park*

FRANKLIN D ROOSEVELT DR

E 109TH ST

Ⓜ 6

E 107TH ST

es A Dana
ery Center

**EAST
HARLEM**

E 105TH ST

*El Museo
del Barrio*

ervatory
en

*Museum of the
City of New York*

Ⓜ 6

E 103RD ST

See
p133
▼

Sheep did indeed graze here until 1934, but they've since been replaced by sunbathers. East of Sheep Meadow, between 66th and 72nd Streets, is the **Mall**, an elm-lined promenade that attracts street performers and in-line skaters. And just east of the Mall's Naumburg Bandshell is Rumsey Playfield – site of the main stage for the citywide **SummerStage** (see p38) series, an eclectic roster of free and benefit concerts.

One of the most popular meeting places in the park is north of the Mall: the grand **Bethesda Fountain & Terrace**, near the midpoint of the 72nd Street Transverse Road. *Angel of the Waters*, the sculpture in the centre of the fountain, was created by Emma Stebbins, the first woman to be granted a major public art commission in New York. Be sure to admire the Minton-tiled ceiling of the ornate passageway that connects the plaza around the fountain to the Mall.

To the west of the fountain, near the W 72nd Street entrance, sits **Strawberry Fields**, a section of the park that memorialises John Lennon, who lived in the nearby Dakota Building. It features a mosaic of the word 'imagine' and more than 160 species of flowers and plants from all over the world. Just north of the Bethesda Fountain is the **Loeb Boathouse** (midpark, at 75th Street). From here, you can take a rowing boat or gondola out on the lake, which is crossed by the elegant Bow Bridge. The Loeb houses the **Central Park Boathouse Restaurant** (Central Park Lake, park entrance on Fifth Avenue, at 72nd Street, 1-212 517 2233, www.thecentral parkboathouse.com, closed dinner Nov-Mar), which commands a great view of the lake, and has a popular outdoor bar.

Further north is **Belvedere Castle**, a restored Victorian structure that sits atop the park's second-highest peak. Besides offering excellent views, it also houses the **Henry Luce Nature Observatory**. The nearby Delacorte Theater hosts **Shakespeare in the Park** (see p38). And further north still sits the **Great Lawn** (midpark, between 79th & 85th Streets), a sprawling stretch of grass that serves as sports fields, a rallying point for political protests, and a summer concert spot. East of the Great Lawn, behind the **Metropolitan Museum of Art** (see p137), is the **Obelisk**, a 69-foot hieroglyphics-covered granite monument dating from around 1500 BC, which was given to the US by the Khedive of Egypt in 1881.

In the mid 1990s, the **Jacqueline Kennedy Onassis Reservoir** (midpark, between 85th & 96th Streets) was renamed in honour of the late first lady, who used to jog around it. The path affords great views of the surrounding skyscrapers.

In the northern section of the park, the exquisite **Conservatory Garden** (entrance on Fifth Avenue, at 105th Street) comprises formal gardens inspired by English, French and Italian styles.

Upper East Side

Although Manhattan's super-rich now live all over town, the air of old money is most pronounced on the Upper East Side. Along Fifth, Madison and Park Avenues, from 61st to 81st Streets, you'll see the great old mansions, many of which are now foreign consulates. Philanthropic gestures made by the moneyed classes over the past 130-odd years have helped create an impressive cluster of art collections, museums and cultural institutions. Indeed, Fifth Avenue from 82nd to 105th Streets is known as Museum Mile because it's lined with more than half a dozen celebrated institutions.

Sights & museums

Cooper-Hewitt, National Design Museum

2 E 91st Street, at Fifth Avenue (1-212 849 8400, www.cooperhewitt. org). Subway 4, 5, 6 to 86th Street. Closed until autumn 2014 (see website for updates and off-site exhibitions). **Map** p133 D2 ❶

Founded in 1897 by the Hewitt sisters, granddaughters of industrialist Peter Cooper, the only museum in the US solely dedicated to design (both historic and modern) has been part of the Smithsonian since the 1960s. In 1976 it took up residence in the former home of steel magnate Andrew Carnegie. The museum is closed until autumn 2014 for a major renovation and expansion project, which will more than double its exhibition space. Meanwhile, the Cooper-Hewitt is staging exhibitions off-site; see the website for information.

Frick Collection

1 E 70th Street, between Fifth & Madison Avenues (1-212 288 0700, www.frick.org). Subway 6 to 68th Street-Hunter College. **Open** 10am-6pm Tue-Sat; 11am-5pm Sun. **Admission** $20; $10-$15 reductions; under-10s not admitted. Pay what you wish 11am-1pm Sun. **Map** p133 D4 ❷

Industrialist, robber baron and collector Henry Clay Frick commissioned this opulent mansion with a view to leaving his legacy to the public. Designed by Thomas Hastings of Carrère & Hastings (the firm behind the New York Public Library) and built in 1914, the building was inspired by 18th-century British and French architecture.

In an effort to preserve the feel of a private residence, labelling is minimal, but you can opt for a free audio guide

or pay $2 for a booklet. Works spanning the 14th to the 19th centuries include masterpieces by Rembrandt, Vermeer, Whistler, Monet and Bellini, and exquisite period furniture and objects. A new gallery in the enclosed garden portico is devoted to decorative arts and sculpture, while the interior fountain court is a serene spot in which to rest your feet.

Event highlights Renaissance and Baroque Bronzes from the Hill Collection (28 Jan-15 June 2014).

Jewish Museum

1109 Fifth Avenue, at 92nd Street (1-212 423 3200, www.thejewish museum.org). Subway 4, 5, 6 to 86th Street; 6 to 96th Street. **Open** 11am-5.45pm Mon, Tue, Sat, Sun; 11am-8pm Thur; 11am-5.45pm Fri (11am-4pm Nov-Mar). Closed on Jewish holidays. **Admission** $15; free-$12 reductions; free Sat. Pay what you wish 5-8pm Thur. **Map** p133 D2 ❸

The Jewish Museum is housed in a magnificent 1908 French Gothic-style mansion – the former home of the financier, collector and Jewish leader Felix Warburg. Inside, 'Culture and Continuity: The Jewish Journey' traces the evolution of Judaism from antiquity to the present day. The two-floor permanent exhibition comprises thematic displays of 800 of the museum's cache of 26,000 works of art, artefacts and media installations. The excellent temporary shows appeal to a broad audience.

Event highlights Chagall: Love, War & Exile (through 2 Feb 2014); Art Spiegelman's Co-Mix: A Retrospective (8 Nov 2013-23 Mar 2014); Helena Rubinstein: Beauty Is Power (31 Oct 2014-22 Mar 2015).

Metropolitan Museum of Art

1000 Fifth Avenue, at 82nd Street (1-212 535 7710, www.metmuseum.org). Subway 4, 5, 6 to 86th Street. **Open** 10am-5.30pm Mon-Thur, Sun; 10am-9pm Fri, Sat. **Admission** suggested

NEW YORK BY AREA

donation (incl same-day admission to the Cloisters) $25; free-$17 reductions. **Map** p133 D3 ④

Now occupying 13 acres of Central Park, the Metropolitan Museum of Art opened in 1880. The original Gothic Revival building was designed by Calvert Vaux and Jacob Wrey Mould, but is now almost completely hidden by subsequent additions. A redesign of the museum's four-block-long plaza is expected to be completed in autumn 2014, bringing new fountains and tree-shaded seating.

The first floor's north wing contains the collection of ancient Egyptian art and the glass-walled atrium housing the Temple of Dendur, moved en masse from its original Nile-side setting and now overlooking a reflective pool. The north-west corner is occupied by the recently revamped American Wing. Its grand Engelhard Court is now more a sculpture court than an interior garden; the light-filled space is flanked by the façade of Wall Street's Branch Bank of the United States (saved when the building was torn down in 1915) and a stunning loggia designed by Louis Comfort Tiffany for his Long Island estate.

In the southern wing are the halls housing Greek and Roman art. Turning west brings you to the Arts of Africa, Oceania and the Americas collection; it was donated by Nelson Rockefeller as a memorial to his son Michael, who disappeared while visiting New Guinea in 1961.

A wider-ranging bequest, the two-storey Robert Lehman Wing, is at the western end of the floor. This eclectic collection is housed in a re-creation of the Lehman family townhouse and features works by Botticelli, Bellini, Ingres and Rembrandt, among others.

Upstairs, the central western section is dominated by the recently expanded and rehung European Paintings galleries, which hold an amazing reserve of old masters; the Dutch section boasts five Vermeers, the largest collection of the artist in the world. To the south, the 19th-century European galleries contain some of the Met's most popular works – in particular the two-room Monet holdings and a colony of Van Goghs that includes his oft-reproduced *Irises*.

Walk eastward and you'll reach the galleries of the Art of the Arab Lands, Turkey, Iran, Central Asia and Later South Asia. In the north-east wing of the floor, you'll find the sprawling collection of Asian art; be sure to check out the ceiling of the Jain Meeting Hall in the South-east Asian gallery. If you're still on your feet, give them a deserved rest in the Astor Court, a tranquil re-creation of a Ming Dynasty garden, or head up to the Iris & B Gerald Cantor Roof Garden (usually open May-late Oct). For the Cloisters, which houses the Met's medieval art collection, see p153.

Event highlights Interwoven Globe: the Worldwide Textile Trade, 1500-1800 (through 5 Jan 2014); Silla: Korea's Golden Kingdom (4 Nov 2013-23 Feb 2014); Jewels by JAR (20 Nov 2013-9 Mar 2014); Ink Art: Past as Present in Contemporary China (11 Dec 2013-6 Apr 2014).

El Museo del Barrio

1230 Fifth Avenue, at 104th Street (1-212 831 7272, www.elmuseo.org). Subway 6 to 103rd Street. **Open** 11am-6pm Wed-Sat. **Admission** suggested donation $9; free-$5 reductions. *Sept-Dec, Feb-May* free 3rd Sat of each month. **Map** p135 D5 ⑤

Founded in 1969 by the artist (and former MoMA curator) Rafael Montañez Ortiz, El Museo del Barrio takes its name from its East Harlem locale. Dedicated to the art and culture of Puerto Ricans and Latin Americans all over the US, El Museo reopened in 2009 following a $35-million renovation. The redesigned spaces within the museum's 1921 Beaux Arts building provide a polished, contemporary showcase for the diversity and vibrancy of Hispanic art. The new galleries allow more space for rotating exhibitions from the museum's 6,500-piece holdings – from pre-Columbian artefacts to contemporary installations – as well as temporary shows.

Museum of the City of New York

1220 Fifth Avenue, between 103rd & 104th Streets (1-212 534 1672, www.mcny.org). Subway 6 to 103rd Street. **Open** 10am-6pm daily. **Admission** suggested donation $10; free-$6 reductions. **Map** p135 D5 ⑥

A great introduction to New York, this institution contains a wealth of city history. *Timescapes*, a 22-minute multimedia presentation that illuminates the history of NYC, is shown free with admission every half hour. The museum's holdings include prints, drawings and photos of the city, decorative arts and furnishings, and a large collection of toys. The undoubted jewel is the amazing Stettheimer Dollhouse: it was created in the 1920s by Carrie Stettheimer, whose artist friends reinterpreted their masterpieces in miniature to hang on the walls. Look closely and you'll even spy a tiny version of Marcel Duchamp's famous *Nude Descending a Staircase*.

A rolling renovation has brought new galleries for temporary exhibitions, which spotlight the city from different angles. Renovations to the museum's North Wing, due to be completed in 2015, will provide space for a core exhibition about the city.

Event highlights I Have Seen the Future: Norman Bel Geddes Designs America (16 Oct 2013-10 Feb 2014); Gilded New York (13 Nov 2013-30 Nov 2014).

Neue Galerie

1048 Fifth Avenue, at 86th Street (1-212 628 6200, www.neuegalerie.org). Subway 4, 5, 6 to 86th Street. **Open** 11am-6pm Mon, Thur-Sun; 11am-8pm 1st Fri of mth. **Admission** $20; $10 reductions. Under-16s must be accompanied by an adult; under-12s not admitted. **Map** p133 D2 ⑦

This elegant gallery is devoted to late 19th- and early 20th-century German and Austrian fine and decorative arts. The creation of the late art dealer Serge Sabarsky and cosmetics mogul Ronald S Lauder, it has the largest concentration of works by Gustav Klimt and Egon Schiele outside Vienna.

Solomon R Guggenheim Museum

1071 Fifth Avenue, at 89th Street (1-212 423 3500, www.guggenheim.org). Subway 4, 5, 6 to 86th Street. **Open** 10am-5.45pm Mon-Wed, Fri, Sun; 10am-7.45pm Sat. **Admission** $22; free-$18 reductions; pay what you wish 5.45-7.15pm Sat. **Map** p133 D2 ⑧

The Guggenheim is as famous for its landmark building – as designed by Frank Lloyd Wright – as it is for its impressive collection and daring temporary shows. The museum opened in 1959, and the addition of a ten-storey tower in 1992 provided space for a sculpture gallery, an auditorium and a café. The institution owns Peggy Guggenheim's trove of Cubist, Surrealist and Abstract Expressionist works, along with the Panza di Biumo Collection of American Minimalist and Conceptual art from the 1960s and '70s. As well as works by Manet, Picasso, Chagall and Bourgeois, the Guggenheim holds the largest collection of Kandinskys in the US.

Event highlights Christopher Wool (25 Oct 2013-22 Jan 2014; Italian Futurism, 1909-1944: Reconstructing the Universe (21 Feb-1 Sept 2014); Countdown to Tomorrow: The International ZERO Network, 1950s-60s (Oct 2014-Jan 2015).

Whitney Museum of American Art

945 Madison Avenue, at 75th Street (1-212 570 3600, www.whitney.org). Subway 6 to 77th Street. **Open** 11am-6pm Wed, Thur, Sat, Sun; 1-9pm Fri. **Admission** $20; free-$16 reductions; pay what you wish 6-9pm Fri. **Map** p133 D3 ⑨

When sculptor and art patron Gertrude Vanderbilt Whitney opened the museum in 1931, she dedicated it to living American artists. Today, the Whitney holds more than 19,000 pieces by around 2,700 artists, including Willem de Kooning, Edward Hopper, Jasper Johns, Georgia O'Keeffe and Claes Oldenburg. Yet its reputation rests primarily on its temporary shows – particularly the Whitney Biennial (see box p141). Launched in 1932 and held in even-numbered years, it's the most prestigious and controversial assessment of contemporary art in the US.

Like the Guggenheim, the Whitney is set apart by its unique architecture, but 2014 is the last year that the museum will occupy the Marcel Breuer-designed granite cube with its all-seeing upper-storey 'eye'. In 2015, the institution will move into its new home at the foot of the High Line (see p93) in the Meatpacking District, a nine-storey building designed by Renzo Piano. For the first time, there will be space for a comprehensive display of the collection.

Event highlights Whitney Biennial (Mar-June 2014); Jeff Koons retrospective (June-Oct 2014).

Eating & drinking

Bar Pleiades

The Surrey, 20 E 76th Street, between Fifth & Madison Avenues (1-212 772 2600, www.danielnyc.com). Subway 6 to 77th Street. **Open** noon-midnight Mon-Thur, Sun; noon-1am Fri, Sat. **Bar**. **Map** p133 D3 ⑩

Designed as a nod to Coco Chanel, Daniel Boulud's bar is framed in black lacquered panels that recall an elegant make-up compact. The luxe setting and moneyed crowd might seem a little stiff, but the drinks are so exquisitely executed, you won't mind sharing your banquette with a suit. Light eats are provided by Café Boulud next door (about $15 a plate).

Bemelmans Bar

The Carlyle, 35 E 76th Street, at Madison Avenue (1-212 744 1600, www.thecarlyle.com). Subway 6 to 77th Street. **Open** 11am-midnight Mon, Sun; 11am-12.30am Tue-Thur; 11am-1am Fri, Sat. **Bar**. **Map** p133 D3 ⑪

The Plaza may have Eloise (the children's book character is a six-year-old girl who lives in the hotel), but the Carlyle has its own children's book connection – the wonderful 1947 murals of Central Park by *Madeline* creator Ludwig Bemelmans in this, the quintessential classy New York bar. A jazz trio adds to the atmosphere every night at 9.30pm (a cover charge of $15-$30 applies when it takes up residence).

Café Sabarsky

Neue Galerie, 1048 Fifth Avenue, at 86th Street (1-212 288 0665, www.cafesabarsky.com). Subway 4, 5, 6 to 86th Street. **Open** 9am-6pm Mon, Wed; 9am-9pm Thur-Sun. **$$**. **Café**. **Map** p133 D2 ⑫

Purveyor of indulgent pastries and whipped-cream-topped *einspänner* coffee for Neue Galerie patrons by day, this sophisticated, high-ceilinged room becomes an upscale restaurant four nights a week. Appetisers are most adventurous – the creaminess of the *spätzle* is a perfect base for sweetcorn, tarragon and wild mushrooms – while main course specials, such as the *wiener schnitzel* tartly garnished with lingonberries, are capable yet ultimately feel like the calm before the *Sturm und Drang* of dessert. Try the *klimttorte*, which masterfully alternates layers of hazelnut cake with chocolate.

Daniel

60 E 65th Street, between Madison & Park Avenues (1-212 288 0033, www.danielnyc.com). Subway F to Lexington Avenue-63rd Street; 6 to 68th Street-Hunter College. **Open** 5.30-11pm Mon-Sat. **$$$$**. **French**. **Map** p133 D5 ⑬

Whitney Bye-ennial

Catch the controversial art show's last uptown stand.

Whitney Biennial 2012

Although its roster has yet to be announced, the 2014 Whitney Biennial is already a landmark show for one reason: it will be the last of the museum's famed contemporary art showcases on the Upper East Side. In 2015, the Whitney (see p139) will decamp the brooding, Marcel Breuer-designed building it has occupied since 1966 for brand-new digs in the crushingly fashionable Meatpacking District.

At 200,000 square feet, the Whitney's future location, designed by Italian starchitect Renzo Piano, will be three times the size of its current one, and was undoubtedly planned with upcoming Biennials in mind. Whether this will prove to be good or bad is very much an open question, given the event's nickname: the show everyone loves to hate.

Launched in 1932 by founder Gertrude Vanderbilt Whitney, the Biennial began as an annual non-juried exhibition of contemporary artists. Historical highlights and low-points include the 1951 show, which introduced works by the Abstract Expressionsts; 1977's show, slagged by critic Hilton Kramer for being too trendy, and having too much photography and video (now a perennial complaint by reviewers); and the infamous 1993 'political' Biennial, which presented a truly multicultural line-up of talent for the first time. This included Daniel Martinez, a Hispanic artist whose contribution (a badge given to visitors that read, 'I Can't Imagine Ever Wanting To Be White') provided a flashpoint of controversy. In 2000, the $100,000 Bucksbaum Award was introduced. The 2012 show was notable for giving considerable space to performing arts.

Over the years, the quality of the Biennial has waxed and waned (many would say mostly the latter). Yet it is one of the city's signature cultural events, and with the added space, there will be a lot more show to hate – and maybe even love – in the coming years.

The cuisine at Daniel Boulud's elegant fine-dining flagship, designed by Adam Tihany, is rooted in French technique with *au courant* flourishes like fusion elements and an emphasis on local produce. Although the menu changes seasonally, it always includes a few signature dishes – Boulud's black truffle and scallops in puff pastry remains a classic, and the duo of beef is a sumptuous pairing of Black Angus short ribs and seared Wagyu tenderloin. His other Upper East Side restaurant, Café Boulud, is at 20 E 76th Street, between Fifth & Madison Avenues (1-212 772 2600).

Earl's Beer & Cheese
1259 Park Avenue, between 97th & 98th Streets (1-212 289 1581, www.earlsny.com). Subway 6 to 96th Street. **Open** 4pm-midnight Mon, Tue; 11am-midnight Wed, Thur, Sun; 11am-2am Fri, Sat. **Bar. Map** p133 D1 ⑭
Tucked into the no-man's land between the Upper East Side and East Harlem, this craft-beer cubby hole has the sort of community-hub vibe that makes you want to settle in and become part of the furniture. The well-priced suds (including rotating craft brews and cheap cans of Genny Light) and slapdash set-up appeal to a neighbourhood crowd, but it's Momofuku Ssäm Bar alum Corey Cova's madcap bar menu that makes it destination-worthy. Try the NY State Cheddar – a grilled cheese featuring an unstoppable combo of braised pork belly, fried egg and house-made kimchi. The crew has since opened a cocktail bar, the Guthrie Inn, next door (at the same address, 1-212 423 9900) and a wine bar, ABV (1504 Lexington Avenue, at 97th Street, 1-212 722 8959, www.abvny.com), a block east.

Lexington Candy Shop
1226 Lexington Avenue, at 83rd Street (1-212 288 0057, www.lexingtoncandyshop.net). Subway 4, 5, 6 to 86th Street. **Open** 7am-7pm Mon-Sat; 8am-6pm Sun. **$. American. Map** p133 D3 ⑮

You won't see much candy for sale at Lexington Candy Shop. Instead, you'll find a wonderfully preserved retro diner (it was founded in 1925), its long counter lined with chatty locals on their lunch hours, tucking into burgers and chocolate malts. If you come for breakfast, order the doorstop slabs of french toast.

Shopping

Madison Avenue, between 57th and 86th Streets, is packed with international designer names: Gucci, Prada, Chloé, Donna Karan, Lanvin, multiple Ralph Lauren outposts and many more.

Barneys New York
660 Madison Avenue, at 61st Street (1-212 826 8900, www.barneys.com). Subway N, R to Fifth Avenue-59th Street; 4, 5, 6 to 59th Street. **Open** 10am-8pm Mon-Fri; 10am-7pm Sat; 11am-6pm Sun. **Map** p133 D5 ⑯
Barneys has a reputation for spotlighting more independent designer labels than other upmarket department stores, and has its own quirky-classic collection. The ground floor showcases luxe accessories, and cult beauty brands are in the basement. Head to the seventh and eighth floors for contemporary designer and denim lines.

Bloomingdale's
1000 Third Avenue, at 59th Street (1-212 705 2000, www.bloomingdales.com). Subway N, Q, R to Lexington Avenue-59th Street; 4, 5, 6 to 59th Street. **Open** 10am-8.30pm Mon-Sat; 11am-7pm Sun. **Map** p133 D5/E5 ⑰
Ranking among the city's top tourist attractions, Bloomie's is a gigantic, glitzy department store stocked with everything from bags to beauty products, home furnishings to designer duds. The beauty hall, which has an outpost of niche-brand apothecary Space NK among the big-name offerings, recently got a glam makeover.

The compact Soho outpost concentrates on contemporary labels, denim and cosmetics.

Fivestory

18 E 69th Street, between Fifth & Madison Avenues (1-212 288 1338, www.fivestoryny.com). Subway 6 to 68th Street-Hunter College. **Open** 10am-6pm Mon-Wed, Fri; 10am-7pm Thur; noon-6pm Sat, Sun. **Map** p133 D4 ⓳

At just 26 (with a little help from her fashion-industry insider dad), Claire Distenfeld opened this glamorous, grown-up boutique, which sprawls over two floors of – yes – a five-storey townhouse. The space is stocked with clothing, shoes and accessories for men, women and children, plus select home items. The emphasis is on less-ubiquitous American and European labels, including New York-based Lyn Devon and Thakoon, and Peter Pilotto, created by two alums of Antwerp's Royal Academy of Fine Arts.

Lisa Perry

988 Madison Avenue, at 77th Street (1-212 334 1956, www.lisaperrystyle.com). Subway 6 to 77th Street. **Open** 10am-6pm Mon-Sat; noon-5pm Sun. **Map** p133 D3 ⓳

Upon graduation from FIT in 1981, designer Lisa Perry launched her line of retro women's threads inspired by her massive personal collection of 1960s and '70s pieces. Ultrabright pieces, such as her signature colour-blocked minidresses, pop against the stark white walls of her Madison Avenue flagship. You'll also find the designer's cheerful accessories, such as candy-coloured duffel bags, and her mod home collection, which includes place mats and throw pillows.

Upper West Side

The gateway to the Upper West Side is Columbus Circle, where Broadway meets 59th Street, Eighth Avenue, Central Park South and Central Park West – a rare roundabout in a city that is largely made up of right angles. The cosmopolitan neighbourhood's seat of culture is **Lincoln Center**, a complex of theatres and concert halls that's home to the New York Philharmonic, the New York City Ballet, the Metropolitan Opera and various other notable arts organisations.

Further uptown, Morningside Heights, between 110th and 125th Streets, from Morningside Park to the Hudson, is dominated by Columbia University. The sinuous Riverside Park, designed by Central Park's Frederick Law Olmsted, starts at 72nd Street and ends at 158th Street, between Riverside Drive and the Hudson River. Below 72nd Street, the first part of a larger riverside redevelopment project, Riverside Park South, is a peaceful urban retreat, with a pier, and landscaped patches of grass.

Sights & museums

American Folk Art Museum

2 Lincoln Square, Columbus Avenue, at 66th Street (1-212 595 9533, www.folkartmuseum.org). Subway 1 to 66th Street-Lincoln Center. **Open** noon-7.30pm Tue-Sat; noon-6pm Sun. **Admission** free. **Map** p132 B4 ⓴

Following a budget crisis that forced the American Folk Art Museum to give up its midtown premises, the institution is still going strong in the small original space it had retained as a second location. Its unparalleled holdings of folk art include more than 5,000 works from the late 18th century to the present. Exhibitions explore the work of self-taught and outsider artists, as well as showing traditional folk art such as quilts and needlework, and other decorative objects. You can purchase original handmade pieces in the large gift shop, and the museum

regularly hosts free musical performances, inexpensive craft workshops and other events.

American Museum of Natural History/Rose Center for Earth & Space

Central Park West, at 79th Street (1-212 769 5100, www.amnh.org). Subway B, C to 81st Street-Museum of Natural History. **Open** 10am-5.45pm daily. **Admission** suggested donation $19; $10.50-$14.50 reductions. **Map** p132 C3 ㉑

The American Museum of Natural History's fourth-floor dino halls are home to the largest and arguably most fabulous collection of dinosaur fossils in the world. Roughly 80% of the bones on display were dug out of the ground by Indiana Jones types, but during the museum's mid 1990s renovation, several specimens were remodelled to incorporate more recent discoveries. The tyrannosaurus rex, for instance, was once believed to have walked upright, *Godzilla*-style; it now stalks prey with its head lowered and tail raised parallel to the ground. A new exhibition devoted to the winged reptiles known as pterosaurs is on view from spring 2014 until January 2015.

The Hall of North American Mammals, part of a two-storey memorial to Theodore Roosevelt, reopened in autumn 2012 after extensive restoration to its formerly faded 1940s dioramas. The Hall of Human Origins houses a fine display of our old cousins, the Neanderthals, and the Hall of Biodiversity examines world ecosystems and environmental preservation. A life-size model of a blue whale hangs from the cavernous ceiling of the Hall of Ocean Life, while in the Hall of Meteorites, the focal point is Ahnighito, the largest iron meteor on display in the world, weighing in at 34 tons.

The spectacular Rose Center for Earth & Space is a giant silvery globe where you can gain insight into recent cosmic discoveries via 3-D shows in the Hayden Planetarium and a simulation of the origins of the Universe in the Big Bang Theater. An IMAX theatre screens larger-than-life nature programmes, and the museum's roster of temporary exhibitions is thought-provoking for all ages.

Event highlights Whales: Giants of the Deep (through 5 Jan 2014); The Power of Poison (16 Nov 2013-10 Aug 2014).

Cathedral Church of St John the Divine

1047 Amsterdam Avenue, at 112th Street (1-212 316 7540, www.stjohn divine.org). Subway B, C, 1 to 110th Street-Cathedral Parkway. **Open** 7am-6pm daily. **Admission** suggested donation $10; $5 reductions. **Map** p134 B4 ㉒

Construction of this massive house of worship, affectionately nicknamed 'St John the Unfinished', began in 1892 in Romanesque style, was put on hold for a Gothic Revival redesign in 1911, then ground to a halt in 1941, when the US entered World War II. It resumed in earnest in 1979, but a fire in 2001 that destroyed the church's gift shop and damaged two 17th-century Italian tapestries further delayed completion. It's still missing a tower and a north transept, among other things, but the nave has been restored and the entire interior reopened and rededicated. No further work is planned… for now.

In addition to Sunday services, the cathedral hosts concerts and tours. It bills itself as a place for all people – and it certainly means it. Annual events include both winter and summer solstice celebrations, and even a Blessing of the Bicycles every spring.

Museum of Arts & Design

2 Columbus Circle, at Broadway (1-212 299 7777, www.madmuseum. org). Subway A, B, C, D, 1 to 59th Street-Columbus Circle. **Open** 11am-6pm Tue, Wed, Sat, Sun; 11am-9pm

Thur, Fri. **Admission** $16; free-$14 reductions; pay what you wish 6-9pm Thur, Fri. **Map** p132 C5 ㉓

This institution brings together contemporary objects created in a wide range of media – including clay, glass, wood, metal and cloth – with a strong focus on materials and process. And in 2008 the museum crafted itself a new home. Originally designed in 1964 by Radio City Music Hall architect Edward Durell Stone to house the Gallery of Modern Art, 2 Columbus Circle was a windowless monolith that had sat empty since 1998. The redesigned ten-storey building now has four floors of exhibition galleries, including the Tiffany & Co Foundation Jewelry Gallery. Curators are able to display more of the 3,000-piece permanent collection, which includes porcelain ware by Cindy Sherman, stained glass by Judith Schaechter and ceramics by James Turrell.

In addition to checking out temporary shows, you can also watch resident artists create works in studios on the sixth floor, while the ninth-floor bistro has views over the park.

Event highlights Out of Hand: Materializing the Postdigital (14 Oct 2013-16 July 2014; Inspired (18 Mar-13 Oct 2014); Multiple Exposures: Jewelry and Photography (24 June 2014-18 Jan 2015).

New-York Historical Society

170 Central Park West, between 76th & 77th Streets (1-212 873 3400, www.nyhistory.org). Subway B, C to 81st Street-Museum of Natural History. **Open** 10am-6pm Tue-Thur, Sat; 10am-8pm Fri; 11am-5pm Sun. **Admission** $15; free-$12 reductions. Pay what you wish 6-8pm Fri. **Map** p132 C3 ㉔

Founded in 1804 by a group of prominent New Yorkers that included Mayor Dewitt Clinton, the New-York Historical Society is the city's oldest museum, originally based at City Hall. In autumn 2011, the society's 1908

building reopened after a three-year, $65-million renovation that opened up the interior spaces to make the collection more accessible to a 21st-century audience. The Robert H and Clarice Smith New York Gallery of American History provides an overview of the collection and a broad sweep of New York's place in American history – Revolutionary-era maps are juxtaposed with a piece of the ceiling mural from Keith Haring's Pop Shop (the artist's Soho store, which closed after his death in 1990). Touch-screen monitors offer insight into artwork and documents, and large HD screens display a continuous slide show of highlights of the museum's holdings, such as original watercolours from *Audubon's Birds of America* and some of its 132 Tiffany lamps. The auditorium screens an 18-minute film tracing the city's development, while downstairs the DiMenna Children's History Museum engages the next generation. The upper floors house changing shows and the Henry Luce III Center for the Study of American Culture, a visible-storage display that spans everything from spectacles and toys to Washington's Valley Forge camp bed.

Event highlights The Armory Show at 100 (11 Oct 2013-23 Feb 2014); Audubon's Aviary: the Complete Flock Part II (14 Mar-26 May 2014); Chinese American: Exclusion/Inclusion (10 Oct 2014-May 2015).

Eating & drinking

Barney Greengrass

541 Amsterdam Avenue, between 86th & 87th Streets (1-212 724 4707, www.barneygreengrass.com). Subway B, C, 1 to 86th Street. **Open** 8.30am-4pm Tue-Fri; 8.30am-5pm Sat, Sun. **$-$$**. No credit cards. **American**. **Map** p132 B2 ㉕

Despite decor that Jewish mothers might call 'schmutzy', this legendary deli is a madhouse at breakfast and brunch. Egg platters come with the usual choice of smoked fish (such as sturgeon or Nova Scotia salmon). Prices are on the high side, but portions are large, and that goes for the sandwiches too. Soup – matzo-ball or cold pink borscht – is a less costly option.

Bouchon Bakery

3rd Floor, Time Warner Center, 10 Columbus Circle, at Broadway (1-212 823 9366, www.bouchonbakery.com). Subway A, B, C, D, 1 to 59th Street-Columbus Circle. **Open** 8am-9pm Mon-Sat; 8am-7pm Sun. **$**. **Café**. **Map** p132 C5 ②⑥

Chef Thomas Keller's café, in the same mall as his lauded fine-dining room Per Se (see p148), lacks ambience, and the menu (soups, tartines, salads, sandwiches) is basic. But prices are much more palatable – a dry-cured ham and emmental baguette is around a tenner. The baked goods, including Keller's takes on American classics like Oreo cookies, are the real highlights.

Boulud Sud

20 W 64th Street, between Broadway & Central Park West (1-212 595 1313, www.danielnyc.com). Subway 1 to 66th Street-Lincoln Center. **Open** noon-2.30pm, 5-11pm Mon-Fri; noon-3pm, 5-11.30pm Sat; noon-3pm, 5-10.30pm Sun. **$$$**. **Mediterranean**. **Map** p132 B5 ②⑦

At his most international restaurant yet, superchef Daniel Boulud highlights the new French cuisine of melting-pot cities like Marseille and Nice. With his executive chef, Aaron Chambers (Café Boulud), he casts a wide net – looking to Israel and Egypt, Turkey and Greece. Budget-minded diners can build a full tapas meal from shareable snacks like octopus *à la plancha*, with marcona almonds and arugula (rocket). Heartier dishes combine Gallic finesse with polyglot flavours: sweet-spicy chicken tagine borrows from the Moroccan pantry. Tunisian-born Ghaya Oliveira's audacious desserts – such as grapefruit

givré (grapefruit stuffed with sorbet), sesame mousse and rose-scented nuggets of Turkish delight – take the exotic mix to even loftier heights.

Ding Dong Lounge

929 Columbus Avenue, between 105th & 106th Street (Duke Ellington Boulevard) (1-212 663 2600, www.dingdonglounge.com). Subway B, C to 103rd Street. **Open** 4pm-4am daily. **Bar**. **Map** p134 B5 ②③

Goth chandeliers and kick-ass music mark this dark dive as punk – with broadened horizons. The tap pulls, dispensing Stella Artois, Guinness and Bass, are sawn-off guitar necks, and the walls are covered with vintage concert posters (from Dylan to the Damned). The affable local clientele and mood-lit conversation nooks make it surprisingly accessible (even without a working knowledge of Dee Dee Ramone).

Hungarian Pastry Shop

1030 Amsterdam Avenue, between 110th & 111th Streets (1-212 866 4230). Subway 1 to 110th Street-Cathedral Parkway. **Open** 7.30am-11.30pm Mon-Fri; 8.30am-11.30pm Sat; 8.30am-10.30pm Sun. **$**. **Café**. **Map** p134 B4 ②⑨

So many theses have been dreamed up, procrastinated over or tossed aside in the Hungarian Pastry Shop since it opened more than five decades ago that the Columbia University neighbourhood institution merits its own dissertation. The java is strong enough to make up for the erratic array of pastries, and the Euro feel is enhanced by the view of St John the Divine cathedral from outdoor tables.

Ouest

2315 Broadway, between 83rd & 84th Streets (1-212 580 8700, www.ouest ny.com). Subway 1 to 86th Street. **Open** 5-9pm Mon, Tue; 5.30-10pm Wed, Thur; 5.30-11pm Fri, Sat; 11am-2pm, 5-8.30pm Sun. **$$$**. **American**. **Map** p132 B3 ③⓪

A prototypical well-heeled clientele calls chef Tom Valenti's Uptown fixture its local canteen. And why not? The friendly servers ferry pitch-perfect cocktails and rich, Italian-inflected cuisine from the open kitchen to immensely comfortable round red booths. Valenti adds some unexpected flourishes to the soothing formula: salmon gravadlax is served with a chickpea pancake topped with caviar and potent mustard oil, while the house-smoked sturgeon presides over frisée, lardons and a poached egg.

Per Se

4th Floor, Time Warner Center, 10 Columbus Circle, at Broadway (1-212 823 9335, www.perseny.com). Subway A, B, C, D, 1 to 59th Street-Columbus Circle. **Open** *5.30-10pm Mon-Thur; 11.30am-1.30pm, 5.30-10pm Fri-Sun.* **$$$$. French. Map** p132 C5 ③①
Expectations are high at Per Se – and that goes both ways. You're expected to wear the right clothes (jackets are required for men), pay a non-negotiable service charge, and pretend you aren't eating in a mall. The restaurant, in turn, is expected to deliver one hell of a tasting menu for $295. And it does. Dish after dish is flawless, beginning with Thomas Keller's signature Oysters and Pearls (a sabayon of pearl tapioca with oysters and caviar). Other hits include a buttery poached lobster and house-made sorbets. An all-vegetable tasting menu is also available. If you can afford it, it's worth every penny.

Shake Shack

366 Columbus Avenue, at 77th Street (1-646 747 8770, www.shakeshack nyc.com). Subway B, C to 81st Street-Museum of Natural History; 1 to 79th Street. **Open** *10.45am-11pm daily.* **$. American. Map** p132 B3 ③②
The spacious offspring of Danny Meyer's popular Madison Square Park concession stand is now one of many locations across the city. Shake Shack gets several local critics' votes for New York's best burger. Sirloin and brisket are ground daily for the prime patties, while franks are served Chicago-style on potato buns with a 'salad' of toppings. Frozen-custard shakes hit the spot, but there's beer and wine if you want something stronger.

Shopping

Alexis Bittar

NEW *410 Columbus Avenue, at 80th Street (1-646 590 4142, www.alexis bittar.com). Subway B, C to 81st Street-Museum of Natural History.* **Open** *11am-7pm Mon-Sat; noon-6pm Sun.* **Map** p132 B3 ③③
Alexis Bittar started out selling his jewellery from a humble Soho street stall, but now the designer has four shops in which to show off his flamboyant pieces, such as sculptural Lucite cuffs and oversized crystal-encrusted earrings. This new boutique is twice the size of the West Village, Upper East Side and Soho locations, and is meant to resemble a 1940s powder room, with silk wallpaper and art deco-style lights.

Levain Bakery

167 W 74th Street, between Columbus & Amsterdam Avenues (1-212 874 6080, www.levainbakery.com). Subway 1 to 79th Street. **Open** *8am-7pm Mon-Sat; 9am-7pm Sun.* **Map** p132 B3 ③④
Levain's cookies are a full 6oz, and the massive mounds stay gooey in the middle. The lush, brownie-like double-chocolate variety, made with extra-dark French cocoa and semi-sweet chocolate chips, is truly decadent.

Magpie

NEW *488 Amsterdam Avenue, between 83rd & 84th Streets (1-646 998 3002, www.magpienewyork.com). Subway 1 to 86th Street.* **Open** *11am-7pm Mon-Sat; 11am-6pm Sun.* **Map** p132 B3 ③⑤
Sylvia Parker worked as a buyer at the American Folk Art Museum gift shop before opening this eco-friendly store. Decorated with no-fume paints and

bamboo shelves, the space is packed with locally made, handcrafted, sustainable and fair-trade items. Finds include vintage quilts, recycled-resin cuff bracelets, and Meow Meow Tweet soaps and candles, handmade in Brooklyn.

Shops at Columbus Circle

Time Warner Center, 10 Columbus Circle, at 59th Street (1-212 823 6300, www.shopsatcolumbuscircle.com). Subway A, B, C, D, 1 to 59th Street-Columbus Circle. **Open** 10am-9pm Mon-Sat; 11am-7pm Sun (hrs vary for some shops, bars and restaurants). **Map** p132 C5 ❸❻

Classier than your average mall, the retail contingent of the 2.8 million-sq-ft Time Warner Center features upscale stores such as Coach, Cole Haan and LK Bennett for accessories and shoes, London shirtmaker Thomas Pink, Bose home entertainment, the fancy kitchenware purveyor Williams-Sonoma, as well as shopping centre staples J Crew, Aveda, and organic grocer Whole Foods. Some of the city's top restaurants (including Thomas Keller's gourmet destination Per Se, see p148, and his café Bouchon Bakery, see p147) have made it a dining destination that transcends the stigma of eating at a mall.

Zabar's

2245 Broadway, at 80th Street (1-212 787 2000, www.zabars.com). Subway 1 to 79th Street. **Open** 8am-7.30pm Mon-Fri; 8am-8pm Sat; 9am-6pm Sun. **Map** p132 B3 ❸❼

Zabar's is more than just a market – it's a New York City landmark. It began in 1934 as a tiny storefront specialising in Jewish 'appetising' delicacies and has gradually expanded to take over half a block of prime Upper West Side real estate. What never ceases to surprise, however, is its reasonable prices, even for high-end foods. Besides the famous smoked fish and rafts of delicacies, Zabar's has fabulous bread, cheese, olives and coffee, and a floor dedicated to homewares.

Nightlife

Beacon Theatre

2124 Broadway, between 74th & 75th Streets (1-212 465 6500, www.beacontheatrenyc.com). Subway 1, 2, 3 to 72nd Street. **Map** p132 B3 ❸❽

This spacious former vaudeville theatre hosts a variety of popular acts, from Aziz Ansari to ZZ Top. While the vastness can be daunting to performers and audience alike, the gilded interior and uptown location make you feel as though you're having a real night out on the town.

Jazz at Lincoln Center

Frederick P Rose Hall, Broadway, at 60th Street (1-212 258 9800, www.jalc.org). Subway A, B, C, D, 1 to 59th Street-Columbus Circle. **Map** p132 C5 ❸❾

The jazz arm of Lincoln Center is several blocks away from the main campus, high atop the Time Warner Center. It features three separate rooms: the Rose Theater is a traditional mid-size space, but the crown jewels are the Allen Room and the smaller Dizzy's Club Coca-Cola, which feel like a Hollywood cinematographer's vision of a Manhattan jazz club. Some of the best players in the business regularly grace the spot, among them Wynton Marsalis, Jazz at Lincoln Center's famed artistic director.

Arts & leisure

Lincoln Center

Columbus Avenue, between 62nd & 65th Streets (1-212 546 2656, www.lincolncenter.org). Subway 1 to 66th Street-Lincoln Center. **Map** p132 B5 ❹❶

Built in the early 1960s, this massive complex is the nexus of Manhattan's performing arts scene, and a recent revamp of its campus included a redesign of the public spaces, refurbishment of the various halls, a new film centre and a visitor centre: the David Rubenstein Atrium (between 62nd & 63rd Streets, Broadway & Columbus

Avenue) sells same-day discounted tickets to Lincoln Center performances and stages free genre-spanning concerts on Thursday nights (see website for details). It's also the starting point for guided tours of the complex (1-212 875 5350, $17, $8-$14 reductions). In addition to the hallowed concert halls, Lincoln Center contains several notable artworks, including Henry Moore's *Reclining Figure* in the plaza near the theatre, and two massive music-themed paintings by Marc Chagall in the lobby of the Metropolitan Opera House.

Event highlights see pp34-42 Calendar.

Alice Tully Hall 1-212 875 5050.

An 18-month renovation turned the cosy home of the Chamber Music Society of Lincoln Center (www.chambermusicsociety.org) into a world-class, 1,096-seat theatre. The new contemporary foyer, with an elegant (if rather pricey) café, is immediately striking, but, more importantly, the revamp brought some dramatic acoustical improvements.

Avery Fisher Hall 1-212 875 5030.

This handsome, comfortable 2,700-seat hall is the headquarters of the New York Philharmonic (1-212 875 5656, www.nyphil.org), the country's oldest symphony orchestra (founded in 1842) – and one of its finest. Depending on who you ask, the sound ranges from good to atrocious (an overhaul is planned for 2017). Inexpensive, early evening 'rush hour' concerts and open rehearsals are presented on a regular basis. The ongoing Great Performers series features top international soloists and ensembles.

David H Koch Theater

1-212 870 5570.

The neoclassical New York City Ballet headlines at this opulent theatre, which Philip Johnson designed to resemble a jewellery box. The company offers its popular *Nutcracker* at the very end of November, carrying on to the beginning of the new year, followed by a winter repertory season. The spring season begins in April. Ballets by

George Balanchine are performed by a wonderful crop of young dancers; there are also plenty by Jerome Robbins, Peter Martins (the company's ballet master in chief) and former resident choreographer Christopher Wheeldon.

Lincoln Center Theater Telecharge 1-212 239 6200, www.lct.org.

The majestic and prestigious Lincoln Center Theater complex has a pair of amphitheatre-style drama venues. The Broadway house, the 1,080-seat Vivian Beaumont Theater, is home to star-studded and elegant major productions. Downstairs from the Beaumont is the 299-seat Mitzi E Newhouse Theater, an Off Broadway space devoted to new work by the upper layer of American playwrights. In an effort to shake off its reputation for stodginess, Lincoln Center launched LCT3, which presents the work of emerging playwrights in the new Claire Tow Theater, built on top of the Beaumont. See box p152.

Metropolitan Opera House 1-212 362 6000, www.metoperafamily.org.

The grandest of the Lincoln Center buildings, the Met is a spectacular place to see and hear opera. It hosts the Metropolitan Opera from September to May, with major visiting companies appearing in summer. Opera's biggest stars appear here regularly, and artistic director James Levine has turned the orchestra into a true symphonic force. Audiences are knowledgeable and fiercely devoted, with subscriptions remaining in families for generations.

The Met had already started becoming more inclusive before current impresario Peter Gelb took the reins in 2006. Now, the company is placing a priority on creating novel theatrical experiences with visionary directors (Robert Lepage, Bartlett Sher, Michael Grandage, David McVicar) and assembling a new company of physically graceful, telegenic stars (Anna Netrebko, Danielle de Niese, Jonas Kaufmann, Erwin Schrott). Its high-definition movie-theatre broadcasts continue to reign supreme outside the opera house.

Lincoln Center

Second acts

To make theatre more affordable, some stately theatrical trees have sprouted smaller branches. **Roundabout Theatre Company** (227 W 42nd Street, Theater District, 1-212 719 1300, www.roundabouttheatre.org) presents $20 shows in the 60-seat Roundabout Underground, and at the Public Lab at **Public Theater** (see p89), you can see works in development for around $15. Three new spaces recently joined their ranks.

BAM Richard B Fisher building

The centrepiece of this new seven-storey building at the Brooklyn Academy of Music (see p164) is the 250-seat Fishman Space, whose flexible structure is intended to respond to the creative needs of individual artists. During the Next Wave Festival, it hosts a series of $20 shows across various disciplines.

Claire Tow Theater

Lincoln Center Theater's LCT3 programme (see p150) now has a dedicated space: the 112-seat Claire Tow, an elegant box of glass and steel that sits on a field of grass atop Lincoln Center's Vivian Beaumont Theater. For $20, you can see works by promising emerging writers.

Studio at Stage II

The Manhattan Theatre Club has reclaimed a site at City Center (see p123) that it had previously abandoned, and dedicated it to works by up-and-coming writers. The Studio can seat up to 150 people; tickets are $30.

Although most tickets are expensive, 200 prime seats for all performances from Monday to Thursday are sold for $20 apiece two hours before curtain up.
Film Society of Lincoln Center
1-212 875 5600, www.filmlinc.com.
Founded in 1969 to promote contemporary film, the FSLC now also hosts the prestigious New York Film Festival, among other annual fests. Programmes are usually thematic, with an international perspective. The $40-million Elinor Bunin Munroe Film Center houses two plush cinemas with built-in cameras for post-screening Q&As. Between these state-of-the-art screens and the operational Walter Reade Theater across the street, a small multiplex has been born. The Bunin also houses a café, Indie Food and Wine.

Symphony Space

2537 Broadway, at 95th Street (1-212 864 5400, www.symphonyspace.org). Subway 1, 2, 3 to 96th Street. **Map** p132 B1 **⊕**
Despite the name, programming here is anything but orchestra-centric: recent seasons have featured sax quartets, Indian classical music, a capella ensembles and HD opera simulcasts from Europe. Annual Wall to Wall marathons (usually in spring) serve up a full day of music free of charge, all focused on a particular composer. The multidisciplinary performing arts centre also stages works by contemporary choreographers and traditional dancers from around the globe.

Harlem & beyond

Extending north from the top of Central Park at 110th Street as far as 155th Street, Harlem is the cultural capital of black America – the legacy of the Harlem Renaissance. By the 1920s, it had become the country's most populous African-American community, attracting some of black America's greatest artists: writers such as Langston

Hughes and musicians like Duke Ellington and Louis Armstrong. West Harlem, between Fifth and St Nicholas Avenues, is the Harlem of popular imagination, and 125th Street is its lifeline. The area around the landmarked Mount Morris Historic District (from 119th to 124th Streets, between Malcolm X Boulevard/Lenox Avenue & Mount Morris Park West) continues to gentrify, and new boutiques, restaurants and cafés dot the double-wide Malcolm X Boulevard. Further uptown, Strivers' Row, from 138th to 139th Streets, between Adam Clayton Powell Jr Boulevard (Seventh Avenue) and Frederick Douglass Boulevard (Eighth Avenue), was developed in 1891. East of Fifth Avenue is East Harlem, better known to its primarily Puerto Rican residents as El Barrio. (For El Museo del Barrio, see p138.)

From 155th Street to Dyckman (200th) Street is Washington Heights, which contains a handful of attractions and, at the tip of Manhattan, picturesque riverside Fort Tryon Park.

Sights & museums

The Cloisters

Fort Tryon Park, Fort Washington Avenue, at Margaret Corbin Plaza (1-212 923 3700, www.metmuseum. org). Subway A to 190th Street, then M4 bus or 10min walk. **Open** *Mar-Oct* 10am-5.15pm daily. *Nov-Feb* 10am-4.45pm daily. **Admission** suggested donation (incl same-day admission to Metropolitan Museum of Art) $25; free-$17 reductions.
Set in a lovely park overlooking the Hudson River, the Cloisters houses the Met's medieval art and architecture collections. A path winds through the peaceful grounds to a castle that seems to date from the Middle Ages; in fact it was built in the 1930s using pieces from five medieval French cloisters.

Highlights include the 12th-century Fuentidueña Chapel, the Unicorn Tapestries and the *Annunciation* triptych by Robert Campin.

Studio Museum in Harlem

144 W 125th Street, between Malcolm X Boulevard (Lenox Avenue) & Adam Clayton Powell Jr Boulevard (Seventh Avenue) (1-212 864 4500, www. studiomuseum.org). Subway 2, 3 to 125th Street. **Open** noon-9pm Thur, Fri; 10am-6pm Sat; noon-6pm Sun. **Admission** suggested donation $7; free-$3 reductions; free Sun. No credit cards. **Map** p134 C3 ㊷
The first black fine arts museum in the country when it opened in 1968, the Studio Museum is an important player in the art scene of the African diaspora. Under the leadership of director and chief curator Thelma Golden, this vibrant institution, housed in a stripped down, three-level space, presents shows in a variety of media by black artists from around the world.

Eating & drinking

Amy Ruth's

113 W 116th Street, between Malcolm X Boulevard (Lenox Avenue) & Adam Clayton Powell Jr Boulevard (Seventh Avenue) (1-212 280 8779, www.amy ruthsharlem.com). Subway 2, 3 to 116th Street. **Open** 11.30am-11pm Mon; 8.30am-11pm Tue-Thur; 8.30am-5pm Fri; 7.30am-5pm Sat; 7.30am-11pm Sun. **$**. **American regional. Map** p134 C4 ㊸
This popular no-reservations spot is the place for soul food. Delicately fried okra is delivered without a hint of slime, and the mac and cheese is gooey inside and crunchy-brown on top. Dishes take their names from notable African-Americans – vote for the President Barack Obama (fried, smothered, baked or barbecued chicken).

Ginny's Supper Club

310 Malcolm X Boulevard (Lenox Avenue), between 125th & 126th

Streets (1-212 421 3821, www.ginnys suppperclub.com). Subway 2, 3 to 125th Street. **Open** 7pm-midnight Thur-Sat. **Bar**. Map p134 C3 ⓮

Red Rooster's sprawling basement lounge is modelled after the Harlem speakeasies of the 1920s. With its own menu, eclectic cocktails and a steady line-up of live music, the venue revives the appealing gentility of the supper-club experience.

Red Rooster

310 Malcolm X Boulevard (Lenox Avenue), between 125th & 126th Streets (1-212 792 9001, www.red roosterharlem.com). Subway 2, 3 to 125th Street. **Open** 11.30am-3pm, 5.30-10.30pm Mon-Thur; 11.30am-3pm, 5.30-11.30pm Fri; 10am-3pm, 5-11.30pm Sat; 10am-3pm, 5-10pm Sun. **$$**. **Eclectic**. Map p134 C3 ⓯

With its hobnobbing bar scrum, potent cocktails and lively jazz, this buzzy eaterie serves as a worthy clubhouse for the new Harlem. Superstar chef Marcus Samuelsson is at his most populist here, drawing on a 'We Are the World' mix of Southern-fried, East African, Scandinavian and French flavours to feed the lively crowd. Harlem politicos mix at the teardrop bar with downtown fashionistas, everyone happily swilling fine cocktails and gorging on rib-sticking food: chicken-liver-enriched dirty rice topped with plump charred shrimp, homey desserts, and crispy fried chicken with hot sauce and white mace gravy. It all adds up to a place that has earned its status as a local hub.

Shrine

2271 Adam Clayton Powell Jr Boulevard (Seventh Avenue), between 133rd & 134th Streets (1-212 690 7807, www.shrinenyc.com). Subway B, C, 2, 3 to 135th Street. **Open** 4pm-4am daily. **Bar**. Map p134 C2 ⓰

Playfully adapting a sign left over from previous tenants (the Black United Foundation), the Shrine deems itself a 'Black United Fun Plaza'. The interior is tricked out with African art and vintage album covers (the actual vinyl adorns the ceiling). Nightly concerts might feature indie rock, jazz, reggae or DJ sets. The cocktail menu aspires to similar diversity: drinks range from a smooth mango mojito to signature tipples like a snappy Afro Trip (lime and ginger enhanced by Jamaican or Brazilian rum).

Shopping

Trunk Show Designer Consignment

NEW *275-277 W 113th Street, between Adam Clayton Powell Jr Boulevard (Seventh Avenue) & Frederick Douglass Boulevard (Eighth Avenue) (1-212 662 0009, www.trunkshowconsignment.com). Subway B, C to 110th Street-Cathedral Parkway.* **Open** 1-8.30pm Tue-Sat; noon-6.30pm Sun. Map p134 C4 ⓱

Modelling agent Heather Jones graduated from hosting oversubscribed pop-up trunk shows to co-opening this small Harlem storefront. Men's and women's threads and accessories range from edgier brands (Margiela, Rick Owens) to Madison Avenue labels (Gucci, Ralph Lauren, Burberry), with in-season items marked down between 20% and 70%.

Nightlife

Apollo Theater

253 W 125th Street, between Adam Clayton Powell Jr Boulevard (Seventh Avenue) & Frederick Douglass Boulevard (Eighth Avenue) (1-212 531 5300, www.apollotheater.org). Subway A, B, C, D, 1 to 125th Street. Map p134 C3 ⓲

This 100-year-old former burlesque theatre has been a hub for African-American artists for decades, and launched the careers of Ella Fitzgerald and D'Angelo, among many others. The now-legendary Amateur Night showcase has been running since 1934. The venue, known for jazz, R&B and soul music, mixes veteran talents such as Dianne Reeves with younger artists such as John Legend.

Brooklyn Bridge p157

Outer Boroughs

Unified in 1898, NYC's five boroughs are more integrated than ever. As non-millionaires have increasingly migrated from Manhattan, the outer boroughs have developed dining, shopping and cultural scenes to rival those on the island. Now that Manhattanites think nothing of crossing the river for a night out in Brooklyn or Queens, these boroughs no longer seem so far out. They hold ample attractions for visitors. Even the most isolated borough, Staten Island, is tipped as the site of construction of the world's tallest ferris wheel, which should break ground in 2014.

The Bronx

The Bronx seems remote to most visitors, partly due to the holdover of the South Bronx's reputation for urban strife in the 1970s. While many neighbourhoods still have an edgy feel, the Bronx is worth visiting for its attractions, the art deco architecture of the Grand Concourse, and the borough's own Little Italy, centred on Arthur Avenue in Belmont.

Sights & museums

Bronx Zoo/Wildlife Conservation Society

Bronx River Parkway, at Fordham Road (1-718 367 1010, www.bronxzoo.com). Subway 2, 5 to E Tremont/W Farms Square, then walk 2 blocks to the zoo's Asia entrance; or Metro-North (Harlem Line local) from Grand Central Terminal to Fordham, then take the Bx9 bus to 183rd Street and Southern Boulevard. **Open** *Apr-Oct* 10am-5pm Mon-Fri; 10am-5.30pm Sat, Sun. *Nov-Mar* 10am-4.30pm daily. **Admission** $16.95; $12-$15 reductions; pay what you wish Wed. Some rides & exhibitions cost extra. The Bronx Zoo shuns cages in favour of indoor and outdoor environments that mimic natural habitats. There are more than 60,000 creatures and more than 600 species here. Monkeys, leopards and tapirs live inside the lush, steamy Jungle World, a re-creation of an Asian rainforest inside a 37,000sq ft building, while lions, giraffes, zebras and other animals roam the African Plains. The popular Congo Gorilla Forest has turned 6.5 acres into a dramatic central African rainforest habitat. A glass-enclosed tunnel winds through the forest, allowing visitors to get close to the dozens of primate families in residence, including majestic western lowland gorillas. Tiger Mountain is populated by Siberian tigers, while the Himalayan Highlands features snow leopards and red pandas.

Bronx Museum of the Arts

1040 Grand Concourse, at 165th Street (1-718 681 6000, www.bronx museum.org). Subway B, D to 167th Street; 4 to 161st Street-Yankee Stadium. **Open** 11am-6pm Thur, Sat, Sun; 11am-8pm Fri. **Admission** free. Featuring more than 1,000 works, this multicultural art museum shines a spotlight on 20th- and 21st-century artists who are either Bronx-based or of African, Asian or Latino ancestry.

New York Botanical Garden

Bronx River Parkway, at Fordham Road (1-718 817 8700, www.nybg. org). Subway B, D, 4 to Bedford Park Boulevard, then Bx26 bus to the garden's Mosholu Gate; or Metro-North (Harlem Line local) from Grand Central Terminal to Botanical Garden. **Open** *Jan, Feb* 10am-5pm Tue-Sun. *Mar-Dec* 10am-6pm Tue-Sun. **Admission** $20-$25; $8-$22 reductions. *Grounds only* $10; $2-$5 reductions; grounds free Wed, 10-11am Sat.

The serene 250 acres comprise 50 gardens and plant collections, including the Rockefeller Rose Garden, the Everett Children's Adventure Garden and the last 50 original acres of a forest that once covered the whole city area. In spring, clusters of lilac, cherry, magnolia and

crab apple trees burst into bloom; in autumn you'll see vivid foliage in the oak and maple groves. The Azalea Garden features around 3,000 vivid azaleas and rhododendrons. The Enid A Haupt Conservatory – the nation's largest greenhouse, built in 1902 – contains the World of Plants, a series of environmental galleries that take you on an eco-tour through tropical rainforests, deserts and a palm tree oasis.

Arts & leisure

Yankee Stadium

River Avenue, at 161st Street (1-718 293 6000, www.yankees.com). Subway B, D, 4 to 161st Street-Yankee Stadium. In 2009, the Yankees vacated the fabled 'House that Ruth Built' and moved into their new $1.3-billion stadium across the street. Monument Park, an open-air museum behind centre field that celebrates the exploits of past Yankee heroes, can be visited as part of a tour ($25, $23 reductions, $20 booked online; 1-646 977 8687), along with the New York Yankees Museum, the dugout, and – when the Yankees are on the road – the clubhouse.

Brooklyn

'Brooklyn' has become shorthand for a particular brand of indie cool. New bars and restaurants continue to proliferate, the music scene is thriving and the borough is now a standard destination on the tour-bus itinerary. For visitors, attractions and cultural draws are concentrated in Brookyn Heights, Dumbo and Prospect Heights, but Williamsburg, Park Slope and Red Hook are great dining and drinking territory.

Sights & museums

Brooklyn Botanic Garden

1000 Washington Avenue, at Eastern Parkway, Prospect Heights (1-718 623 7200, www.bbg.org). Subway B, Q,

Franklin Avenue S to Prospect Park; 2, 3 to Eastern Parkway-Brooklyn Museum. **Open** *Mar-Oct* 8am-6pm Tue-Fri; 10am-6pm Sat, Sun. *Nov-Feb* 8am-4.30pm Tue-Fri; 10am-4.30pm Sat, Sun. **Admission** $10; free-$5 reductions; free Tue, 10am-noon Sat. This 52-acre haven of luscious greenery was founded in 1910. In spring, when Sakura Matsuri, the annual Cherry Blossom Festival, takes place, prize buds and Japanese culture are in full bloom. Linger in serene spots like the Japanese Hill-and-Pond Garden, the first Japanese-inspired garden built in the US, and the Shakespeare Garden, brimming with plants mentioned in the Bard's works. Start your stroll at the eco-friendly visitor centre (it has a green roof filled with 45,000 plants).

Brooklyn Bridge

Subway A, C to High Street; J, Z to Chambers Street; 4, 5, 6 to Brooklyn Bridge-City Hall.
Even if you don't have time to spend a day in Brooklyn, it's worth walking to the centre of the bridge along its wide, wood-planked promenade. Designed by civil engineer John Augustus Roebling, the Brooklyn Bridge was constructed in response to the harsh winter of 1867 when the East River froze over, severing the connection between Manhattan and what was then the nation's third most populous city. When it opened in 1883, the 5,989ft-long structure was the world's longest bridge, and the first in the world to use steel suspension cables. From it, there are striking vistas of the Statue of Liberty, the skyline of Lower Manhattan and New York Harbor.

Brooklyn Bridge Park

Riverside, from the Manhattan Bridge, Dumbo, to Atlantic Avenue, Brooklyn Heights (www.brooklynbridgepark.org). Subway A, C to High Street; F to York Street.
The views of Manhattan from this still-evolving riverside strip are spectacular. Brooklyn Bridge Park has been undergoing a rolling redesign that includes lawns, freshwater gardens, a water fowl-attracting salt marsh and the Granite Prospect, a set of stairs fashioned from salvaged granite facing the Downtown skyline. There's also an open-air wine bar and cult food carts. The restored vintage merry-go-round known as Jane's Carousel (www.janescarousel.org) made its long-awaited debut in a Jean Nouvel-designed pavilion in 2011.

Brooklyn Museum

200 Eastern Parkway, at Washington Avenue, Prospect Heights (1-718 638 5000, www.brooklynmuseum.org). Subway 2, 3 to Eastern Parkway-Brooklyn Museum. **Open** 11am-6pm Wed, Fri-Sun; 11am-10pm Thur; 11am-11pm 1st Sat of mth (except Sept). **Admission** suggested donation $12; free-$8 reductions; free 5-11pm 1st Sat of mth (except Sept).
Among the many assets of Brooklyn's premier institution are the third-floor Egyptian galleries. Highlights include the Mummy Chamber, an installation of 170 objects, including human and animal mummies. Also on this level, works by Cézanne, Monet and Degas, part of an impressive European art collection, are displayed in the museum's skylighted Beaux-Arts Court. The Elizabeth A Sackler Center for Feminist Art on the fourth floor is dominated by Judy Chicago's monumental mixed-media installation, *The Dinner Party*. The fifth floor is mainly devoted to American works, including Albert Bierstadt's immense *A Storm in the Rocky Mountains, Mt Rosalie*, and the Visible Storage-Study Center, where paintings, furniture and other objects are intriguingly juxtaposed.
Event highlights The Fashion World of Jean Paul Gaultier: from the Sidewalk to the Catwalk (25 Oct 2013-23 Feb 2014); Witness: Art & Civil Rights in the Sixties (7 Mar-6 July 2014); Ai Weiwei: According to What? (18 Apr-10 Aug 2014).

NEW YORK BY AREA

BrisketTown

Green-Wood Cemetery

Fifth Avenue, at 25th Street, Sunset Park (1-718 768 7300, www.green-wood.com). Subway M, R to 25th Street. **Open** varies by season; usually 8am-5pm daily. **Admission** free.

Filled with Victorian mausoleums, cherubs and gargoyles, Green-Wood is the resting place of some half-million New Yorkers, among them Jean-Michel Basquiat, Leonard Bernstein, Boss Tweed and Horace Greeley.

New York Transit Museum

Corner of Boerum Place & Schermerhorn Street, Brooklyn Heights (1-718 694 1600, www.mta.info/mta/museum). Subway A, C, G to Hoyt-Schermerhorn; 2, 3, 4, 5 to Borough Hall. **Open** 10am-4pm Tue-Fri; 11am-5pm Sat, Sun. **Admission** $7; free-$5 reductions.

Located in a historic 1936 IND subway station, this is the largest museum in the United States devoted to urban public transport history. Exhibits explore the social and practical impact of public transport on the development of greater New York; among the highlights is an engrossing walk-through display charting the construction of the city's century-old subway system. But the best part is down another level to a real platform where you can board an exceptional collection of vintage subway and El ('Elevated') cars.

Eating & drinking

Al di là

248 Fifth Avenue, at Carroll Street, Park Slope (1-718 783 4565, www.aldilatrattoria.com). Subway R to Union Street. **Open** noon-3pm, 6-10.30pm Mon-Thur; noon-3pm, 6-11pm Fri; 11am-3.30pm, 5.30-11pm Sat; 11am-3.30pm, 5-10pm Sun. **$$. Italian**

A fixture on the Slope's Fifth Avenue for more than a decade, this convivial, no-reservations restaurant is still wildly popular. Affable owner Emiliano Coppa orchestrates the inevitable wait with panache. Coppa's wife, co-owner and chef, Anna Klinger, produces northern Italian dishes with a Venetian slant. It would be hard to better her braised rabbit with black olives atop polenta, and even simple pastas, such as the own-made tagliatelle al ragù, are superb.

BrisketTown

NEW *359 Bedford Avenue, between South 4th & 5th Streets, Williamsburg (1-718 701 8909, http://delaneybbq.com).* **Open** 11am-midnight Mon-Thur, Sun; 11am-2am Fri, Sat. **$$. Barbecue**

New Jersey-born Daniel Delaney – a former journalist – might not seem like an obvious poster child for purist Texan 'cue. But the Yankee is turning out some seriously crave-worthy meat. Delaney takes the traditionalist route, coating chunks of heritage beef in salt and pepper before smoking them over oak-fuelled fire for 16 hours. That deep-pink brisket, along with remarkably tender pork ribs, draws Williamsburg's jeans-and-plaid set, who tuck in while indie tunes jangle over the speakers.

Clover Club

210 Smith Street, between Baltic & Butler Streets, Cobble Hill (1-718 855 7939, www.cloverclubny.com). Subway F, G to Bergen Street. **Open** 4pm-2am Mon-Thur; noon-4am Fri; 11am-4am Sat; 11am-2am Sun. **Bar**

Classic cocktails are the signature tipples at maven Julie Reiner's Victorian-styled cocktail parlour. Sours, fizzes, mules, punches and cobblers all get their latter-day due at the 19th-century mahogany bar. Highbrow snacks (fried oysters, steak tartare) accompany drinks like the eponymous Clover Club (with gin, raspberry syrup, egg whites, dry vermouth and lemon juice).

Donna

27 Broadway at Dunham Place, Williamsburg (1-646 568 6622, www.donnabklyn.com). Subway J, M to Marcy Avenue. **Open** 6pm-2am Mon-Thur; 4pm-4am Fri, Sat; 4pm-2am Sun. **Bar**

This breezy, rum-soaked drinkery hidden away near the Williamsburg waterfront feels worlds away from the industrial streets outside. The interior is a fever-dream vision of Central America that takes its inspiration from Spanish-colonial cathedrals, art nouveau parlours and the sailor's flophouse that existed on this site in the 1800s. Rum anchors the cocktail list: the OJ-splashed Brancolada elevates that tiki warhorse, the piña colada, with herbal and minty Branca Menta – with sophisticated and dangerously easygoing results. If you're making an evening of it, you can keep yourself moored with tapas-style snacks.

Maison Premiere

298 Bedford Avenue, between Grand & South 1st Streets, Williamsburg (1-347 335 0446, www.maisonpremiere.com). Subway L to Bedford Avenue. **Open** 4pm-3am Mon-Fri; 11am-3am Sat, Sun. **Bar**
Most of NYC's New Orleans-inspired watering holes choose debauched Bourbon Street as their muse, but this gorgeous salon embraces the romance found in the Crescent City's historic haunts. Belly up to the oval, marble-topped bar and get familiar with the twin pleasures of oysters and absinthe: two French Quarter staples with plenty of appeal in Brooklyn. The mythical anise-flavoured liqueur appears in 19 international varieties, in addition to a trim list of cerebral cocktails.

Marlow & Sons

81 Broadway, between Berry Street & Wythe Avenue, Williamsburg (1-718 384 1441, www.marlowandsons.com). Subway J, M, Z to Marcy Avenue. **Open** 8am-midnight daily. **$$**.
American creative
This popular place serves as an old-time oyster bar, quaint general store and daytime café. Seated in the charming front-room shop, diners survey the gourmet olive oils and honeys while wolfing down market-fresh salads, succulent brick chicken and the creative crostini

of the moment (such as goat's cheese with flash-fried strawberries). In the back room, an oyster shucker cracks open the catch of the day, while the bartender mixes the kind of potent drinks that helped to make the owners' earlier ventures (including next-door Diner, a tricked-out 1920s dining car) successes.

Peter Luger

178 Broadway, at Driggs Avenue, Williamsburg (1-718 387 7400, www.peterluger.com). Subway J, M, Z to Marcy Avenue. **Open** 11.45am-9.45pm Mon-Thur; 11.45am-10.45pm Fri, Sat; 12.45-9.45pm Sun. **$$$**.
No credit cards. **Steakhouse**
At Luger's old-school steakhouse, the choice is limited, but the porterhouse is justly famed. Choose from various sizes, from a small single steak to 'steak for four'. Although a slew of Luger copycats have prospered in the last several years, none has captured the elusive charm of this stucco-walled, beer hall-style eatery, with worn wooden floors and tables, and waiters in waistcoats and bow ties.

Pok Pok NY

127 Columbia Street, between DeGraw & Kane Streets, Red Hook (1-718 923 9322, www.pokpokny.com). Subway F, G to Bergen Street. **Open** 5.30-10.30pm daily. **$**. **Thai**
James Beard Award-winning chef Andy Ricker's restaurant replicates the dives of Chiang Mai – a tented dining room out back is festooned with dangling plants, colourful oilcloths on the tables and second-hand seats. But what separates Pok Pok from other cultish Thai restaurants is the curatorial role of its minutiae-mad chef. Ricker highlights a host of surprisingly mild northern-Thai dishes, including a lovely sweet-and-sour Burmese-inflected pork curry, *kaeng hung leh*. His *khao soi*, the beloved meal-in-a-bowl from Chiang Mai – chicken noodle soup delicately spiced with yellow curry and topped with fried noodles for crunch – is accompanied

here by raw shallots and pickled mustard greens. The restaurant is expected to move to a larger space nearby at press time, so call before venturing out.

Roberta's

261 Moore Street, between Bogart & White Streets, Bushwick (1-718 417 1118, www.robertaspizza.com). Subway L to Morgan Avenue. **Open** 11am-midnight Mon-Fri; 10am-midnight Sat, Sun. **$$-$$$**. **Italian**

This sprawling hangout has become the unofficial meeting place for Brooklyn's sustainable-food movement. Opened in 2008 by a trio of friends, Roberta's has its own on-site garden that provides some of the ingredients for its locally sourced dishes. The pizzas – like the Cheeses Christ, topped with mozzarella, taleggio, parmesan, black pepper and cream – are among Brooklyn's finest. The team recently opened Blanca, a sleek spot in the back garden, to showcase chef Carlo Mirarchi's acclaimed evening-only tasting menu (6-10pm Wed-Sat, $180).

Spuyten Duyvil

359 Metropolitan Avenue, at Havermeyer Street, Williamsburg (1-718 963 4140, www.spuytenduyvilnyc.com). Subway L to Lorimer St; G to Metropolitan Avenue. **Open** 5pm-2am Mon-Thur; 5pm-4am Fri; 1pm-4am Sat; 1pm-2am Sun. **Bar**

Don't arrive thirsty. It takes at least ten minutes to choose from roughly 150 beers. Most selections are middle-European regionals, and bartenders are eager to tell you about them. The cosy interior is full of fleamarket finds, most of which are for sale. There's also a tasty bar menu of smoked meats, pâtés, cheeses and terrines.

Vinegar Hill House

72 Hudson Avenue, between Front & Water Streets, Dumbo (1-718 522 1018, www.vinegarhillhouse.com). Subway A, C to High Street; F to York Street. **Open** 6-11pm Mon-Thur;

11am-3.30pm, 6-11.30pm Fri, Sat; 11am-3.30pm, 5.30-11pm Sun. **$$**. **American**

As it's hidden in a residential street in the forgotten namesake neighbourhood (now essentially part of Dumbo), tracking down Vinegar Hill House engenders a treasure-hunt thrill. A daily-changing menu focuses on seasonal comfort foods, and the cosy, tavern-like spot has a limited reservation policy (see website for details), but waiting in the secluded garden with drinks is a pleasure. You can also try the tiny next-door wine-bar-cum-café offshoot, Hillside.

Union Hall

702 Union Street, between Fifth & Sixth Avenues, Park Slope (1-718 638 4400, www.unionhallny.com). Subway R to Union Street. **Open** 4pm-4am Mon-Fri; 1pm-4am Sat, Sun. **Bar**

Upstairs, customers chomp on mini burgers and sip microbrews in the gentlemen's club-style anteroom (decorated with Soviet-era globes, paintings of fez-capped men, fireplaces) – before battling it out on the clay bocce courts. Downstairs, in the taxidermy-filled basement, the stage hosts bands, comedians and offbeat events.

Shopping

By Brooklyn

261 Smith Street, between DeGraw & Douglass Streets, Carroll Gardens (1-718 643 0606, www.bybrooklyn.com). Subway F, G to Carroll Street. **Open** 11am-7pm Mon-Wed, Sun; 11am-8pm Thur-Sat.

Gaia DiLoreto's modern-day general store offers an array of New York-made goods, including pickles, soaps, T-shirts, jewellery and books by Brooklyn authors. Look out for Purch ceramic homeware, Natural Abstract nature-inspired silver earrings and necklaces, and Lola Falk colour-block handbags.

CB I Hate Perfume

93 Wythe Avenue, between North 10th & North 11th Streets, Williamsburg

(1-718 384 6890, www.cbihateperfume. com). Subway L to Bedford Avenue.
Open noon-6pm Tue-Sat.
Contrary to the name of his shop, Christopher Brosius doesn't actually hate what he sells; he just despises the concept of mass-produced fragrances. Although there's currently a hold on bespoke collaborations due to high demand, you can choose from 43 evocative ready-made fragrances, such as Gathering Apples or At the Beach 1966.

Modern Anthology
68 Jay Street, between Front & Water Streets, Dumbo (1-718 522 3020, www. modernanthology.com). Subway A, C to High Street; F to York Street. **Open** 11am-7pm Mon-Sat; noon-6pm Sun.
Owners Becka Citron and John Marsala – the creative force behind the DIY Network's *Man Caves* series – have created a one-stop lifestyle shop where dudes can find items that walk the line between vintage and contemporary: check out pillows made from fabric route signs from British buses from the 1930s to '50s, and sturdy steel task lamps. And what hip bachelor pad is complete without a stack of vintage issues of *Playboy* and barware?

Tiger Blanket Records & Vintage Boutique
NEW *421 Graham Avenue, between Frost & Withers Streets, Williamsburg (1-520 977 6913, www.tigerblanket records.com). Subway L to Graham Avenue.* **Open** 1-8pm Tue-Sun.
Singer-songwriter Emmy Wildwood infuses her twin loves of fashion and rock'n' roll into her indie record label's storefront. Stock includes print dresses from the 1970s through '90s, men's concert tees and leather jackets, plus $5 records from retro favourites such as the B-52s and Debbie Harry. Wildwood also puts out one seven-inch by a local unsigned band each month, available exclusively at the store, and hosts free monthly performances.

Nightlife

Barbès
376 9th Street, between Sixth & Seventh Avenues, Park Slope (1-347 422 0248, www.barbesbrooklyn.com). Subway F to Seventh Avenue. **Open** 5pm-2am Mon-Thur; noon-4am Fri; 2pm-4am Sat; 2pm-2am Sun.
Show up early if you want to get into Park Slope's global-bohemian club – it's tiny. Run by musically inclined French expats, this *boîte* brings in traditional swing and jazz of more daring stripes – depending on the night, you could catch African, French, Brazilian or Colombian music or acts that often defy categorisation.

Music Hall of Williamsburg
66 North 6th Street, between Kent & Wythe Avenues, Williamsburg (1-718 486 5400, www.musichall ofwilliamsburg.com). Subway L to Bedford Avenue.
When, in 2007, the local promoter Bowery Presents found itself in need of a Williamsburg outpost, it gave the former Northsix a facelift and took over the bookings. It's basically a Bowery Ballroom (see p79) in Brooklyn – and bands such as Sonic Youth, Hot Chip and Real Estate headline, often on the day after they've played Bowery Ballroom or Terminal 5.

Output
NEW *74 Wythe Avenue, at North 12th Street, Williamsburg (no phone, www.outputclub.com). Subway L to Bedford Avenue.*
With the opening of Output in early 2013, New York nightlife's centre of gravity continues its eastward push into Brooklyn. Akin in ethos to such underground-music headquarters as Berlin's Berghain/Panorama Bar complex or London's Fabric, the club boasts a warehouse-party vibe and a killer sound system. Top-shelf DJs (both international hotshots and local

heroes) spin the kind of left-field house, techno and bass music you rarely hear in more commercially oriented spots. If the weather's nice, head to the rooftop bar – the view of the Manhattan skyline is a stunner.

Pete's Candy Store

709 Lorimer Street, between Frost & Richardson Streets, Williamsburg (1-718 302 3770, www.petescandy store.com). Subway L to Lorimer Street. **Open** 5pm-2am Mon-Wed; 5pm-4am Thur; 4pm-4am Fri, Sat; 4pm-2am Sun. An overlooked gem tucked away in an old candy shop, Pete's is beautifully ramshackle, tiny and almost always free. The performers are generally unknown and crowds can be thin, but it can be a charming place to catch a singer-songwriter. Worthy underdogs may stop by for casual sets.

This n' That (TNT)

NEW 108 North 6th Street, between Berry Street & Wythe Avenue, Williamsburg (1-718 599 5959, www. thisnthatbrooklyn.com). Subway L to Bedford Avenue. **Open** 4pm-4am daily. The latest addition to the Brooklyn queer-bar scene is parked in the middle of the most hipstery block of the city's most hipstery neighbourhood. Still, most nights you'll find a surprisingly unpretentious crowd here, enjoying various parties (trivia, movie nights, sweaty dance fests).

Arts & leisure

Barclays Center

NEW 620 Atlantic Avenue, at Flatbush Avenue, Prospect Heights (1-917 618 6700, www.barclayscenter.com). Subway B, D, N, Q, R, 2, 3, 4, 5 to Atlantic Avenue-Barclays Center. The city's newest arena, home of the rechristened Brooklyn Nets basketball team, opened in autumn 2012. Although controversy over the construction still causes tensions among locals, the venue opened with a series

of concerts by native son and Nets investor Jay-Z, and continues to secure a slate of splashy shows.

Bargemusic

Fulton Ferry Landing, between Old Fulton & Water Streets, Dumbo (1-718 624 4924, www.bargemusic.org). Subway A, C to High Street; F to York Street; 2, 3 to Clark Street. No credit cards. This former coffee-bean barge usually presents four chamber concerts a week set against a panoramic view of lower Manhattan. It's a magical experience (and the programming has recently grown more ambitious), but be sure to dress warmly in the winter. In less chilly months, enjoy a drink on the upper deck during the interval.

Brooklyn Academy of Music

Peter Jay Sharp Building 30 Lafayette Avenue, between Ashland Place & St Felix Street, Fort Greene. Subway B, Q, 2, 3, 4, 5 to Atlantic Avenue; C to Lafayette Avenue; D, N, R to Pacific Street; G to Fulton Street. **BAM Harvey Theater** 651 Fulton Street, at Rockwell Place, Fort Greene. Subway B, Q, R to DeKalb Avenue; C to Lafayette Avenue; G to Fulton Street; 2, 3, 4, 5 to Nevins Street. **BAM Richard B Fisher Building** 321 Ashland Place, between Ashland Place & Lafayette Avenue, Fort Greene. Subway B, Q, 2, 3, 4, 5 to Atlantic Avenue; C to Lafayette Avenue; D, N, R to Pacific Street; G to Fulton Street. **All** 1-718 636 4100, www.bam.org. America's oldest performing-arts academy continues to present some of the freshest programming in the city. Every year in autumn and winter, the Next Wave Festival provides avant-garde music, dance and theatre in its grand old opera house in the Peter Jay Sharp Building and the smaller BAM Harvey Theater. The newest facility, BAM Fisher, houses an intimate performance space and studios. BAM Rose Cinemas (in the Peter Jay Sharp building) does double duty as a rep house for well-programmed classics on 35mm and a first-run multiplex for indie films.

Brooklyn Bowl

61 Wythe Avenue, between North 11th & 12th Streets, Williamsburg (1-718 963 3369, www.brooklynbowl.com). Subway L to Bedford Avenue. **Open** (over-21s only except noon-6pm Sat) 6pm-midnight Mon-Wed; 6pm-2am Thur, Fri; noon-2am Sat; noon-midnight Sun.

Brooklyn Bowl turns bowling into a complete night out, with a menu from popular local eaterie Blue Ribbon and a full-size concert venue. The block-long former ironworks foundry takes its design cues from the Coney Island of the 1930s and '40s, with reproductions of old freak-show posters and carnival-game relics. All the beer – by Sixpoint, Kelso and next-door Brooklyn Brewery – is made in the borough.

Coney Island

Luna Park & Cyclone *1000 Surf Avenue, at W 10th Street (1-718 373 5862, www.lunaparknyc.com).*
Deno's Wonder Wheel Amusement Park *1025 Boardwalk, at W 12th Street (1-718 372 2592, www.wonderwheel.com).*
Both *Subway D, F, N, Q to Coney Island-Stillwell Avenue.* **Open** late Mar-Oct; hrs vary (see websites).

In its heyday, from the turn of the century to World War II, Coney Island was New York City's playground. Years of neglect followed, but the arrival of the new Luna Park amusement hub – and the staying power of the iconic Wonder Wheel and teeth-rattling 1927 Cyclone rollercoaster – are drawing a new generation of pleasure seekers. Coney Island USA (1208 Surf Avenue, at 12th Street, 1-718 372 5159, http://coney island.com) stages seasonal sideshow and burlesque diversions.

Nitehawk Cinema

136 Metropolitan Avenue, between Berry Street & Wythe Avenue, Williamsburg (1-718 384 3980, www.nitehawkcinema. com). Subway L to Bedford Avenue.
At this cinema-restaurant-bar hybrid, you can have dinner and a movie at the same time. Seats are arranged in pairs with tables, and viewers order from a menu created by Michelin-starred chef Saul Bolton. Just write down your order at any point during the movie on a piece of paper for a server to pick up. The comfort-food grub includes a tasty burger, but the real highlights are the chef's variations on concession-stand staples, like popcorn tossed with parmesan, black pepper and garlic butter.

Queens

Sights & museums

MoMA PS1

22-25 Jackson Avenue, at 46th Avenue, Long Island City (1-718 784 2084, www.momaps1.org). Subway E, M to Court Square-23rd Street; G to 21st Street; 7 to 45th Road-Court House Square. **Open** noon-6pm Mon, Thur-Sun. **Admission** suggested donation $10; $5 reductions.

Housed in a Romanesque Revival former public school, MoMA PS1 mounts cutting-edge shows and hosts an acclaimed international studio programme. The contemporary art centre became an affiliate of MoMA in 1999, and the two institutions sometimes stage collaborative exhibitions. The museum's DJed summer Warm Up parties are an unmissable fixture of the city's dance-music scene, and its new eaterie, M Wells Dinette, is a foodie destination.

Museum of the Moving Image

35th Avenue, at 36th Street, Astoria (1-718 777 6888, www.movingimage. us). Subway M, R to Steinway Street; N, Q to 36th Avenue. **Open** *Galleries* 10.30am-5pm Wed, Thur; 10.30am-8pm Fri; 11.30am-7pm Sat, Sun. **Admission** $12; free-$9 reductions; free 4-8pm Fri. No pushchairs/strollers.

Nitehawk Cinema

World-class Queens

A revamped museum helps to revive the World's Fair site.

Facing the Unisphere – the 140ft stainless steel globe created for the 1964 World's Fair – in Flushing Meadows Corona Park, the **Queens Museum** (see p167) occupies the former New York City Building, a Gotham-themed pavilion built for the earlier World's Fair in 1939. In the 1940s, the structure was the first home of the United Nations while its permanent Manhattan home was being constructed. During the 1964 World's Fair, the New York City Building showcased the *Panorama of the City of New York*, a 9,335sq ft scale model of the city dreamed up by powerful urban planner Robert Moses. Still on display in the museum, it includes every one of the 895,000 buildings constructed before 1992.

Now, after more than two years, the Queens Museum is wrapping up an expansion-cum-renovation project that will double its size and help to revitalise the neglected World's Fair site.

The centrepiece of the 50,000sq ft addition, which used to house a public ice-skating rink, is an airy atrium flanked by roofless art galleries designed to be illuminated by the enormous skylight. The extra space will accommodate studios for Queens-based artists, a café and a museum shop selling original World's Fair memorabilia. The *Panorama* is getting a modest makeover of its own. Its day-to-night cycle, which allowed it to be viewed as a city at night, is being restored, and once 1 World Trade Center is complete, the Twin Towers will be removed to a display case and replaced with a replica of the new skyscraper.

The inaugural exhibitions reflect both the building's history and the institution's present. Photographer Jeff Chien-Hsing Liao's series of large-scale images of the project will be displayed alongside archive photographs and other materials documenting the building's past. In 'The People's UN (pUN)', Mexican artist Pedro Reyes stages humorous performances by 'representatives'. Both shows run until December 2013. The Queens International, the museum's sixth biennial (until January 2014), showcases the work of artists in NYC's most multicultural borough.

The Museum of the Moving Image reopened in 2011 after a major renovation that doubled its size and made it one of the foremost museums in the world dedicated to TV, film and video. The collection and state-of-the-art screening facilities are housed in the Astoria Studios complex, which was once the New York production headquarters of Paramount Pictures. The upgraded core exhibition, 'Behind the Screen', on the second and third floors, contains artefacts from more than 1,000 productions (including the super creepy stunt doll used in *The Exorcist*, with full head-rotating capabilities, and a miniature skyscraper from *Bladerunner*) and interactive displays. A new gallery devoted to Muppets creator Jim Henson is expected to open in late 2014 or early 2015.

Noguchi Museum

9-01 33rd Road, between Vernon Boulevard & 10th Street, Long Island City (1-718 204 7088, www.noguchi. org). Subway N, Q to Broadway, then 15min walk or Q104 bus to 11th Street; 7 to Vernon Boulevard-Jackson Avenue, then Q103 bus to 10th Street. **Open** 10am-5pm Wed-Fri; 11am-6pm Sat, Sun. **Admission** $10; free-$5 reductions; pay what you wish 1st Fri of mth. No pushchairs/strollers.

When Japanese-American sculptor and designer Isamu Noguchi (1904-88) opened his Queens museum in 1985, he became the first living artist in the US to establish such an institution. The Noguchi Museum occupies a former photo-engraving plant across the street from the studio he had occupied since the 1960s; its location allowed him to be close to stone and metal suppliers along Vernon Boulevard. Noguchi designed the entire building to be a meditative oasis amid its gritty, industrial setting. Eleven galleries – spread over two floors – and an outdoor space are filled with his sculptures, as well as drawn, painted and collaged studies, architectural models, and stage and furniture designs.

Queens Museum

New York City Building, park entrance on 49th Avenue, at 111th Street, Flushing Meadows Corona Park (1-718 592 9700, www.queensmuseum.org). Subway 7 to 111th Street, then walk south on 111th Street, turning left on to 49th Avenue; continue into the park and over Grand Central Parkway Bridge. **Open** noon-6pm Wed-Sun. **Admission** suggested donation $8; free-$4 reductions. See box p166.
Event highlights Queens International 2013 (11 Oct 2013-Jan 2014); Andy Warhol's 13 Most Wanted Men & the 1964 World's Fair (Apr-Aug 2014).

Eating & drinking

Bohemian Hall & Beer Garden

29-19 24th Avenue, between 29th & 30th Streets, Astoria (1-718 274 4925, www.bohemianhall.com). Subway N, Q to Astoria Boulevard. **Open** 5pm-1am Mon-Thur; 3pm-2am Fri; noon-3am Sat, Sun. **Bar**
This authentic Czech beer garden features plenty of mingle-friendly picnic tables, where you can sample cheap, robust platters of sausage and 14 mainly European draughts. Though the huge, tree-canopied garden is open year-round (in winter, the area is tented and heated), summer is prime time to visit.

Dutch Kills

27-24 Jackson Avenue, at Dutch Kills Street, Long Island City (1-718 383 2724, www.dutchkillsbar.com). Subway E, R to Queens Plaza. **Open** 5pm-2am daily. **Bar**
What separates Dutch Kills from other mixology temples modelled after vintage saloons is the abundance of elbow room. Settle into one of the deep, dark-wood booths in the front, or perch at the bar. Cocktails are mostly classic, with prices slightly lower than in similar establishments in Manhattan.

NEW YORK BY AREA

M Wells Dinette

22-25 Jackson Avenue, at 46th Avenue, Long Island City (1-718 786 1800). Subway E, M to Court Square-23rd Street; G to 21st Street; 7 to 45th Road-Court House Square. **Open** noon-6pm Mon, Thur-Sun. **$$. Eclectic**

M Wells, the irreverent Queens diner that closed in 2011, was roundly cheered by the city's critics for playing with its food (foie gras on meatloaf, tripe cut in the shape of noodles). So it's fitting that husband-and-wife team Hugue Dufour and Sarah Obraitis have resurrected their brand in a former elementary-school space at MoMA PS1. At this museum cafeteria, Dufour puts his trademark cockeyed spin on seafood dishes (oyster Bolognese) as well as classic French dishes like the rich rabbit and foie gas terrine. In a nod to the space's educational past, the menu is scrawled on a blackboard and school desk-styled communal tables are stocked with pencils and playing cards.

Sripraphai

64-13 39th Avenue, between 64th & 65th Streets, Woodside (1-718 899 9599, www.sripraphairestaurant.com). Subway 7 to 61st Street-Woodside. **Open** 11.30am-9.30pm Mon, Tue, Thur-Sun. **$. Thai**

Woodside's destination eaterie offers distinctive, traditional Thai dishes such as catfish salad or green curry with beef: a thick, piquant broth filled out with roasted Thai aubergine. The dining areas, which sprawl over two levels and a garden (open in summer), are packed with Manhattanites who can be seen eyeing the plates enjoyed by the Thai regulars, mentally filing away what to order the next time.

Sweet Afton

30-09 34th Street, at 30th Avenue, Astoria (1-718 777 2570, www.sweet aftonbar.com). Subway N, Q to 30th Avenue. **Open** 4pm-3.30am Mon-Thur; 3pm-3.30am Fri; 11am-3.30am Sat, Sun. **Bar**

This gastropub combines an industrial feel – lots of concrete and massive beams – with the dim, dark-wood cosiness of an Irish pub. The bar's smartly curated array of reasonably priced suds includes strong selections from craft breweries like Kelso, Six Point and Captain Lawrence, but the bartender will just as happily crack open a cheap everyman ale such as Amstel or Miller. The satisfying food menu is highlighted by the beer-battered McClure's pickles – an epic bar snack.

Nightlife

Creek & the Cave

10-93 Jackson Avenue, at 11th Street, Long Island City (1-718 706 8783, www.creeklic.com). Subway 7 to Vernon Boulevard-Jackson Avenue.

This hardworking venue offers all the things comedians and their fans need to survive: multiple performance spaces, convivial environs, a fully stocked bar, cheap Mexican food and a patio on which to rant and laugh late into the night. As if this weren't enough, owner Rebecca Trent also shows her appreciation for all who make the trek to Queens by making nearly every show free.

Arts & leisure

Chocolate Factory Theater

5-49 49th Avenue, at Vernon Boulevard, Long Island City (1-718 482 7069, www. chocolatefactorytheater.org). Subway G to 21st Street; 7 to Vernon Boulevard-Jackson Avenue.

Brian Rogers and Sheila Lewandowski founded this 5,000sq ft performance venue in 2005, converting a one-time hardware store into two spaces: a low-ceilinged downstairs room and a loftier, brighter upstairs white box that caters to the interdisciplinary and the avant-garde. Past choreographers include Beth Gill, Jillian Peña, Big Dance Theater and Tere O'Connor. Rogers, an artist in his own right, also presents work here.

Essentials

Wythe Hotel p182

Hotels

Accommodation is more expensive in New York City than in the rest of the country, and while the average room rate dipped sharply in the wake of the financial crisis, reports from industry research specialist STR show it has been creeping up steadily since then, nearing $300 in the autumn high season. The hotel business is booming – both new construction and conversions of old buildings – and the city now has more than 90,000 rooms, representing an increase of around 20 per cent over the past five years. Unfortunately for bargain-seeking travellers, the figures show most of them are full year-round.

Hotel hotspots

Hip mini chain **Ace Hotel** (see p176) colonised a northern corner of the Flatiron District, which is emerging as a hotel (and restaurant) hotspot – the long-awaited **NoMad Hotel** (see p178), from the same developer, debuted in 2012. There is now more boutique choice in desirable areas like Chelsea and Greenwich Village with the arrival of the **High Line Hotel** (see box p177) and the **Jade Hotel** (see p174) in 2013. Perhaps the strongest indication of the economic recovery is a cluster of new luxury properties tipped to open on, or around, midtown's West 57th Street, including outposts of **Viceroy** (October 2013, www.viceroyhotel group.com) and **SLS** (spring/summer 2014, www.slshotels.com). The **Quin** (1-212 245 7846, www.thequinhotel. com), a deluxe transformation of the 1929 Buckingham Hotel, featuring amped-up amenities like Dux by Duxiana beds, Fresh toiletries and a personal concierge service, is due to open by publication of this guide.

It's also worth looking to the outer boroughs for competitively priced accommodation – Brooklyn, especially, is an increasingly desirable place to stay. Even the Bronx is tipped to get a boutique hotel; a 60-room conversion of the borough's former Beaux Arts opera house (1-718 407 2800, www.opera househotel.com) near Yankee Stadium should be open by the time you read this.

Prices & information

Rates within a single property can vary considerably according to room type and season, and special deals are often available, especially if you book on the hotel's website. When budgeting, don't forget to factor in the hefty 14.75 per cent tax – which includes city, state and hotel-room occupancy tax – plus an extra $3.50 per night for most rooms.

Downtown

Financial District

Andaz Wall Street

75 Wall Street, at Water Street (1-212 590 1234, www.wallstreetandaz.com). Subway 2, 3, 4, 5 to Wall Street. **$$$**.
The New York outpost of this Hyatt subsidiary occupies the first 17 floors of a former Barclays Bank building. Inside, the vibe is anything but corporate: upon entering the spacious bamboo-panelled lobby-lounge, you're greeted by a free-range 'host', who acts as a combination check-in clerk and concierge. Chic, loft-style rooms are equally casual and user-friendly. The restaurant (Wall & Water), bar and spa are welcome attributes in an area with little action at weekends.

Conrad New York

102 North End Avenue, at Vesey Street (1-212 945 0100, www. conradnewyork.com). Subway A, C to Chambers Street; 1, 2, 3 to

SHORTLIST

Best new
- High Line Hotel (p177)
- Jade Hotel (p174)
- Refinery Hotel (p180)
- Wythe Hotel (p182)

Design statements
- Dream Downtown (p175)
- Hôtel Americano (p176)
- NoMad Hotel (p178)
- Yotel New York (p179)

Best budget chic
- 414 Hotel (p179)
- Bowery House (p173)
- Jane (p175)
- New York Loft Hostel (p182)
- Pod 39 (p178)
- Wythe Hotel (p182)

Rooms with a view
- Conrad New York (left)
- On the Ave Hotel (p181)
- Standard (p175)
- Z NYC Hotel (p182)

Best spas
- Gansevoort Meatpacking NYC (p175)
- Greenwich Hotel (p172)
- Surrey (p181)

Best restaurants
- Ace Hotel (p178)
- Gramercy Park Hotel (p178)
- Greenwich Hotel (p172)
- NoMad Hotel (p178)

Best pools
- Gansevoort Meatpacking NYC (p175)
- Greenwich Hotel (p172)
- Hôtel Americano (p176)

Best classic style
- Hotel Elysée (p181)
- Plaza (p181)
- Surrey (p181)

ESSENTIALS

Chambers Street; E to World Trade Center; R to Cortlandt Street; 2, 3 to Park Place. **$$$**.

This sophisticated Hilton offshoot fronts Battery Park City's riverside Nelson A Rockefeller Park. West-facing rooms have views of the Hudson, but there's also plenty to see within the art-rich property. Sol LeWitt's vivid 100ft by 80ft painting *Loopy Doopy (Blue and Purple)* graces the dramatic 15-storey, glass-ceilinged, granite-floored lobby, and coolly understated guestrooms are adorned with pieces by the likes of Elizabeth Peyton and Mary Heilmann. Nespresso machines and marble bathrooms with Aromatherapy Associates products are indulgent touches. Above the rooftop bar (open May-Oct), with views of the Statue of Liberty, is a vegetable patch providing fresh produce for the hotel's restaurant.

Tribeca & Soho

60 Thompson

60 Thompson Street, between Broome & Spring Streets (1-212 431 0400, www.thompsonhotels.com). Subway C, E to Spring Street. **$$$$**.

The first property of the boutique chain Thompson Hotels, this stylish spot has been luring the film, fashion and media elite since it opened in 2001. British designer Tara Bernerd, who created the classy contemporary interiors for the group's new London hotel, Belgraves, is behind a redesign planned for early 2014. Indulgent details include Sferra linens and REN products. The hotel's acclaimed restaurant, Kittichai, serves creative Thai cuisine beside a pool filled with floating orchids, while A60, the exclusive guests-only rooftop bar, offers magnificent city views and a Moroccan-inspired decor.

Cosmopolitan

95 West Broadway, at Chambers Street (1-212 566 1900, www.cosmohotel. com). Subway A, C, 1, 2, 3 to Chambers Street. **$$**.

Despite the name, you won't find the legendary pink cocktail at this well-maintained hotel in two adjacent 1850s buildings, let alone a bar in which to drink it, though there is a café. Open continuously since the mid 19th century, the hotel remains a tourist favourite for its address, clean rooms and reasonable rates. A wide range of configurations is available, including a suite with two queen beds and a sofa bed, ideal for families.

Crosby Street Hotel

79 Crosby Street, between Prince & Spring Streets (1-212 226 6400, www.firmdalehotels.com). Subway N, R to Prince Street; 6 to Spring Street. **$$$$**.

In 2009, Britain's hospitality power couple, Tim and Kit Kemp, brought their super-successful Firmdale formula across the Atlantic with the warehouse-style Crosby Street Hotel. Design director Kit's signature style – a fresh, contemporary take on classic English decor characterised by an oft-audacious mix of patterns, bold colours and judiciously chosen antiques – is instantly recognisable. Other Firmdale imports include a carefully selected art collection, a guests-only drawing room as well as a public restaurant and bar, a slick, 99-seat screening room and a private garden.

Greenwich Hotel

377 Greenwich Street, between Franklin & North Moore Streets (1-212 941 8900, www.thegreenwichhotel.com). Subway 1 to Franklin Street. **$$$$**.

The design inspiration at this Tribeca retreat, co-owned by Robert De Niro, is as international as the jet-set clientele. Individually decorated rooms combine custom-made English leather seating, Tibetan rugs and gorgeous Moroccan or Carrara-marble-tiled bathrooms, most outfitted with capacious tubs that fill up in a minute flat (bath salts from Nolita spa Red Flower are provided). Breaststroke meditatively beneath the frame of a 250-year-old Kyoto farmhouse in the Shibui Spa's underground pool, then unwind with a bottle of wine by the water's edge. For dinner, there's no need to rub shoulders with the masses at the always-mobbed house restaurant, Locanda Verde. Have your meal delivered to the cloistered courtyard, where travertine floors and terracotta pots evoke a Florentine villa.

James New York

27 Grand Street, at Thompson Street (1-212 465 2000, www.jameshotels. com). Subway A, C, E to Canal Street. **$$$**.

Hotel art displays are usually limited to eye-catching lobby installations or forgettable in-room prints. Not so at the James, which maintains a substantial showcase of local talent. The corridor of each guest floor is dedicated to the work of an individual artist, selected by a house curator and complete with museum-style notes. Although compact, bedrooms make the most of the available space with high ceilings and wall-spanning windows. Natural materials warm up the clean contemporary lines and bathroom products are courtesy of Intelligent Nutrients. A two-level 'urban garden' houses an outdoor bar and eaterie. The rooftop bar, Jimmy, opens on to the (admittedly tiny) pool.

Mercer

147 Mercer Street, at Prince Street (1-212 966 6060, www.mercerhotel. com). Subway N, R to Prince Street. **$$$$**.

Opened in 2001 by trendsetting hotelier André Balazs, the Mercer still has ample attractions that appeal to a celeb-heavy clientele. The lobby, with oversized white couches and chairs, acts as a bar, library and lounge, and is exclusive to hotel guests. Loft-like rooms are large by New York standards and feature furniture by Christian Liaigre. The restaurant, Mercer Kitchen, serves Jean-Georges Vongerichten's stylish version of casual American cuisine.

Chinatown, Little Italy & Nolita

Bowery House

220 Bowery, between Prince & Spring Streets (1-212 837 2373, www.theboweryhouse.com). Subway J, Z to Bowery. **$**.

Two young real-estate developers transformed a 1927 Bowery flophouse into this stylish take on a hostel. Corridors with original wainscotting lead to cubicles (singles are a cosy 35sq ft and not all have windows) with latticework ceilings to allow air circulation. It might not be the best bet for light sleepers, but the place is hopping with pretty young things attracted to the hip aesthetic and the location, between Soho and the Lower East Side. Quarters are decorated with vintage prints and historical photographs, and towels and robes are courtesy of Ralph Lauren. The (gender-segregated) communal bathrooms have rain showerheads and products from local spa Red Flower, while the guest lounge is outfitted with chesterfield sofas and a huge LCD TV.

Nolitan

30 Kenmare Street, at Elizabeth Street (1-212 925 2555, www. nolitanhotel.com). Subway J, Z to Bowery; 6 to Spring Street. **$$$**.

The 55 airy rooms of this boutique hotel feature floor-to-ceiling windows, wooden floors, custom-made walnut beds and toiletries from Prince Street spa Red Flower. The emphasis on keeping it local is reflected in numerous guest perks: the luxuriously laid-back property lends out bikes and lays on free local calls and discounts at neighbourhood boutiques. Admire views of Nolita and beyond from the 2,400sq ft roof deck, complete with fire pit, or your private perch – more than half the guest quarters have balconies. Standard checkout is 2pm.

Sohotel

341 Broome Street, between Bowery & Elizabeth Street (1-212 226 1482, www.thesohotel.com). Subway J, Z to Bowery; 6 to Spring Street. **$$**.

Housed in a renovated late 18th-century building, Sohotel has charming touches – exposed-brick walls, ceiling fans, hardwood floors and bathroom products from venerable NYC apothecary CO Bigelow – that place it a rung above similarly priced establishments. The many Regency Plus rooms, which can accommodate four to five guests, are the best bargain. Guests get a 10% discount at the on-site craft-brew emporium, Randolph Beer.

Lower East Side

Hotel on Rivington

107 Rivington Street, between Essex & Ludlow Streets (1-212 475 2600, www.hotelonrivington.com). Subway F to Delancey Street; J, Z to Delancey-Essex Streets. **$$$**.

When the Hotel on Rivington opened in 2005, its ultra-modern glass-covered façade was a novelty on the largely low-rise Lower East Side. Now, with condos popping up everywhere, the building seems less out of place, but it remains one of the few luxury hotels in the neighbourhood. Rooms are super-sleek, with black and white decorative touches, Frette bed linen and robes, and floor-to-ceiling windows. A stylish crowd congregates in the hotel's two restaurants, Coop Food & Drink, which serves sushi alongside modern American fare, and Viktor & Spoils, a contemporary *taqueria* and tequila bar.

East Village

Bowery Hotel

335 Bowery, at 3rd Street (1-212 505 9100, www.theboweryhotel.com). Subway B, D, F, M to Broadway-Lafayette Street; 6 to Bleecker Street. **$$$$**.

This fanciful boutique property from prominent hoteliers Eric Goode and Sean MacPherson is the capstone in the gentrification of the Bowery. Shunning minimalism, they created plush rooms that pair old-world touches (oriental rugs, wood-beamed ceilings, marble washstands) with modern amenities (flatscreen TVs, Wi-Fi).

East Village Bed & Coffee

110 Avenue C, between 7th & 8th Streets (1-917 816 0071, www.bedandcoffee.com). Subway F to Lower East Side-Second Avenue; L to First Avenue. **$**.

This East Village B&B (minus the breakfast) embodies quirky downtown culture. Each of the guest rooms has a unique theme, reflected in their names: for example, the Black and White Room or the Treehouse (the latter has an ivory and olive colour scheme, animal-print linens and a whitewashed brick wall). When the weather's nice, sip your complimentary morning java in the private garden.

Hotel 17

225 E 17th Street, between Second & Third Avenues (1-212 475 2845, www.hotel17ny.com). Subway L to Third Avenue; L, N, Q, R, 4, 5, 6 to 14th Street-Union Square. **$**.

Shabby chic is the best way to describe this hotel a few blocks from Union Square. Rooms are a study in contrast: antique dressers are paired with paisley bedspreads and vintage wallpaper. In most cases, bathrooms are shared, but they're kept immaculately clean. Over the years, the building has been featured in numerous films – including Woody Allen's *Manhattan Murder Mystery* – and has put up Madonna and, more recently, transgender downtown diva Amanda Lepore.

Greenwich Village

Jade Hotel

NEW *52 W 13th Street, between Fifth & Sixth Avenues (1-212 375 1300, www.thejadenyc.com). Subway F, M, 1, 2, 3 to 14th Street; L to Sixth Avenue; L, N, Q, R, 4, 5, 6 to 14th Street-Union Square.* **$$$**.

With its Georgian-style portico and decorative brickwork, the Jade Hotel is indistinguishable from the pre-war apartment buildings in its Greenwich Village locale. But the sensitively conceived 18-storey structure was built from scratch. The rooms, designed by Andres Escobar in an art deco style, feature marble-inlaid Macassar ebony desks, chrome period lamps and champagne satin poufs – to preserve the period illusion, the TV is hidden behind a decorative cabinet. The classic black-and-white tiled bathrooms are stocked with toiletries from venerable Village pharmacy CO Bigelow. Some rooms have private terraces, floor-to-ceiling windows or cosy window seats.

West Village & Meatpacking District

Gansevoort Meatpacking NYC

18 Ninth Avenue, at 13th Street (1-212 206 6700, www.hotelgansevoort.com). Subway A, C, E to 14th Street; L to Eighth Avenue. **$$$**.
This Meatpacking District pioneer is known for its rooftop-pool-lounge playgrounds at two NYC locations (a Park Avenue property opened in 2010). By day, you can soak up the sun, and the Hudson River panorama, on a lounger by the 45ft heated open-air pool. After dark, the wraparound terrace bar becomes a DJed outdoor party with a glittering Manhattan backdrop. The guest quarters recently received a glam makeover, which brought Studio 54-inspired photography that plays on the hotel's reputation as a party hub. Plush feather-bed layers atop excellent mattresses and marble bathrooms amp up the luxury. The Exhale spa is a candlelit subterranean sanctuary.

Jane

113 Jane Street, at West Street (1-212 924 6700, www.thejane nyc.com). Subway A, C, E to 14th Street; L to Eighth Avenue. **$-$$**.
Opened in 1907 as the American Seaman's Friend Society Sailors Home, the six-storey landmark was a residential hotel when hoteliers Eric Goode and Sean MacPherson took it over. The

Jane's wood-panelled, 50sq ft rooms were inspired by vintage train sleeper compartments – there's a single bed with built-in storage and brass hooks for hanging up your clothes, but also iPod docks and wall-mounted flatscreen TVs. If entering the hotel feels like stepping on to a film set, there's good reason. Inspiration came from various celluloid sources, including *Barton Fink*'s Hotel Earle for the lobby.

Standard

848 Washington Street, at 13th Street (1-212 645 4646, www.standard hotels.com). Subway A, C, E to 14th Street; L to Eighth Avenue. **$$$**.
André Balazs's lauded West Coast mini-chain arrived in New York in 2009. Straddling the High Line, the retro 18-storey structure has been configured to give each room an exhilarating view, either of the river or a midtown cityscape. Quarters are compact (from 230sq ft) but the combination of floor-to-ceiling windows, curving tambour wood panelling and 'peekaboo' bathrooms (with Japanese-style tubs or huge showerheads) give a sense of space. Eating and drinking options include a chop house, a beer garden and an exclusive top-floor bar with a massive jacuzzi.

Midtown

Chelsea

Dream Downtown

355 W 16th Street, between Eighth & Ninth Avenues (1-212 229 2559, www.dreamdowntown.com). Subway A, C, E to 14th Street; L to Eighth Avenue. **$$$**.
Be sure to pack your totem: staying at the latest property from hotel wunderkind Vikram Chatwal may make you wonder if you're in a dream within a Dream. The expansive, tree-shaded lobby, furnished with curvy, metallic-lizard banquettes, and presided over by a DJ every evening, has an overhead view of swimmers doing laps in the

glass-bottomed pool on the terrace above. Housed in the former annex of the New York Maritime Union (now the adjacent Maritime Hotel, see right), the surreal building is riddled with round windows. Quarters combine classic elements (white chesterfield chairs or sofas, Tivoli radios, Turkish rugs) with futuristic touches like shiny steel bathtubs in some rooms.

High Line Hotel

NEW *180 Tenth Avenue, at 20th Street (1-212 929 3888, www.thehighlinehotel. com). Subway C, E to 23rd Street.* $$$. See box p177.

Hôtel Americano

518 W 27th Street, between Tenth & Eleventh Avenues (1-212 216 0000, www.hotel-americano.com). Subway C, E to 23rd Street. $$$.
You won't find any Talavera tiles in Grupo Habita's first property outside Mexico. Mexican architect Enrique Norten's sleek, mesh-encased structure stands alongside the High Line. Decor evokes classic mid-century American style, interpreted by a European (Colette designer Arnaud Montigny). The minimalist rooms have Japanese-style platform beds, iPads and, in one of several subtle nods to US culture, super-soft denim bathrobes. After a day of gallery-hopping, get an elevated view of the neighbourhood from the rooftop bar and grill, where a petite pool does double duty as a hot tub in winter.

Inn on 23rd

131 W 23rd Street, between Sixth & Seventh Avenues (1-212 463 0330, www.innon23rd.com). Subway F, M, 1 to 23rd Street. $$.
This renovated 19th-century townhouse offers the charm of a traditional bed and breakfast with enhanced amenities (a lift, pillow-top mattresses, private bathrooms and white-noise machines). Owners Annette and Barry Fisherman have styled each bedroom with a unique theme, such as Maritime, Bamboo and

1940s. One of the Inn's best attributes is the 'library', a cosy jumble of tables and chairs that's open 24/7 to guests for coffee and tea. Another nice perk: guests receive 25% off the bill at the Guilty Goose, the owners' modern American brasserie on the ground floor.

Maritime Hotel

363 W 16th Street, between Eighth & Ninth Avenues (1-212 242 4300, www.themaritimehotel.com). Subway A, C, E to 14th Street; L to Eighth Avenue. $$$.
Once the headquarters of the New York Maritime Union, this nautically themed hotel is outfitted with self-consciously hip details befitting a Wes Anderson film. Standard rooms are modelled on cruise cabins, lined with teak panelling and sporting a single porthole window. The hotel's busy Italian restaurant, La Bottega, also supplies room service, and the adjoining bar hosts a crowd of models and mortals, who throng the umbrella-lined patio in warmer weather.

Flatiron District & Union Square

Ace Hotel New York

20 W 29th Street, at Broadway (1-212 679 2222, www.acehotel.com). Subway N, R to 28th Street. $$$.
Bourgeois hipsters tired of crashing on couches will appreciate the New York outpost of the cool chainlet founded in Seattle by a pair of DJs. The music influence is clear: many rooms in the 1904 building have playful amenities such as functioning turntables, stacks of vinyl and gleaming Gibson guitars. The buzzing lobby bar is sheltered within a panelled library salvaged from a Madison Avenue apartment. Guests can also score a table at chef April Bloomfield and Ken Friedman's popular restaurants, the Breslin Bar & Dining Room and the John Dory Oyster Bar (for both, see p111). There's even an outpost of one of the city's hippest boutiques, Opening Ceremony (see p70).

Divine digs

Stay in a serene sanctuary in the heart of the city.

In the early 19th century, Chelsea was a country estate owned by Clement Clarke Moore, author of the poem 'A Visit from St Nicholas' (''Twas the Night Before Christmas'). The man of letters gifted a chunk of land to the Episcopal Church to establish the General Theological Seminary, which remains a bastion of religious study. These days, however, it's across the street from one of the city's most popular attractions: the High Line. And the railway line-turned-park lends its name to a new boutique hotel on the seminary grounds.

Previously run by the institution, the old guest wing and conference centre has been transformed into the **High Line Hotel** (p176), with interiors by Roman and Williams, the fashionable design firm behind the Ace Hotel New York's eclectic decor. In keeping with the institution's intellectual purview, the lobby of the imposing 1895 neo-Gothic landmark is home to NYC's first outpost of Chicago's Intelligentsia Coffee. Exuding an old-fashioned residential vibe, the 60 guest quarters feature antique Persian rugs on hardwood floors, custom-designed wallpaper and a mix of vintage furnishings and reproductions of pieces sourced by the designers. Many rooms retain original fireplaces – though these days the eco-friendly property is heated and cooled by a geothermal system. Rewired 1930s Western Electric rotary phones and desk-top embossers for customising your snail mail may seem like an antidote to the digital age, but don't panic: there's also free in-room Wi-Fi, and you can connect your iPod to the retro Tivoli radio by the bed.

NoMad Hotel

1170 Broadway, at 28th Street (1-212 796 1500, www.thenomadhotel.com). Subway N, R to 28th Street. **$$$**.

Like nearby hipster hub the Ace Hotel, the NoMad (which shares a developer) is also a self-contained microcosm encompassing destination dining – courtesy of Daniel Humm and Will Guidara, of Michelin-three-starred Eleven Madison Park (see p111) – and the first stateside outpost of Parisian concept store Maison Kitsuné. Jacques Garcia, designer of Paris celeb hangout Hôtel Costes, transformed the interior of a 1903 New York office building into this convincing facsimile of a grand hotel. The chic rooms, furnished with vintage Heriz rugs and distressed-leather armchairs, are more personal – Garcia based the design on his old Paris apartment. Many feature old-fashioned claw-foot tubs for a scented soak in Côté Bastide bath salts.

Gramercy Park & Murray Hill

Carlton Arms Hotel

160 E 25th Street, at Third Avenue (1-212 679 0680, www.carltonarms.com). Subway 6 to 23rd Street. **$**.

The Carlton Arms Art Project started in the late 1970s, when a small group of creative types brought fresh paint and new ideas to a run-down shelter. Today, the site is a bohemian backpackers' hub and a live-in gallery, festooned with outré artwork. Themed quarters include the Money Room and a tribute to a traditional English cottage. Roughly half of the quarters have shared bathrooms. Reserve well in advance.

Gramercy Park Hotel

2 Lexington Avenue, at 21st Street (1-212 920 3300, www.gramercy parkhotel.com). Subway 6 to 23rd Street. **$$$$**.

Many NYC hotels have exclusive terraces or gardens, but only one boasts access to the city's most storied private outdoor space: Gramercy Park. The hotel's interior resembles a baronial manor occupied by a rock star, with rustic wooden beams and a roaring fire in the lobby; a $65 million art collection, including works by Richard Prince, Damien Hirst and Andy Warhol; and studded velvet headboards and mahogany drink cabinets in the bedrooms. Get a taste of the Eternal City in the restaurant, Maialino, Danny Meyer's tribute to Roman trattorias.

Morgans

237 Madison Avenue, between 37th & 38th Streets (1-212 686 0300, www.morganshotel.com). Subway S, 4, 5, 6, 7 to 42nd Street-Grand Central. **$$$**.

New York's original boutique hotel, Morgans opened in 1984. Some 25 years later, its designer, Andrée Putman, returned to officiate over a revamp that softened its stark monochrome appearance. Unfussy bedrooms, cast in a calming palette of silver, grey, cream and white, are hung with original Robert Mapplethorpe prints; window seats are piled with linen cushions. The classic black-and-white-tiled bathrooms offer products from NYC's Malin + Goetz.

Pod 39

145 E 39th Street, between Lexington & Third Avenues (1-212 865 5700, www.thepodhotel.com). Subway S, 4, 5, 6, 7 to 42nd Street-Grand Central. **$**.

The city's second Pod occupies a 1918 residential hotel for single men – you can hang out by the fire or play ping-pong in the redesigned gents' sitting room. As the name suggests, rooms are snug, but not oppressively so; some have queen-size beds, others stainless-steel bunk beds with individual TVs and bedside shelves inspired by air-storage. But you should probably know your roommate well since the utilitarian, subway-tiled bathrooms are partitioned off with sliding frosted-glass doors. Restaurant dream team April Bloomfield and Ken Friedman is behind on-site eaterie Salvation Taco (see p115).

Herald Square & Garment District

Refinery Hotel

NEW *63 W 38th Street, between Fifth & Sixth Avenues (1-646 664 0310, www.refineryhotelnewyork.com). Subway B, D, F, M, N, Q, R to 34th Street-Herald Square; 7 to Fifth Avenue.* **$$$**.
See box p180.

Theater District & Hell's Kitchen

414 Hotel

414 W 46th Street, between Ninth & Tenth Avenues (1-212 399 0006, www.414hotel.com). Subway A, C, E to 42nd Street-Port Authority. **$$**.
Tucked into a residential yet central neighbourhood, this budget boutique hotel is a real find. The place is twice as big as it looks, as it consists of two walk-up buildings separated by a leafy courtyard, which in warmer months is a lovely place to eat your complimentary breakfast. Rooms are simple yet chic, with a modern colour scheme that pairs grey headboards and red accents, and equipped with fridges, flatscreen TVs and iPod docks.

Out NYC

510 W 42nd Street, between Tenth & Eleventh Avenues (1-212 947 2999, www.theoutnyc.com). Subway A, C, E to 42nd Street-Port Authority. **$-$$**.
Homo hotspot Hell's Kitchen is the location of New York's first specifically gay (but 'straight-friendly') luxury hotel. Built in the husk of a 1960s motel, the sprawling all-in-one playground also houses XL, a club operated by nightlife bigwigs John Blair and Beto Sutter, and Tony Fornabaio and Brandon Voss of FV Events; a restaurant, KTCHN; and a 5,000sq ft spa. The complex is designed around three courtyards, including the faux-ivy-lined sundeck, which leads to a glass-ceilinged area with two hot tubs. Despite a few style statements, the monochrome room decor is on the spare side. The quad rooms, with four curtained cubby-bunks reminiscent of sleeper compartments – upgraded with double beds and TVs – are a budget option for those who are travelling with a crowd or want to make new friends.

Yotel New York

570 Tenth Avenue, at 42nd Street (1-646 449 7700, www.yotel.com). Subway A, C, E to 42nd Street-Port Authority. **$$**.
The British team behind this futuristic hotel is known for airport-based capsule accommodation that gives travellers just enough space to get horizontal between flights. Yotel New York has ditched the 75sq ft cubbies in favour of 'premium cabins' more than twice the size. Adaptable furnishings (such as beds that fold up futon-style) maximise space, and the bathroom has streamlined luxuries such as a heated towel rail and monsoon shower. If you want to unload excess baggage, the 20ft tall robot (or Yobot, in the hotel's playful lingo) will stash it for you in a lobby locker. In contrast with the compact quarters, the sprawling public spaces include a wraparound terrace so large it's serviced by two bars.

Fifth Avenue & around

Chambers Hotel

15 W 56 Street, between Fifth & Sixth Avenues (1-212 974 5656, www.chambershotel.com). Subway E, M to Fifth Avenue-53rd Street. **$$$**.
Room design at this small boutique hotel takes its cue from upscale loft apartments, combining designer furniture with raw concrete ceilings, exposed pipes, floor-to-ceiling windows and either polished walnut floorboards or Tibetan wool carpeting. Everything is designed to make you feel at home, from the soft terrycloth slippers in bright colours to the architect's desks stocked with a roll of paper and coloured pencils should artistic inspiration hit. There's no need to leave the hotel for meals,

ESSENTIALS

Fashion house

A design-conscious hotel opens in the Garment District.

Be sure to pack your vintage fedora for a stay at the **Refinery Hotel** (see p179). Stonehill & Taylor Architects, the firm behind the 1912 neo-Gothic building's conversion and design, took inspiration from its former life as a hat-making workshop. Milliners once toiled on the upper floors, while the ground level was devoted to showrooms and a genteel tea salon for shoppers. 'It created this duality, almost an *Upstairs, Downstairs* kind of thing,' explains Stonehill & Taylor principal Christina Zimmer. 'We thought that was really interesting and brought it to bear on our new hotel.' (The firm's CV also includes the NoMad Hotel, see p178, and Ace Hotel New York, see p176.)

With exposed pipes, concrete ceilings and oak floors, the rooms have an industrial aesthetic that echoes the former factory space, while the public areas on the ground floor are more – dare we say it – *refined*. Screened off from the lobby with leaded-glass panels, Winnie's Tea Lounge takes its name from Winifred McDonald, who owned a ladies' tearoom in the building in the early 20th century – but today, cocktails are served. Other eating and drinking options include American bistro Parker & Quinn, and a sprawling indoor-outdoor space with a direct view of the Empire State Building. The 3,500-square-foot roof is a year-round destination, comprising three distinct spaces: an indoor bar with a fireplace, a semi-open atrium featuring a retractable skylight and a fountain, and an outdoor deck. To lend the space some gritty NYC cred, the architects used wood salvaged from the building's dismantled water tower to build the ceiling and an interior wall.

In the guest rooms, furnishings subtly reference the garment industry for a look that's more sophisticated than steampunk. Wall coverings riff on linen, super-soft bed throws mimic burlap, coffee tables are modelled on early 20th-century factory carts, and desks are reproductions of vintage Singer sewing-machine tables.

since David Chang's Má Pêche and an outpost of his Milk Bar are on site.

Plaza

768 Fifth Avenue, at Central Park South (1-212 759 3000, www.the plaza.com). Subway N, Q, R to Fifth Avenue-59th Street. **$$$$**.
This 1907 French Renaissance-style landmark building reopened in spring 2008 following a $400 million renovation. Although 152 rooms were converted into private condo units, guests can still check into one of 282 quarters complete with Louis XV-inspired furnishings and white-glove butler service. The opulent vibe extends to the bathrooms, which feature 24-carat gold-plated sink fittings and chandeliers.

Midtown East

Hotel Elysée

60 E 54th Street, between Madison & Park Avenues (1-212 753 1066, www.elyseehotel.com). Subway E, M to Lexington Avenue-53rd Street; 6 to 51st Street. **$$$**.
Since 1926, this discreet but opulent hotel has attracted luminaries. You may bump into one while going from your antique-appointed room to the second-floor lounge for the complimentary wine and cheese served every evening, or in the exclusive Monkey Bar (see p130), *Vanity Fair* editor Graydon Carter's restaurant that shares the building – a few tables are set aside for guests.

Uptown

Upper East Side

Surrey

20 E 76th Street, between Fifth & Madison Avenues (1-212 288 3700, 1-800 978 7739). Subway 6 to 77th Street. **$$$$**.
Occupying an elegant 1920s building given a $60 million overhaul, the Surrey pitches at both traditionalists and the

trend-driven. The coolly elegant limestone and marble lobby showcases museum-quality contemporary art, and rooms are dressed in a refined palette of cream, grey and beige, with luxurious white marble bathrooms. But the centrepiece is undoubtedly the incredibly comfortable DUX by Duxiana bed, swathed in sumptuous Sferra linens. The hotel is flanked by top chef Daniel Boulud's Café Boulud and his chic cocktail destination, Bar Pleiades; there's also a luxurious spa.

Upper West Side

On the Ave Hotel

222 W 77th St, at Broadway (1-212 362 1100, www.ontheave-nyc.com). Subway 1 to 79th Street. **$$**.
Given the affluent area, it's hardly surprising that On the Ave's rooms are stylish (industrial-style bathroom sinks, ergonomic Herman Miller chairs). On the upper floors, panoramic deluxe rooms and penthouse suites have fantastic private-balcony views of Central Park or the Hudson, but all guests have access to terraces on the 14th and 16th floors. The hotel houses the second location of acclaimed modern Chinese spot RedFarm (see p95).

Harlem

Harlem Flophouse

242 W 123rd Street, between Adam Clayton Powell Jr Boulevard (Seventh Avenue) & Frederick Douglass Boulevard (Eighth Avenue) (1-347 632 1960, www.harlemflophouse.com). Subway A, B, C, D to 125th Street. **$**.
The dark-wood interior, moody lighting and lilting jazz make musician Rene Calvo's Harlem inn feel more like a 1930s speakeasy than a 21st-century B&B. The airy suites have restored tin ceilings, a quirky mix of junk-store furnishings and period knick-knacks, and working sinks in antique cabinets. There are just two suites per floor; each pair shares a bathroom.

Outer Boroughs

Brooklyn

New York Loft Hostel

249 Varet Street, at Bogart Street, Bushwick (1-718 366 1351, www. nylofthostel.com). Subway L to Morgan Avenue. $.

Set in an arty enclave, this budget lodging fuses the traditional youth hostel set-up (dorm-style rooms with single beds and lockers, communal kitchen and lounging areas) with a fashionable loft aesthetic. In the former clothing warehouse, linen curtains billow in front of huge windows, and there's plenty of industrial-chic exposed brick and piping. The large patio is the site of summer barbecues.

Nu Hotel

85 Smith Street, between Atlantic Avenue & State Street, Boerum Hill, (1-718 852 8585, www.nuhotelbrooklyn.com). Subway A, C, F to Jay Street-Borough Hall; F, G to Bergen Street; R to Court Street; 2, 3, 4, 5 to Borough Hall. $$.

Conveniently placed for the shops and restaurants of BoCoCa (Boerum Hill, Cobble Hill and Carroll Gardens), Nu Hotel has bundled quirky niceties into a classy, eco-friendly package. Cork flooring, organic linens and recycled teak furniture mix it up with 32in flatscreen TVs and Sangean audio systems, free Wi-Fi and AV docks for multimedia devices. Friends Suites have bunk beds, and the lofty Urban Suites are outfitted with hammocks and a padded-leather sleeping alcove. Cyclists can borrow one of the hotel's loaner bikes to pedal around Brooklyn, and iPads are available for guest use. The lobby bar offers a tapas menu designed by *Next Iron Chef* runner-up Jehangir Mehta.

Wythe Hotel

80 Wythe Avenue, at North 11th Street, Williamsburg (1-718 460 8000, www.wythehotel.com). Subway L to Bedford Avenue. $$.

A 1901 cooperage near the waterfront topped with a three-storey glass-and-aluminium addition, the Wythe perfectly captures the neighbourhood's elusive hip factor. Since the launch team includes Andrew Tarlow, the restaurateur behind popular local eateries Diner and Marlow & Sons, it's not surprising that the ground-floor restaurant, Reynard, was an instant hit. In many of the guest rooms, floor-to-ceiling windows offer a panorama of the Manhattan skyline. Heated concrete floors, exposed brick, reclaimed-timber beds and witty custom wallpaper create a rustic-industrial vibe, offset by fully plugged-in technology: a cable by the bed turns your iPhone into a surround-sound music system. For non-couple travelling companions, compact bunk rooms are equipped with individual TVs, and some even have cute terraces.

Queens

Z NYC Hotel

11-01 43rd Avenue, at 11th Street, Long Island City (1-212 319 7000, www.zhotelny.com). Subway E, M to Court Square-23rd Street; F to 21st Street-Queensbridge; N, Q, 7 to Queensboro Plaza. $$.

The Z shares a gritty industrial side street with tool suppliers and flooring wholesalers, but the Queensboro Bridge-side setting and largely low-rise neighbours facilitate its most stunning feature: knock-your-socks-off midtown views through floor-to-ceiling windows. Offbeat details, such as lightbulbs encased in mason jars dangling over the bed, wall stencils of iconic New York images and black flip-flops instead of the standard white slippers, enliven the stock boutique luxury of the accommodation. The public spaces are more dramatic: in the lobby, an old-school train-station-style 'departure board' spells out welcome in 18 languages, and the sprawling roof bar offers 360-degree panoramas.

Getting Around

By air

John F Kennedy International Airport

1-718 244 4444, www.panynj.gov/ airports/jfk.html.

The **subway** (see p184) is the cheapest option. The **AirTrain** ($5, www.airtrainjfk.com) links to the A train at Howard Beach or the E, J and Z trains at Sutphin Boulevard-Archer Avenue ($2.50-$2.75).

NYC Airporter buses (1-718 777 5111, www.nycairporter.com; one way $16, round trip $29) connect JFK and Manhattan, with stops near Grand Central Terminal, Penn Station and Port Authority Bus Terminal. Buses run every 30mins from 5am to 11.30pm daily.

A **yellow cab** to Manhattan will charge a flat $52.50 fare, plus toll (usually $5) and tip (15 per cent is the norm). The fare to JFK from Manhattan is not a set rate, but is usually roughly the same (see p186).

La Guardia Airport

1-718 533 3400, www.panynj.gov/ airports/laguardia.html.

Seasoned New Yorkers take the **M60 bus** ($2.50), to 106th Street at Broadway. The ride takes 40-60mins, depending on traffic, and runs 24 hrs daily. The route crosses Manhattan at 125th Street in Harlem. Get off at Lexington Avenue for the 4, 5 and 6 trains; at Malcolm X Boulevard (Lenox Avenue) for the 2 and 3; or at St Nicholas Avenue for the A, B, C and D trains.

Less time-consuming options include **NYC Airporter** buses (one way $13, round trip $23). **Taxis** and **car services** charge about $30, plus toll and tip.

Newark Liberty International Airport

1-973 961 6000, www.panynj.gov/ airports/newark-liberty.html.

The best bet is the $12.50, half-hour trip via **New Jersey Transit** to or from Penn Station. The airport's monorail, **AirTrain Newark** (www.airtrainnewark.com), is linked to the NJ Transit and Amtrak train systems.

Bus services operated by **Coach USA** (1-877 894 9155, www. coachusa.com) run to Manhattan, stopping outside Grand Central Terminal, and inside the Port Authority Bus Terminal (one way $16, round trip $28); buses leave every 15-30mins. A **car** or **taxi** will run at $60-$75, plus toll and tip.

By bus

Most out-of-town buses come and go from the Port Authority Bus Terminal (see below). **Greyhound** (1-800 231 2222, www.greyhound. com) runs long-distance travel to US destinations. The company's **BoltBus** (1-877 265 8287, www.bolt bus.com), booked online, serves several East Coast cities. **New Jersey Transit** (1-973 275 5555, www.njtransit.com) runs services to most of New Jersey and parts of New York State. Finally, **Peter Pan** (1-800 343 9999, www.peterpanbus. com) runs extensive services to cities across the North-east; its tickets are also valid on Greyhound buses.

Port Authority Bus Terminal

625 Eighth Avenue, between 40th & 42nd Streets, Garment District (1-212 564 8484, www.panynj.gov/ bus-terminals/port-authority-bus-terminal.html). Subway A, C, E to 42nd Street-Port Authority.

ESSENTIALS

By rail

Grand Central Terminal *42nd to 44th Streets, between Vanderbilt & Lexington Avenues, Midtown East. Subway S, 4, 5, 6, 7 to 42nd Street-Grand Central.*
Home to Metro-North, which runs trains to more than 100 stations in New York State and Connecticut.

Penn Station *31st to 33rd Streets, between Seventh & Eighth Avenues, Garment District. Subway A, C, E, 1, 2, 3 to 34th Street-Penn Station.*
Amtrak, Long Island Rail Road and New Jersey Transit trains depart from this terminal.

Public transport

Metropolitan Transportation Authority (MTA)

511 local, 1-877 690 5116 outside New York State, 1-212 878 7000 international, www.mta.info.
The MTA runs the subway and bus lines, as well as services to points outside Manhattan. News of service interruptions and MTA maps are on its website. Be warned: backpacks, handbags and large containers may be subject to random searches.

Fares & tickets

Although you can pay with exact change (no dollar bills) on buses, to enter the subway system you'll need either a single-ride ticket ($2.75, available from station vending machines only) or a MetroCard. You can buy MetroCards from booths or vending machines in the stations, from the Official NYC Information Center, from the New York Transit Museum in Brooklyn or Grand Central Terminal, and from many hotels.

The standard base fare across the subway and bus network on a MetroCard is $2.50. Free transfers between the subway and buses are available only with a MetroCard (for bus-to-bus transfers on cash fares, see p185). Up to four people can use a pay-per-ride MetroCard, sold in denominations from $5 to $80. If you put $5 or more on the card, you'll receive a five per cent bonus – or 25 cents for every $5 – thus reducing the cost of each ride. However, if you're planning to use the subway or buses often, an Unlimited Ride MetroCard is great value. These cards are offered in two denominations, available at station vending machines but not at booths: a seven-day pass ($30) and a 30-day pass ($112). Both are good for unlimited rides within those periods, but you can't share a card with your travel companions.

Subway

Far cleaner and safer than it was 20 years ago, the subway system is one of the world's largest and cheapest. For fares and MetroCards, see above. Trains run around the clock. If you are travelling late at night, board the train from the designated off-peak waiting area, usually near the middle of the platform; this is more secure than the ends of the platform, which are often less populated in the wee hours.

Stations are most often named after the street on which they're located. Entrances are marked with a green and white globe (open 24 hours) or a red and white globe (limited hours). Many stations have separate entrances for the uptown and downtown platforms – look before you pay. Trains are identified by letters or numbers, colour-coded according to the line on which they run. Local trains stop at every station on the line; express trains stop at major stations only.

The most current Manhattan subway map is reprinted at the back of this guide; you can also ask MTA workers in service booths for a free copy, or refer to enlarged maps displayed in each subway station.

City buses

White and blue MTA buses are usually the best way to travel crosstown and a pleasant way to travel up- or downtown, as long as you're not in a hurry. They have a digital destination sign on the front, along with a route number preceded by a letter (M for Manhattan, B for Brooklyn, Bx for the Bronx, Q for Queens and S for Staten Island). Maps are posted on most buses and at all subway stops; they're also available from the Official NYC Information Center (see p189). The Manhattan bus map is printed in the back of this guide. All local buses are equipped with wheelchair lifts. The fare is payable with a MetroCard (see p184) or exact change ($2.50 in coins only; no pennies or dollar bills). MetroCards allow for an automatic transfer from bus to bus, and between bus and subway. If you pay cash, and you're travelling uptown or downtown and want to go crosstown (or vice versa), ask the driver for a transfer when you get on – you'll be given a ticket for use on the second leg of your journey, valid for two hours. MTA's express buses usually head to the outer boroughs for a $6 fare.

Rail

The following commuter trains serve NY's hinterland.
Long Island Rail Road *511 local, 1-718 217 5477 outside New York State, www.mta.info/lirr*.
Rail services from Penn Station, Brooklyn and Queens to towns throughout Long Island.

Metro-North Railroad *511 local, 1-212 532 4900 outside New York State, www.mta.info/mnr*.
Serves towns north of Manhattan, leaving from Grand Central Terminal.
New Jersey Transit *1-973 275 5555, www.njtransit.com*.
Services from Penn Station reach most of New Jersey, some points in NY State and Philadelphia.
PATH Trains *1-800 234 7284, www.panynj.gov/path*.
PATH trains run from six stations in Manhattan to various New Jersey destinations, including Hoboken, Jersey City and Newark. The 24-hour service costs $2.25.

Boat

NY Waterway (1-800 533 3779, www.nywaterway.com) runs a water-transport service that connects Manhattan to Queens, Brooklyn and some New Jersey cities. The East River Ferry runs between Midtown East at 34th Street and downtown Manhattan at Pier 11 via Long Island City in Queens and Greenpoint, Williamsburg and Dumbo in Brooklyn (from $4 one way, $12 day pass). On the West Side of the island, NY Waterway's Hudson River ferries link Pier 79 on 39th Street and the World Financial Center in lower Manhattan to destinations in New Jersey, including Hoboken and Jersey City ($7-$21.50 one-way). Visit the website for ferry routes and schedules.

Taxis

If the centre light atop the taxi is lit, the cab is available and should stop if you flag it down. Get in and then tell the driver where you're going. (New Yorkers generally give cross-streets rather than addresses.) By law, taxis cannot refuse to take you anywhere inside the five boroughs or to New York airports. Use only

ESSENTIALS

yellow medallion (licensed) cabs; avoid unregulated 'gypsy cabs'.

Taxis will carry up to four passengers for the same price: $2.50 plus 50¢ per fifth of a mile or per minute idling, with an extra 50¢ charge (a new state tax), another 50¢ from 8pm to 6am and a $1 surcharge during rush hour (4-8pm Mon-Fri). The average fare for a three-mile ride is $14, but this will vary depending on the time and traffic.

If you have a problem, take down the medallion and driver's numbers, posted on the partition. Always ask for a receipt – there's a meter number on it. To complain or to trace lost property, call the **Taxi & Limousine Commission** (1-212 227 0700, 8.30am-5pm Mon-Fri) or visit www.nyc.gov/taxi. Tip 15-20 per cent, as in a restaurant. All taxis now accept major credit cards.

Car services are regulated by the Taxi & Limousine Commission. Unlike cabs, drivers can make only pre-arranged pickups. Don't try to hail one, and be wary of those that offer you a ride. These companies will pick you up anywhere in the city for a set fare.
Carmel *1-212 666 6666.*
Dial 7 *1-212 777 7777.*
GroundLink *1-877 227 7260.*

Driving

Car hire

You need a credit card to rent a car in the US, and usually must be at least 25 years old. Car hire is cheaper in the city's outskirts and further afield than in Manhattan. NYC companies add 19.875 per cent in taxes.

If you just want a car for a few hours, **Zipcar** (US: 1-866 494 7227, www.zipcar.com; UK: 0333 240 9000, www.zipcar.co.uk) is cost effective.
Alamo *US: 1-877 222 9075, www. alamo.com. UK: 0871 384 1086, www.alamo.co.uk.*

Avis *US: 1-800 230 4898, www.avis.com. UK: 0844 581 0147, www.avis.co.uk.*
Budget *US: 1-800 527 0700, www.budget.com. UK: 0844 581 2231, www.budget.co.uk.*
Enterprise *US: 1-800 261 7331, www.enterprise.com. UK: 0800 800 227, www.enterprise.co.uk.*
Hertz *US: 1-800 654 3131, www.hertz.com. UK: 0843 309 3099, www.hertz.co.uk.*

Parking

Make sure you read parking signs and never park within 15 feet of a fire hydrant (to avoid a $115 ticket and/or having your car towed). Parking is off-limits on most streets for at least a few hours daily. The Department of Transportation provides information on daily changes to regulations (dial 311). If precautions fail, call 1-212 971 0771 for Manhattan towing and impoundment information; go to www.nyc.gov for phone numbers in other boroughs.

Cycling

While biking on NYC's streets is only recommended for experienced cyclists, the new **Citi Bike** system (www.citibikenyc.com, 1-855 245 3311) gives you temporary access to bikes at 600 stations in Manhattan and Brooklyn. Visitors can purchase a 24-hour ($9.95) or seven-day ($25) Access Pass at a station kiosk with a credit or debit card. You'll then receive a 'ride code' that will allow you to undock and ride for 30 minutes at a stretch. A longer trip will incur an extra fee.

Bike & Roll (1-212 260 0400, www.bikeandroll.com/newyork) is the city's biggest cycle-hire company, with nine outposts. Rates (incl helmet) start at $10 per hour.

Resources A-Z

Accident & emergency

In an emergency only, dial 911 for an ambulance, police or the fire department, or call the operator (dial 0). The following hospitals have emergency rooms:

Downtown Hospital *83 Gold Street, between Spruce & Beekman Streets, Financial District (1-212 312 5000). Subway 4, 5, 6 to Brooklyn Bridge-City Hall.*

Mount Sinai Hospital *Madison Avenue, at 100th Street, Upper East Side (1-212 241 6500). Subway 6 to 103rd Street.*

New York – Presbyterian Hospital/ Weill Cornell Medical Center *525 E 68th Street, at York Avenue, Upper East Side (1-212 746 5454). Subway 6 to 68th Street-Hunter College.*

Roosevelt Hospital *1000 Tenth Avenue, at 59th Street, Upper West Side (1-212 523 4000). Subway A, B, C, D, 1 to 59th Street-Columbus Circle.*

Customs

US Customs allows foreigners to bring in $200 worth of gifts (the limit is $800 for returning Americans) without paying duty. One carton of 200 cigarettes (or 50 cigars) and one litre of liquor (spirits) are allowed. Plants, meat and fresh produce of any kind cannot be brought into the country. You will have to fill out a form if you carry more than $10,000 in currency. You will be handed a white form on your inbound flight to fill in, confirming that you haven't exceeded any of these allowances.

If you need to bring prescription drugs with you into the US, make sure the container is clearly marked, and bring your doctor's statement or a prescription. Marijuana, cocaine and most opiate derivatives, along with a number of other drugs and chemicals, are not permitted: the possession of them is punishable by a stiff fine and/or imprisonment. Check in with the US Customs Service (www.cbp.gov) before you arrive if you're unsure.

Disabled

Under New York City law, facilities constructed after 1987 must provide complete access for the disabled – restrooms, entrances and exits included. In 1990, the Americans with Disabilities Act made the same requirement federal law. Many older buildings have added disabled-access features. There has been widespread compliance with the law, but call ahead to check facilities. For information on accessible cultural institutions, contact the **Mayor's Office for People with Disabilities** (1-212 788 2830, 9am-5pm Mon-Fri). All Broadway theatres are equipped with devices for the hearing-impaired; call **Sound Associates** (1-888 772 7686, www.soundassociates.com) for more information. For the visually impaired, **HAI** (1-212 575 7676, www.hainyc.org) offers live audio descriptions of selected theatre performances.

Electricity

The US uses 110-120V, 60-cycle alternating current rather than the 220-240V, 50-cycle AC used in Europe. The transformers that power or recharge newer electronic devices such as laptops are designed to handle either current and may need nothing more than an adaptor for the wall outlet. Other appliances may also require a power converter. Adaptors and converters can be purchased at airport shops, pharmacies, department stores and at branches of electronics chain Radio Shack (www.radioshack.com).

Embassies & Consulates

Australia *1-212 351 6500.*
Canada *1-212 596 1628.*
United Kingdom *1-212 745 0200.*
Ireland *1-212 319 2555.*
New Zealand *1-212 832 4038.*

Internet

Cycle Café *250 W 49th Street, between Broadway & Eighth Avenue, Theater District (1-212 380 1204). Subway C, E, 1 to 50th Street; N, Q, R to 49th Street.* **Open** *8am-midnight daily.* A bike-rental shop and internet café rolled into one.
NYCWireless *www.nycwireless.net.* This group has established dozens of hotspots in the city for free wireless access. (For example, most parks below 59th Street are covered.) Visit the website for information and a map.
New York Public Library *1-212 592 7000, www.nypl.org.* Branches of the NYPL are great places to get online for free, offering both Wi-Fi and computers for public use. (Ask for an out-of-state card, for which you need proof of residence, or a guest pass.). The **Science, Industry & Business Library** (188 Madison Avenue, at 34th Street, Midtown East), part of the Public Library system, has about 50 computers. All libraries have a computer limit of 45 minutes per day.
Starbucks *www.starbucks.com.* Many branches offer free Wi-Fi; there's a search facility on the website.

Opening hours

These are general guidelines.
Banks 9am-6pm Mon-Fri; generally also Sat mornings.
Businesses 9am or 10am to 5pm or 6pm Mon-Fri.
Pubs & bars 4pm-2am Mon-Thur, Sun; noon-4am Fri, Sat (but hours vary widely).
Shops 9am, 10am or 11am to 7pm or 8pm Mon-Sat (some open at noon and/or close at 9pm). Many also open on Sun, usually 11am or noon to 6pm.

Police

The NYPD stations below are in central, tourist-heavy areas of Manhattan. To find the nearest police precinct or for information about police services, call 1-646 610 5000 or visit www.nyc.gov.
Sixth Precinct *233 W 10th Street, between Bleecker & Hudson Streets, West Village (1-212 741 4811).*
Seventh Precinct *19½ Pitt Street, at Broome Street, Lower East Side (1-212 477 7311).*
Midtown North Precinct *306 W 54th Street, between Eighth & Ninth Avenues, Hell's Kitchen (1-212 760 8300).*
17th Precinct *167 E 51st Street, between Lexington & Third Avenues, Midtown East (1-212 826 3211).*
Central Park Precinct *86th Street & Transverse Road, Central Park (1-212 570 4820).*

Post

Post offices are usually open 9am-5pm Mon-Fri (a few open as early as 7.30am and close as late as 8.30pm); some are open Sat until 3pm or 4pm. The James A Farley Post Office (421 Eighth Avenue, between 31st & 33rd Streets, Garment District, 1-800 275 8777, 24hr information, www.usps.com) is open 24 hours daily for automated services.

Smoking

The 1995 NYC Smoke-Free Air Act makes it illegal to smoke in virtually all indoor public places. Since 2011 smoking has also been prohibited in New York City parks, pedestrian plazas (such as the ones in Times Square and Herald Square) and on beaches. Violators could face a $50 fine.

Telephones

As a rule, you must dial 1 + the area code before a number, even if the place you are calling is in the same area code. The area codes for Manhattan are 212 and 646; Brooklyn, Queens, Staten Island and the Bronx are 718 and 347; 917 is now mostly for mobile phones and pagers. Numbers preceded by 800, 877 and 888 are free of charge when dialled from within the US. To dial abroad, dial 011 followed by the country code, then the number. For the operator dial 0. Mobile phone users from other countries will need a tri-band handset. Public pay phones take coins and credit cards. The best way to make long-distance calls is with a phone card, available from the post office and chain stores such as Duane Reade and Rite Aid.

Time

New York is on Eastern Standard Time. This is five hours behind Greenwich Mean Time. Clocks are set forward one hour in early March for Daylight Saving Time (Eastern Daylight Time) and back one hour at the beginning of November. Going from east to west, Eastern Time is one hour ahead of Central Time, two hours ahead of Mountain Time and three hours ahead of Pacific Time.

Tipping

In restaurants, it's customary to tip at least 15 per cent; a quick way to calculate the tip is to double the tax.

Tourist information

Official NYC Information Center
810 Seventh Avenue, between 52nd & 53rd Streets, Theater District (1-212 484 1222, www.nycgo.com). Subway B, D, E to Seventh Avenue. **Open** 8.30am-6pm Mon-Fri; 9am-5pm Sat, Sun.

What's on

The weekly *Time Out New York* magazine (www.timeout.com/newyork), which hits newsstands on Wednesdays, is NYC's essential arts and entertainment guide. The best source for all things gay is *Next* (www.nextmagazine.com); the monthly *Go!* (www.gomag.com) is geared towards girls.

Visas

Currently, 37 countries participate in the Visa Waiver Program (VWP; www.cbp.gov/esta) including Australia, Ireland, New Zealand, and the UK. Citizens of these countries do not need a visa for stays in the US shorter than 90 days (business or pleasure) as long as they have a machine-readable passport (e-passport) valid for the full 90-day period, a return ticket, and authorisation to travel through the ESTA (Electronic System for Travel Authorization) scheme. Visitors must fill in the ESTA form at least 24 hours before travelling (72 hours is recommended) and pay a $14 fee; the form can be found at www.cbp.gov/xp/cgov/travel/id_visa/esta/).

If you do not qualify for entry under the VWP, you will need a visa; leave plenty of time to check before travelling.

ESSENTIALS

Index

Sights & Areas

ESSENTIALS

ESSENTIALS